Hard Press

HELEN OF THE OLD HOUSE

BY HAROLD BELL WRIGHT

1921

Contents

THE INTERPRETER

"Take up our quarrel with the foe:
To you from failing hands we throw
* The torch; be yours to hold it high.*
* If ye break faith with us who die*
We shall not sleep, though poppies grow
*   In Flanders fields."*

CHAPTER I

THE HUT ON THE CLIFF

No well informed resident of Millsburgh, when referring to the principal industry of his little manufacturing city, ever says "the mills"—it is always "the Mill."

The reason for this common habit of mind is that one mill so overshadows all others, and so dominates the industrial and civic life of this community, that in the people's thought it stands for all.

The philosopher who keeps the cigar stand on the corner of Congress Street and Ward Avenue explained it very clearly when he answered an inquiring stranger, "You just can't think Millsburgh without thinkin' mills; an' you can't think mills without thinkin' *the* Mill."

As he turned from the cash register to throw his customer's change on the scratched top of the glass show case, the philosopher added with a grin that was a curious blend of admiration, contempt and envy, "An' you just can't think the Mill without thinkin' Adam Ward."

That grin was another distinguishing mark of the well informed resident of Millsburgh. Always, in those days, when the citizens mentioned the owner of the Mill, their faces took on that curious half-laughing expression of mingled admiration, contempt and envy.

But it has come to pass that in these days when the people speak of Adam Ward they do not smile. When they speak of Adam Ward's daughter, Helen, they smile, indeed, but with quite a different meaning.

The history of Millsburgh is not essentially different from that of a thousand other cities of its class.

Born of the natural resources of the hills and forests, the first rude mill was located on that wide sweeping bend of the river. About this industrial beginning a settlement gathered. As the farm lands of the valley were developed, the railroad came, bringing more mills. And so the town grew up around its smoky heart.

It was in those earlier days that Adam Ward, a workman then, patented and introduced the new process. It was the new process, together with its owner's native genius for "getting on," that, in time, made Adam the owner of the Mill. And, finally, it was this combination of Adam and the new process that gave this one mill dominion over all others.

As the Mill increased in size, importance and power, and the town grew into the city, Adam Ward's material possessions were multiplied many times.

Then came the year of this story.

It was midsummer. The green, wooded hills that form the southern boundary of the valley seemed to be painted on shimmering gauze. The grainfields on the lowlands across the river were shining gold. But the slate-colored dust from the unpaved streets of that section of Millsburgh known locally as the "Flats" covered the wretched houses, the dilapidated fences, the hovels and shanties, and everything animate or inanimate with a thick coating of dingy gray powder. Shut in as it is between a long curving line of cliffs on the south and a row of tall buildings on the river bank, the place was untouched by the refreshing breeze that stirred the trees on the hillside above. The hot, dust-filled atmosphere was vibrant with the dull, droning voice of the Mill. From the forest of tall stacks the smoke went up in slow, twisting columns to stain the clean blue sky with a heavy cloud of dirty brown.

The deep-toned whistle of the Mill had barely called the workmen from their dinner pails and baskets when two children came along the road that for some distance follows close to the base of that high wall of cliffs. By their ragged, nondescript clothing which, to say the least, was scant enough to afford them comfort and freedom of limb, and by the dirt, that covered them from the crowns of their bare, unkempt heads to the bottoms of their bare, unwashed feet, it was easy to identify the children as belonging to that untidy community.

One was a sturdy boy of eight or nine neglected years. On his rather heavy, freckled face and in his sharp blue eyes there was, already, a look of hardness that is not good to see in the countenance of a child. The other, his sister, was two years younger—a thin wisp of a girl, with tiny stooping shoulders, as though, even in her babyhood, she had found a burden too heavy. With her tired little face and grave, questioning eyes she looked at the world as if she were wondering, wistfully, why it should bother to be so unkind to such a helpless mite of humanity.

As they came down the worn road, side by side they chose with experienced care those wheel ruts where the black dust lay thickest and, in solemn earnestness, plowed the hot tracks with their bare feet, as if their one mission in life were to add the largest possible cloud of powdered dirt to the already murky atmosphere of the vicinity.

Suddenly they stood still.

For a long, silent moment they gazed at a rickety old wooden stairway that, at this point in the unbroken line of cliffs, climbs zigzag up the face of the rock-buttressed wall. Then, as if moved by a common impulse, they faced each other. The quick fire of adventure kindled in the eyes of the boy as he met the girl's look of understanding.

8

"Let's go up—stump yer," he said, with a daredevil grin.

"Huh, yer wouldn't dast."

Womanlike, she was hoping that he would "dast" and, with the true instinct of her sex, she chose unerringly the one way to bring about the realization of her hope.

Her companion met the challenge like a man. With a swaggering show of courage, he went to the stairway and climbed boldly up—six full steps. Then he paused and looked down, "I don't dast, don't I?"

From the lower step she spurred his faltering spirit, "Dare yer—dare yer—dare yer."

He came reluctantly down two steps, "Will yer go up if I do?"

She nodded, "Uh-huh—but yer gotter go first."

He looked doubtfully up at the edge of the cliff so far above them. "Shucks," he said, with conviction, "ain't nobody up there 'cept old Interpreter, an' that dummy, Billy Rand. I know 'cause Skinny Davis an' Chuck Wilson, they told me. They was up—old Interpreter, he can't do nothin' to nobody—he ain't got no legs."

Gravely she considered with him the possible dangers of the proposed adventure. "Billy Rand has got legs."

"He can't hear nothin', though—can't talk neither," said the leader of the expedition. "An' besides maybe he ain't there—we might catch him out. What d'yer say? Will we chance it?"

She looked up doubtfully toward the unknown land above. "I dunno, will we?"

"Skinny an' Chuck, they said the Interpreter give 'em cookies—an' told 'em stories too."

"Cookies, Gee! Go ahead—I'm a-comin'."

That tiny house high on the cliff at the head of the old, zigzag stairway, up which the children now climbed with many doubtful stops and questioning fears, is a landmark of interest not only to Millsburgh but to the country people for miles around.

Perched on the perilous brink of that curving wall of rocks, with its low, irregular, patched and weather-beaten roof, and its rough-boarded and storm-beaten walls half hidden in a tangle of vines and bushes, the little hut looks, from a distance, as though it might once have been the strange habitation of some gigantic winged creature of prehistoric ages. The place may be reached from a seldom-used road that leads along the steep hillside, a quarter of a mile back from the edge of the precipice, but the principal connecting link between the queer habitation and the world is that flight of rickety wooden steps.

Taking advantage of an irregularity in the line of cliffs, the upper landing of the stairway is placed at the side of the hut. In the rear, a small garden is protected from the uncultivated life of the hillside by a fence of close-set pickets. Across the front of the curious structure, well out on the projecting point of rocks, and reached only through the interior, a wide, strongly railed porch overhangs the sheer wall like a balcony.

With fast-beating hearts, the two small adventurers gained the top of the stairway. Cautiously they looked about—listening, conferring in whispers, ready for instant, headlong retreat.

The tall grasses and flowering weeds on the hillside nodded sleepily in the sunlight. A bird perched on a near-by bush watched them with bright eyes for a moment, then fearlessly sought the shade of the vines that screened the side of the hut. Save the distant, droning, moaning voice of the Mill, there was no sound.

Calling up the last reserves of their courage, the children crept softly along the board walk that connects the landing of the stairway with the rude dwelling. Once again they paused to look and listen. Then, timidly, they took the last cautious steps and stood in the open doorway. With big, wondering eyes they stared into the room.

It was a rather large room, with a low-beamed ceiling of unfinished pine boards and gray, rough-plastered walls, and wide windows. A green-shaded student lamp with a pile of magazines and papers on the table caught their curious eyes, and they gazed in awe at the long shelves of books against the wall. Opposite the entrance where they stood they saw a strongly made workbench. And beneath this bench and piled in that corner of the room were baskets—dozens of them—of several shapes and sizes; while brackets and shelves above were filled with the materials of which the baskets were woven. There was very little furniture. The floors were bare, the windows without hangings. It was all so different from anything that these children of the Flats had ever seen that they felt their adventure assuming proportions.

For what seemed a long time, the boy and the girl stood there, hesitating, on the threshold, expecting something—anything—to happen. Then the lad ventured a bold step or two into the room. His sister followed timidly.

They were facing hungrily toward an open door that led, evidently, to the kitchen, when a deep voice from somewhere behind them said, "How do you do?"

Startled nearly out of their small wits, the adventurers whirled to escape, but the voice halted them with, "Don't go. You came to see me, didn't you?"

10

The voice, though so deep and strong, was unmistakably kind and gentle—quite the gentlest voice, in fact, that these children had ever heard.

Hesitatingly, they went again into the room, and now, turning their backs upon the culinary end of the apartment, they saw, through the doorway opening on to the balcony porch, a man seated in a wheel chair. In his lap he held a half-finished basket.

For a little while the man regarded them with grave, smiling eyes as though, understanding their fears, he would give them time to gain courage. Then he said, gently, "Won't you come out here on the porch and visit with me?"

The boy and the girl exchanged questioning looks.

"Come on," said the man, encouragingly.

Perhaps the sight of that wheel chair recalled to the boy's mind the reports of his friends, Skinny and Chuck. Perhaps it was something in the man himself that appealed to the unerring instincts of the child. The doubt and hesitation in the urchin's freckled face suddenly gave way to a look of reckless daring and he marched forward with the swaggering air of an infant bravado. Shyly the little girl followed.

Invariably one's first impression of that man in the wheel chair was a thought of the tremendous physical strength and vitality that must once have been his. But the great trunk, with its mighty shoulders and massive arms, that in the years past had marked him in the multitude, was little more than a framework now. His head with its silvery white hair and beard—save that in his countenance there was a look of more venerable age—reminded one of the sculptor Rodin. These details of the man's physical appearance held one's thoughts but for a moment. One look into the calm depths of those dark eyes that were filled with such an indescribable mingling of pathetic courage, of patient fortitude, and of sorrowful authority, and one so instantly felt the dominant spiritual and mental personality of this man that all else about him was forgotten.

Squaring himself before his host, the boy said, aggressively, "I know who *yer* are. Yer are the Interpreter. I know 'cause yer ain't got no legs."

"Yes," returned the old basket maker, still smiling, "I am the Interpreter. At least," he continued, "that is what the people call me." Then, as he regarded the general appearance of the children, and noted particularly the tired face and pathetic eyes of the little girl, his smile was lost in a look of brooding sorrow and his deep voice was sad and gentle, as he added, "But some things I find very hard to interpret."

The girl, with a shy smile, went a little nearer.

11

The boy, with his eyes fixed upon the covering that in spite of the heat of the day hid the man in the wheel chair from his waist down, said with the cruel insistency of childhood, "Ain't yer got no legs—honest, now, ain't yer?"

The Interpreter laughed understandingly. Placing the unfinished basket on a low table that held his tools and the material for his work within reach of his hand, he threw aside the light shawl. "See!" he said.

For a moment the children gazed, breathlessly, at those shrunken and twisted limbs that resembled the limbs of a strong man no more than the empty, flapping sleeves of a scarecrow resemble the arms of a living human body.

"They are legs all right," said the Interpreter, still smiling, "but they're not much good, are they? Do you think you could beat me in a race?"

"Gee!" exclaimed the boy.

Two bright tears rolled down the thin, dirty cheeks of the little girl's tired face, and she turned to look away over the dirty Flats, the smoke-grimed mills, and the golden fields of grain in the sunshiny valley, to something that she seemed to see in the far distant sky.

With a quick movement the Interpreter again hid his useless limbs.

"And now don't you think you might tell me about yourselves? What is your name, my boy?"

"I'm Bobby Whaley," answered the lad. "She's my sister, Maggie."

"Oh, yes," said the Interpreter. "Your father is Sam Whaley. He works in the Mill."

"Uh-huh, some of the time he works—when there ain't no strikes ner nothin'."

The Interpreter, with his eyes on that dark cloud that hung above the forest of grim stacks, appeared to attach rather more importance to Bobby's reply than the lad's simple words would justify.

Then, looking gravely at Sam Whaley's son, he said, "And you will work in the Mill, too, I suppose, when you grow up?"

"I dunno," returned the boy. "I ain't much stuck on work. An' dad, he says it don't git yer nothin', nohow."

"I see," mused the Interpreter, and he seemed to see much more than lay on the surface of the child's characteristic expression.

12

The little girl was still gazing wistfully at the faraway line of hills.

As if struck by a sudden thought, the Interpreter asked, "Your father is working now, though, isn't he?"

"Uh-huh, just now he is."

"I suppose then you are not hungry."

At this wee Maggie turned quickly from contemplating the distant horizon to consider the possible meaning in the man's remark.

For a moment the children looked at each other. Then, as a grin of anticipation spread itself over his freckled face, the boy exclaimed, "Hungry! Gosh! Mister Interpreter, we're allus hungry!"

For the first time the little girl spoke, in a thin, piping voice, "Skinny an' Chuck, they said yer give 'em cookies. Didn't they, Bobby?"

"Uh-huh," agreed Bobby, hopefully.

The man in the wheel chair laughed. "If you go into the house and look in the bottom part of that cupboard near the kitchen door you will find a big jar and—"

But Bobby and Maggie had disappeared.

The children had found the jar in the cupboard and, with their hands and their mouths filled with cookies, were gazing at each other in unbelieving wonder when the sound of a step on the bare floor of the kitchen startled them. One look through the open doorway and they fled with headlong haste back to the porch, where they unhesitatingly sought refuge behind their friend ha the wheel chair.

The object of their fears appeared a short moment behind them.

"Oh," said the Interpreter, reaching out to draw little Maggie within the protecting circle of his arm, "it is Billy Rand. You don't need to fear Billy."

The man who stood looking kindly down upon them was fully as tall and heavy as the Interpreter had been in those years before the accident that condemned him to his chair. But Billy Rand lacked the commanding presence that had once so distinguished his older friend and guardian. His age was somewhere between twenty and thirty; but his face was still the face of an overgrown and rather slow-witted child.

Raising his hands, Billy Rand talked to the Interpreter in the sign language of the deaf and dumb. The Interpreter replied in the same manner and, with a smiling nod to the children, Billy returned to the garden in the rear of the house.

Tiny Maggie's eyes were big with wonder.

"Gee!" breathed Bobby. "He sure enough can't talk, can he?"

"No," returned the Interpreter. "Poor Billy has never spoken a word."

"Gee!" said Bobby again. "An' can't he hear nothin,' neither?"

"No, Bobby, he has never heard a sound."

Too awe-stricken even to repeat his favorite exclamation, the boy munched his cooky in silence, while Maggie, enjoying her share of the old basket maker's hospitality, snuggled a little closer to the wheel of the big chair.

"Billy Rand, you see," explained the Interpreter, "is my legs."

Bobby laughed. "Funny legs, I'd say."

"Yes," agreed the Interpreter, "but very good legs just the same. Billy runs all sorts of errands for me—goes to town to sell our baskets and to bring home our groceries, helps about the house and does many things that I can't do. He is hoeing the garden this afternoon. He comes in every once in a while to ask if I want anything. He sleeps in a little room next to mine and sometimes in the night, when I am not resting well, I hear him come to my bedside to see if I am all right."

"An' yer keep him an' take care of him?" asked Bobby.

"Yes," returned the Interpreter, "I take care of Billy and Billy takes care of me. He has fine legs but not much of a—but cannot speak or hear. I can talk and hear and think but have no legs. So with my reasonably good head and his very good legs we make a fairly good man, you see."

Bobby laughed aloud and even wee Maggie chuckled at the Interpreter's quaint explanation of himself and Billy Rand.

"Funny kind of a man," said Bobby.

"Yes," agreed the Interpreter, "but most of us men are funny in one way or another— aren't we, Maggie?" He looked down into the upturned face of that tiny wisp of humanity at his side.

14

Maggie smiled gravely in answer.

Very confident now in his superiority over the Interpreter, whose deaf and dumb legs were safely out of sight in the garden back of the house, Bobby finished the last of his cookies, and began to explore. Accompanying his investigations with a running fire of questions, he fingered the unfinished basket and the tools and material on the table, examined the wheel chair, and went from end to end of the balcony porch. Hanging over the railing, he looked down from every possible angle upon the rocks, the stairway and the dusty road below. Exhausting, at last, the possibilities of the immediate vicinity, he turned his inquiring gaze upon the more distant landscape.

"Gee! Yer can see a lot from here, can't yer?"

"Yes," returned the Interpreter, gravely, "you can certainly see a lot. And do you know, Bobby, it is strange, but what you see depends almost wholly on what you are?"

The boy turned his freckled face toward the Interpreter. "Huh?"

"I mean," explained the Interpreter, "that different people see different things. Some who come to visit me can see nothing but the Mill over there; some see only the Flats down below; others see the stores and offices; others look at nothing but the different houses on the hillsides; still others can see nothing but the farms. It is funny, but that's the way it is with people, Bobby."

"Aw—what are yer givin' us?" returned Bobby, and, with an unmistakably superior air, he faced again toward the scene before them. "I can see the whole darned thing—I can."

The Interpreter laughed. "And that," he said, "is exactly what every one says, Bobby. But, after all, they don't see the whole darned thing—they only think they do."

"Huh," retorted the boy, scornfully, "I guess I can see the Mill, can't I?—over there by the river—with the smoke a-rollin' out of her chimneys? Listen, I can hear her, too."

Faintly, on a passing breath of air, came the heavy droning, moaning voice of the Mill.

"Yes," agreed the Interpreter, with an odd note in his deep, kindly voice, "I can nearly always hear it. I was sure you would see the Mill."

"An' look-ee, look-ee," shouted the boy, forgetting, in his quick excitement, to maintain this superior air, "look-ee, Mag! Come here, quick." With energetic gestures he beckoned his sister to his side. "Look-ee, right over there by that bunch

15

of dust, see? It's our house—where we live. That there's Tony's old place on the corner. An' there's the lot where us kids plays ball. Gee, yer could almost see mom if she'd only come outside to talk to Missus Grafton er somethin'!"

From his wheel chair the Interpreter watched the children at the porch railing. "Of course you would see your home," he said, gravely. "The Mill first, and then the place where you live. Nearly every one sees those things first. Now tell what else you see."

"I see, I see—" The boy hesitated. There was so much to be seen from the Interpreter's balcony porch.

The little girl's thin voice piped up with shrill eagerness, "Look at the pretty yeller fields an' the green trees away over there across the river, Bobby. Gee, but wouldn't yer just love to be over there an'—an'—roll 'round in the grass, an' pick flowers, an' everything?"

"Huh," retorted Bobby. "Look-ee, that there's McIver's factory up the river there. It's 'most as big as the Mill. An' see all the stores an' barber shops an' things downtown—an' look-ee, there's the courthouse where the jail is an'—"

Maggie chimed in with, "An' all the steeples of the churches—an' everythin'."

"An' right down there," continued the boy, pointing more toward the east where, at the edge of the Flats, the ground begins to rise toward the higher slope of the hills, "in that there bunch of trees is where Pete Martin lives, an' Mary an' Captain Charlie. Look-ee, Mag, yer can see the little white house a-showin' through the green leaves."

"You know the Martins, do you?" asked the Interpreter.

"You bet we do," returned Bobby, without taking his gaze from the scene before him, while Maggie confirmed her brother's words by turning to look shyly at her new-found friend. "Pete and Charlie they work in the Mill. Charlie he was a captain in the war. He's one of the head guys in our union now. Mary she used to give us stuff to eat when dad was a-strikin' the last time."

"An' look-ee," continued the boy, "right there next to the Martins' yer can see the old house where Adam Ward used to live before the Mill made him rich an' he moved to his big place up on the hill. I know 'cause I heard dad an' another man talkin' 'bout it onct. Ain't nobody lives in the old house now. She's all tumbled down with windows broke an' everything. I wonder—" He paused to search the hillside to the east. "Yep," he shouted, pointing, "there she is—there's the castle—there's where old Adam an' his folks lives now. Some place to live I'd say. Gee, but wouldn't I like to put a chunk o' danermite er somethin' under there! I'd blow the whole darned thing into nothin' at all an that old devil Adam with it. I'd—"

16

Little Maggie caught her warlike brother's arm. "But, Bobby—Bobby, yer wouldn't dast to do that, yer know yer wouldn't!"

"Huh," returned the boy, scornfully. "I'd show yer if I had a chanct."

"But, Bobby, yer'd maybe kill the beautiful princess lady if yer was to blow up the castle an' every-thin'."

"Aw shucks," returned the boy, shaking off his sister's hand with manly impatience. "Couldn't I wait 'til she was away somewheres else 'fore I touched it off? An', anyway, what if yer wonderful princess lady *was* to git hurt, I guess she's one of 'em, ain't she?"

Poor Maggie, almost in tears, was considering this doubtful reassurance when Bobby suddenly pointed again toward that pretentious estate on the hillside, and cried in quick excitement: "Look-ee, Mag, there's a autermobile a-comin' out from the castle, right now—see? She's a-goin' down the hill toward town. Who'll yer bet it is? Old Adam Ward his-self, heh?"

Little Maggie's face brightened joyously. "Maybe it's the princess lady, Bobby."

"And who is this that you call the princess lady, Maggie?" asked the Interpreter.

Bobby answered for his sister. "Aw, she means old Adam's daughter. She's allus a-callin' her that an' a-makin' up stories about her."

"Oh, so you know Miss Helen Ward, too, do you?" The Interpreter was surprised.

The boy turned his back on the landscape as though it held nothing more of interest to him. "Naw, we've just seen her, that's all."

Stealing timidly back to the side of the wheel chair, the little girl looked wistfully up into the Interpreter's face. "Do yer—do yer know the princess lady what lives in the castle?" she asked.

The old basket maker, smiling down at her, answered, "Yes, dear, I have known your princess lady ever since she was a tiny baby—much smaller than you. And did you know, Maggie, that she was born in the old house down there, next door to Charlie and Mary Martin?"

"An'—an' did she live there when she was—when she was as big as me?"

Bobby interrupted with an important "Huh, I know her brother John is a boss in the Mill. He was in the war, too, with Captain Charlie. Did he live in the old house when he was a kid?"

"Yes."

"An'—an' when the princess lady was little like me, an' lived in the old house, did yer play with her?" asked Maggie.

The Interpreter laughed softly. "Yes, indeed, often. You see I worked in the Mill, too, in those days, Maggie, with her father and Peter Martin and—"

"That was when yer had yer real, sure-nuff legs, wasn't it?" the boy interrupted.

"Yes, Bobby. And every Sunday, almost, I used to be at the old house where the little princess lady lived, or at the Martin home next door, and Helen and John and Charlie and Mary and I would always have such good times together."

Little Maggie's face shone with appreciative interest. "An' did yer tell them fairy stories sometimes?"

"Sometimes."

The little girl sighed and tried to get still closer to the man in the wheel chair. "I like fairies, don't yer?"

"Indeed, I do," he answered heartily.

"Skinny and Chuck, they said yer tol' *them* stories, too."

The Interpreter laughed quietly. "I expect perhaps I did."

"I don't suppose yer know any fairy stories right now, do yer?"

"Let me see," said the Interpreter, seeming to think very hard. "Why, yes, I believe I do know one. It starts out like this: Once upon a time there was a most beautiful princess, just like your princess lady, who lived in a most wonderful palace. Isn't that the way for a fairy story to begin?"

"Uh-huh, that's the way. An' then what happened?"

With a great show of indifference the boy drew near and stretched himself on the floor on the other side of the old basket maker's chair.

"Well, this beautiful princess in the story, perhaps because she was so beautiful herself, loved more than anything else in all the world to have lots and lots of jewels. You know what jewels are, don't you?"

18

"Uh-huh, the princess lady she has 'em—heaps of 'em. I seen her onct close, when she was a-gettin' into her autermobile, in front of one of them big stores."

"Well," continued the story-teller, "it was strange, but with all her diamonds and pearls and rubies and things there was *one* jewel that the princess did *not* have. And, of course, she wanted that one particular gem more than all the others. That is the way it almost always is, you know."

"Huh," grunted Bobby.

"What was that there jewel she wanted?" asked Maggie.

"It was called the jewel of happiness," answered the Interpreter, "because whoever possessed it was sure to be always as happy as happy could be. And so, you see, because she did not have that particular jewel the princess did not have as good times as such a beautiful princess, living in such a wonderful palace, with so many lovely things, really ought to have.

"But because this princess' heart was kind, a fairy appeared to her one night, and told her that if she would go down to the shore of the great sea that was not far from the castle, and look carefully among the rocks and in the sand and dirt, she would find the jewel of happiness. Then the fairy disappeared—poof! just like that."

Little Maggie squirmed with thrills of delight. "Some story, I'd say. An' then what happened?"

"Why, of course, the very next day the princess went to walk on the seashore, just as the fairy had told her. And, sure enough, among the rocks and in the sand and dirt, she found hundreds and hundreds of bright, shiny jewels. And she picked them up, and picked them up, and picked them up, until she just couldn't carry another one. Then she began to throw away the smaller ones that she had picked up at first, and to hunt for larger ones to take instead. And then, all at once, right there beside her, was a poor, ragged and crooked old woman, and the old woman was picking up the ugly, dirt-colored pebbles that the princess would not touch.

"'What are you doing, mother?' asked the beautiful princess, whose heart was kind.

"And the crooked old woman answered, 'I am gathering jewels of happiness on the shore of the sea of life.'

"'But those ugly, dirty pebbles are not jewels, mother,' said the lady. 'See, these are the jewels of happiness.' And she showed the poor, ignorant old woman the bright, shiny stones that she had gathered.

"And the crooked old crone looked at the princess and laughed—a curious, creepy, crawly, crooked laugh.

19

"Then the old woman offered to the princess one of the ugly, dirt-colored pebbles that she had gathered. 'Take this, my dear,' she croaked, 'and wear it, and you shall see that I am right—that this is the jewel of happiness.'

"Now the beautiful princess did not want to wear that ugly, dirt-colored stone—no princess would, you know. But, nevertheless, because her heart was kind and she saw that the poor, crooked old woman would feel very bad if her gift was not accepted, she took the dull, common pebble and put it with the bright, shiny jewels that she had gathered.

"And that very night the fairy appeared to the princess again.

"'Did you do as I told you?' the fairy asked. 'Did you look for the jewel of happiness on the shore of the sea of life?'

"'Oh, yes,' cried the princess. 'And see what a world of lovely ones I found!'

"The fairy looked at all the pretty, shiny stones that the princess had gathered. 'And what is this?' the fairy asked, pointing to the ugly, dirt-colored pebble.

"'Oh, that,' replied the princess, hanging her head in embarrassment,—'that is nothing but a worthless pebble. A poor old woman gave it to me to wear because she thinks it is beautiful.'

"'But you will not wear the ugly thing, will you?' asked the fairy. 'Think how every one would point at you, and laugh, and call you strange and foolish.'

"'I know,' answered the princess, sadly, 'but I must wear it because I promised, and because if I did not and the poor old lady should see me without it, she would be so very, very unhappy.'

"And, would you believe it, no sooner had the beautiful princess said those words than the fairy disappeared—poof! just like that! And right there, on the identical spot where she had been, was that old ragged and crooked woman.

"'Oh!' cried the princess.

"And the old woman laughed her curious, creepy, crawly, crooked laugh. 'Don't be afraid, my dear,' she said, 'you shall have your jewel of happiness. But look!' She pointed a long, skinny, crooked finger at the shiny jewels on the table and there, right before the princess' eyes, they were all at once nothing but lumps of worthless dirt.

"'Oh!' screamed the princess again. 'All my lovely jewels of happiness!'

"'But look,' said the old woman again, and once more pointed with her skinny finger. And would you believe it, the princess saw that ugly, dirt-colored pebble turn into the most wonderfully splendid jewel that ever was—the true jewel of happiness.

"And so," concluded the Interpreter, "the beautiful princess whose heart was kind lived happy ever after."

Little Maggie clapped her thin hands with delight.

"Gee," said Bobby, "wish I knowed where that there place was. I'd get me enough of them there jewel things to swap for a autermobile an' a—an' a flyin' machine."

"If you keep your eyes open, Bobby," answered the old basket maker, "you will find the place all right. Only," he added, looking away toward the big house on the hill, "you must be very careful not to make the mistake that the princess lady is making— I mean," he corrected himself with a smile, "you must be careful not to pick up only the bright and shiny pebbles as the princess in the story did."

"Huh—I guess I'd know better'n that," retorted the boy. "Come on, Mag, we gotter go."

"You will come to see me again, won't you?" asked the Interpreter, as the children stood on the threshold. "You have legs, you know, that can easily bring you."

"Yer bet we'll come," said Bobby, "won't we, Mag?"

The little girl, looking back at the man in the wheel chair, smiled.

* * * * *

For some time after the children had gone the Interpreter sat very still. His dark eyes were fixed upon the Mill with its tall, grim stacks and the columns of smoke that twisted upward to form that overshadowing cloud. The voices of the children, as they started down the stairway to the dusty road and to their wretched home in the Flats, came to him muffled and indistinct from under the cliff.

Perhaps the man in the wheel chair was thinking of the days when Maggie's princess lady was a little girl and lived in the old house next door to Mary and Charlie Martin. Perhaps his mind still dwelt on the fairy story and the princess who found her jewel of happiness. It may have been that he was listening to the droning, moaning voice of the Mill, as one listens to the distant roar of the surf on a dangerous coast.

With a weary movement he took the unfinished basket from the table and began to work. But it was not his basket making that caused the weariness of the Interpreter—it was not his work that put the light of sorrow in his dark eyes.

* * * * *

As Bobby and Maggie went leisurely down the zigzag steps, proud of the tremendous success of their adventure, the boy paused several times to execute an inspirational "stunt" that would in some degree express his triumphant emotions.

"Gee!" he exulted. "Wait 'til I see Skinny and Chuck an' the rest of the gang! Gee, won't I tell 'em! Just yer wait. I'll knock 'em dead. Gee!"

On the bottom step they deliberately seated themselves as if they had suddenly found the duty of leaving the charmed vicinity of that hut on the cliff above impossible.

Suddenly, from around the curve in the road followed by a whirling cloud of dust, came an automobile. It was a big car, very imposing with its shiny black body, its gleaming metal, and its liveried chauffeur.

The children gazed in open-mouthed wonder. The car drew nearer, and they saw, behind the dignified personality at the wheel, a lady who might well have been the beautiful princess of the Interpreter's fairy tale.

Little Maggie caught her brother's arm. "Bobby! It's—it's *her*—it's the princess lady herself."

"Gee!" gasped the boy. "She's a slowin' down—what d'yer—"

The automobile stopped not thirty feet from where the children sat on the lower step of the old stairway. Springing to the ground, the chauffeur, with the dignity of a prime minister, opened the door.

But the princess lady sat motionless in her car. With an expression of questioning disapproval she looked at the Interpreter's friends on that lower step of the Interpreter's stairway.

CHAPTER II

LITTLE MAGGIE'S PRINCESS LADY

By nine out of ten of the Millsburgh people, the Interpreter would be described as a strange character. But the judge once said to the cigar-store philosopher, when that worthy had so spoken of the old basket maker, "Sir, the Interpreter is more than a character; he is a conviction, a conscience, an institution."

It was about the time when the patents on the new process were issued that the Interpreter—or Wallace Gordon, as he was then known—appeared from no one knows where, and went to work in the Mill. Because of the stranger's distinguished appearance, his evident culture, and his slightly foreign air, there were many who sought curiously to learn his history. But Wallace Gordon's history remained as it, indeed, remains still, an unopened book. Within a few months his ability to speak several of the various languages spoken by the immigrants who were drawn to the manufacturing city caused his fellow workers to call him the Interpreter.

Working at the same bench in the Mill with Adam Ward and Peter Martin, the Interpreter naturally saw much of the two families that, in those days, lived such close neighbors. Sober, hard working, modest in his needs, he acquired, during his first year in the Mill, that little plot of ground on the edge of the cliff, and built the tiny hut with its zigzag stairway. But often on a Sunday or a holiday, or for an hour of the long evenings after work, this man who was so alone in the world would seek companionship in the homes of his two workmen friends. The four children, who were so much together that their mothers used to say laughingly they could scarcely tell which were Wards and which were Martins, claimed the Interpreter as their own. With his never-failing fund of stories, his ultimate acquaintance with the fairies, his ready understanding of their childish interests, and his joyous comradeship in their sports, he won his own peculiar place in their hearts.

It was during the second year of his residence in Millsburgh that he adopted the deaf and dumb orphan boy, Billy Rand.

That such a workman should become a leader among his fellow workers was inevitable. More and more his advice and counsel were sought by those who toiled under the black cloud that rolled up in ever-increasing volumes from the roaring furnaces.

The accident which so nearly cost him his life occurred soon after the new process had taken Adam from his bench to a desk in the office of the Mill. Helen and John were away at school. At the hospital they asked him about his people. He smiled grimly and shook his head. When the surgeons were finally through with him, and it was known that he would live but could never stand on his feet again, he was still silent as to his family and his life before he came to the Mill. So they carried him around by the road on the hillside to his little hut on the top of the cliff where, with

Billy Rand to help him, he made baskets and lived with his books, which he purchased as he could from time to time during the more profitable periods of his industry.

As the years passed and the Mill, under Adam Ward's hand, grew in importance, Millsburgh experienced the usual trials of such industrial centers. Periodic labor wars alternated with times of industrial peace. Months of prosperity were followed by months of "hard times," and want was in turn succeeded by plenty. When the community was at work the more intelligent and thrifty among those who toiled with their hands and the more conservative of those who labored in business were able to put by in store enough to tide them over the next period of idleness and consequent business depression.

From his hut on the cliff the Interpreter watched it all with never-failing interest and sympathy. Indeed, although he never left his work of basket making, the Interpreter was a part of it all. For more and more the workers from the Mill, the shops and the factories, and the workers from the offices and stores came to counsel with this white-haired man in the wheel chair.

The school years of John and Helen, the new home on the hill, and all the changes brought by Adam Ward's material prosperity separated the two families that had once been so intimate. But, in spite of the wall that the Mill owner had built between himself and his old workmen comrades, the children of Adam Ward and the children of Peter Martin still held the Interpreter in their hearts. To the man condemned to his wheel chair and his basket making, little Maggie's princess lady was still the Helen of the old house.

Sam Whaley's children sitting on the lower step of the zigzag stairway that afternoon had no thought for the Interpreter's Helen of the old house. Bobby's rapt attention was held by that imposing figure in uniform. Work in the Mill when he became a man! Not much! Not as long as there were automobiles like that to drive and clothes like those to wear while driving them! Little Maggie's pathetically serious eyes saw only the beautiful princess of the Interpreter's story—the princess who lived in a wonderful palace and who because her heart was so kind was told by the fairy how to find the jewel of happiness. Only this princess lady did not look as though she had found her jewel of happiness yet. But she would find it—the fairies would be sure to help her because her heart was kind. How could any princess lady—so beautiful, with such lovely clothes, and such a grand automobile, and such a wonderful servant—how could any princess lady like that help having a kind heart!

"Tom, send those dirty, impossible children away!"

The man touched his cap and turned to obey.

Poor little Maggie could not believe. It was not what the lady said; it was the tone of her voice, the expression of her face, that hurt so. The princess lady must be very unhappy, indeed, to look and speak like that. And the tiny wisp of humanity, with

24

her thin, stooping shoulders and her tired little face—dirty, half clothed and poorly fed—felt very sorry because the beautiful lady in the automobile was not happy.

But Bobby's emotions were of quite a different sort. Sam Whaley would have been proud of his son had he seen the boy at that moment. Springing to his feet, the lad snarled with all the menacing hate he could muster, "Drive us away, will yer! I'd just like to see yer try it on. These here are the Interpreter's steps. If the Interpreter lets us come to see him, an' gives us cookies, an' tells us stories, I guess we've got a right to set on his steps if we want to."

"Go on wid ye—git out o' here," said the man in livery. But Bobby's sharp eyes saw what the lady in the automobile could not see—a faint smile accompanied the chauffeur's attempt to obey his orders.

"Go on yerself," retorted the urchin, defiantly, "I'll go when I git good an' ready. Ain't no darned rich folks what thinks they's so grand—with all their autermobiles, an' swell drivers, 'n' things—can tell *me* what to do. I know her—she's old Adam Ward's daughter, she is. An' she lives by grindin' the life out of us poor workin' folks, that's what she does; 'cause my dad and Jake Vodell they say so. Yer touch me an' yer'll see what'll happen to yer, when I tell Jake Vodell."

Unseen by his mistress, the smile on the servant's face grew more pronounced; and the small defender of the rights of the poor saw one of the man's blue Irish eyes close slowly in a deliberate wink of good fellowship. In a voice too low to be heard distinctly in the automobile behind him, he said, "Yer all right, kid, but fer the love o' God beat it before I have to lay hands on ye." Then, louder, he added gruffly, "Get along wid ye or do ye want me to help ye?"

Bobby retreated in good order to a position of safety a little way down the road where his sister was waiting for him.

With decorous gravity the imposing chauffeur went back to his place at the door of the automobile.

"Gee!" exclaimed Bobby. "What do yer know about that! Old Adam Ward's swell daughter a-goin' up to see the Interpreter. Gee!"

On the lower step of the zigzag stairway, with her hand on the railing, the young woman paused suddenly and turned about. To the watching children she must have looked very much indeed like the beautiful princess of the Interpreter's fairy tale.

"Tom—" She hesitated and looked doubtfully toward the children.

"Yes, Miss."

"What was it that boy said about his rights?"

"He said, Miss, as how they had just been to visit the Interpreter an' the old man give 'em cookies, and so they thought they was privileged to sit on his steps."

A puzzled frown marred the really unusual loveliness of her face. "But that was not all he said, Tom."

"No, Miss."

She looked upward to the top of the cliff where one corner of the Interpreter's hut was just visible above the edge of the rock. And then, as the quick light of a smile drove away the trouble shadows, she said to the servant, "Tom, you will take those children for a ride in the car. Take them wherever they wish to go, and return here for me. I shall be ready in about an hour."

The man gasped. "But, Miss, beggin' yer pardon,—the car—think av the upholsterin'—an' the dirt av thim little divils—beggin' yer pardon, but 'tis ruined the car will be—an' yer gowns! Please, Miss, I'll give them a dollar an' 'twill do just as well—think av the car!"

"Never mind the car, Tom, do as I say, please."

In spite of his training, a pleased smile stole over the Irish face of the chauffeur; and there was a note of ungrudging loyalty and honest affection in his voice as he said, touching his cap, "Yes, Miss, I will have the car here in an hour—thank ye, Miss."

A moment later the young woman saw her car stop beside the wondering children. With all his high-salaried dignity the chauffeur left the wheel and opened the door as if for royalty itself.

The children stood as if petrified with wonder, although the boy was still a trifle belligerent and suspicious.

In his best manner the chauffeur announced, "Miss Ward's compliments, Sir and Miss, an' she has ordered me to place her automobile at yer disposal if ye would be so minded as to go for a bit of a pleasure ride."

"Oh!" gulped little Maggie.

"Aw, what are yer givin' us!" said Bobby.

The man's voice changed, but his manner was unaltered. "'Tis the truth I'm a-tellin' ye, kids, wid the lady herself back there a-watchin' to see that I carry out her orders. So hop in, quick, and don't keep her a-waitin'."

"Gee!" exclaimed the boy.

26

Maggie looked at her brother doubtfully. "Dast we, Bobby? Dast we?"

"Dast we!—Huh! Who's afraid? I'll say we dast."

Another second and they were in the car. The chauffeur gravely touched his cap. "An' where will I be drivin' ye, Sir?"

"Huh?"

"Where is it ye would like for to go?"

The two children looked at each other questioningly. Then a grin of wild delight spread itself over the countenance of the boy and he fairly exploded with triumphant glee, "Gee! Mag, now's our chance." To the man he said, eagerly, "Just you take us all 'round the Flats, mister, so's folks can see. An'—an', mind yer, toot that old horn good an' loud, so as everybody'll know we're a-comin'." As the automobile moved away he beamed with proud satisfaction. "Some swells we are—heh? Skinny an' Chuck an' the gang'll be plumb crazy when they see us. Some class, I'll tell the world."

"Well, why not?" demanded the cigar-stand philosopher, when Tom described that triumphant drive of Sam Whaley's children through the Flats. "Them kids was only doin' what we're all a-tryin' to do in one way or another."

The lawyer, who had stopped for a light, laughed. "I heard the Interpreter say once that 'to live on some sort of an elevation was to most people one of the prime necessities of life.'"

"Sure," agreed the philosopher, reaching for another box for the real-estate agent, "I'll bet old Adam Ward himself is just as human as the rest of us if you could only catch him at it."

For some time after her car, with Bobby and Maggie, had disappeared in its cloud of dust, among the wretched buildings of the Flats, Helen stood there, on the lower step of the zigzag stairway, looking after them. She was thinking, or perhaps she was wondering a little at herself. She might even have been living again for the moment those old-house days when, with her brother and Mary and Charlie Martin, she had played there on these same steps.

Those old-house days had been joyous and carefree. Her school years, too, had been filled with delightful and satisfying activities. After her graduation she had been content with the gayeties and triumphs of the life to which she had been arbitrarily removed by her father and the new process, and for which she had been educated. She had felt the need of nothing more. Then came the war, and, in her brother's enlistment and in her work with the various departments of the women forces at home, she had felt herself a part of the great world movement. But now when the victorious soldiers—brothers and sweethearts and husbands and friends—had returned, and the days of excited rejoicing were past, life had suddenly presented to her a different front. It would have been hard to find in all Millsburgh, not excepting the most wretched home in the Flats, a more unhappy and discontented person than this young woman who was so unanimously held to have everything in the world that any one could possibly desire.

Slowly she turned to climb the zigzag stairway to the Interpreter's hut.

CHAPTER III

THE INTERPRETER

The young woman announced her presence at the open door of the hut by calling, "Are you there?"

The deep voice of the Interpreter answered, "Helen! Here I am, child—on the porch. Come!" As she passed swiftly through the house and appeared in the porch doorway, he added, "This is a happy surprise, indeed. I thought you were not expected home for another month. It seems ages since you went away."

She tried bravely to smile in response to the gladness in her old friend's greeting. "I had planned to stay another month," she said, "but I—" She paused as if for some reason she found it hard to explain why she had returned to Millsburgh so long before the end of the summer season. Then she continued slowly, as if remembering that she must guard her words, "Brother wrote me that they were expecting serious labor troubles, and with father as he is—" Her voice broke and she finished lamely, "Mother is *so* worried and unhappy. I—I felt that I really ought not to be away."

She turned quickly and went to stand at the porch railing, where she watched the cloud of dust that marked the progress of Bobby and Maggie through the Flats.

"I can't understand father's condition at all," she said, presently, without looking at the Interpreter. "He is so—so—" Again she paused as if she could not find courage to speak the thought that so disturbed her mind.

From his wheel chair the Interpreter silently watched the young woman who was so envied by the people. And because the white-haired old basket maker knew many things that were hidden from the multitude, his eyes were as the eyes of the Master when He looked upon the rich young ruler whom He loved.

Then, as if returning to a thought that had been interrupted by the unwelcome intrusion of a forbidden subject, Helen said, "I can't understand how you tolerate such dirty, rude and vicious little animals as those two children."

The Interpreter smiled understandingly at the back of her very becoming and very correctly fashioned hat. "You met my little friends, did you?"

"I did," she answered, with decided emphasis, "at the foot of your stairs, and I was forced to listen to the young ruffian's very frank opinion of me and of all that he is taught to believe I represent. I wonder *you* did not hear. But I suppose you can guess what he would say."

"Yes," said the man in the wheel chair, gently, "I can guess Bobby's opinion of you, quite as accurately as Bobby guesses your opinion of him."

At that she turned on him with a short laugh that was rather more bitter than mirthful. "Well, the little villain is guessing another guess just now. I sent Tom to take them for a ride in the car."

"And why did you do that?"

She waited a little before she answered. "I don't know exactly. Perhaps it was your Helen of the old house that did it. She may have been a little ashamed of me and wanted to make it up to them. I am afraid I really wasn't very kind at first."

"I see," said the Interpreter, gravely.

"There might possibly have been the shade of another reason," she continued, after a moment, and there was a hint of bitterness in her voice now.

"Yes?"

"Yes, it is conceivable, perhaps, that, in spite of the prevailing opinions of such people, even *I* might have felt a wee bit sorry for the poor kiddies—especially for the girl. She is such a tiny, tired-looking mite."

The old basket maker was smiling now, as he said, "I have known for a long time that there were *two* Helens. Little Maggie, it seems, has found still another."

"How interesting!"

"Yes, Maggie has discovered, somehow, that you are really a beautiful princess, living on most intimate terms with the fairies. She will think so more than ever now."

The young woman laughed at this. "And the boy—what do you suppose *he* will think after his ride with Tom in the limousine?"

The Interpreter shook his head doubtfully. "Bobby will probably reserve his judgment for a while, on the possible chance of another ride in your car."

"Tell me about them," said Helen.

"Are you really interested?"

She flushed a little as she answered, "I am at least curious."

30

"Why?"

"Perhaps because of your interest in them," she retorted. "Who are they?"

The Interpreter did not answer for a moment; then, with his dark eyes fixed on the heavy cloud of smoke that hung above the Mill and overshadowed the Flats, he said, slowly, "They are Sam Whaley's children. Their father works—when he works—in your father's Mill. I knew both Sam and his wife before they were married. She was a bright girl, with fine instincts for the best things of life and a capacity for great happiness. Sam was a good worker in those days, and their marriage promised well. Then he became interested in the wrong sort of what is called socialism, and began to associate with a certain element that does not value homes and children very highly. The man is honest, and fairly capable, up to a certain point; but there never was much capacity there for clear thinking. He is one of those who always follow the leader who yells the loudest and he mistakes vituperation for argument. He is strong on loyalty to class, but is not so particular as he might be when it comes to choosing his class. And so, for several years now, in every little difference between the workmen and the management, Sam has been too ready to quit his job and let his wife and children go hungry for the good of the cause, while he vociferates loudly against the cruelty of all who refuse to offer their families as sacrifice on the altar of his particular and impracticable ideas."

"And his wife—the mother of his children—the girl with fine instincts for the best things and a capacity for great happiness—what of her?" demanded Helen.

The Interpreter pointed toward the Flats. "She lives down there," he said, sadly. "You have seen her children."

The young woman turned again to the porch railing and looked down on the wretched dwellings of the Flats below.

"It is strange," she said, presently, as if speaking to herself, "but that poor woman makes me think of mother. Mother is like that, isn't she? I mean," she added, quickly, "in her instincts and in her capacity for happiness."

"Yes," agreed the Interpreter, "your mother is like that."

She faced him once more, to say thoughtfully, but with decisive warmth, "It is a shame the way such children—I mean the children of such people as this man Whaley—are being educated in lawlessness. Those youngsters are nothing less than juvenile anarchists. They will grow up a menace to our government, to society, to our homes, and to everything that is decent and right. They are taught to hate work. And they fairly revel in their hatred of every one and every thing that is not of their own miserable class."

There was a note of gentle authority in the Interpreter's deep voice, and in his dark eyes there was a look of patient sorrow, as he replied, "Yes, Helen, all that you say of our Bobbies and Maggies is true. But have you ever considered whether it might not be equally true of the children of wealth?"

"Is the possession of what we call wealth a crime?" the young woman asked, bitterly. "Is poverty *always* such a virtue?"

The Interpreter answered, "I mean, child, that wealth which comes unearned from the industries of life—that wealth for which no service is rendered—for which no equivalent in human strength, mental or physical, is returned. Are not the children of such conditions being educated in lawlessness when the influence of their money so often permits them to break our laws with impunity? Are they not a menace to our government when they coerce and bribe our public servants to enact laws and enforce measures that are for the advantage of a few favored ones and against the welfare of our people as a whole? Are they not a menace to society when they would limit the meaning of the very word to their own select circles and cliques? Are they not a menace to our homes by the standards of morals that too often govern their daily living? For that hatred of class taught the Bobbies and Maggies of the Flats, Helen, these other children are taught an intolerance and contempt for everything that is not of their class—an intolerance and contempt that breed class hatred as surely as blow flies breed maggots."

For some time the silence was broken only by the dull, droning voice of the Mill. They listened as they would have listened to the first low moaning of the wind that might rise later into a destructive storm.

The Interpreter spoke again. "Helen, this nation cannot tolerate one standard of citizenship for one class and a totally different standard for another. Whatever is right for the children of the hill, yonder, is right for the children of the Flats, down there."

Helen asked, abruptly, "Is there any truth in all this talk about coming trouble with the labor unions?"

The man in the wheel chair did not answer immediately. Then he replied, gravely, with another question, "And who is it that says there is going to be trouble again, Helen?"

"John says everybody is expecting it. And Mr. McIver is so sure that he is already preparing for it at his factory. *He* says it will be the worst industrial war that Millsburgh has ever experienced—that it must be a fight to the finish this time—that nothing but starvation will bring the working classes to their senses."

"Yes," agreed the Interpreter, thoughtfully, "McIver would say just that. And many of our labor agitators would declare, in exactly the same spirit, that nothing but the final and absolute downfall of the employer class can ever end the struggle. I wonder what little Bobby and Maggie Whaley and their mother would say if they could have their way about it, Helen?"

Helen Ward's face flushed as she said in a low, deliberate voice, "Father agrees with Mr. McIver—you know how bitter he is against the unions?"

"Yes, I know."

"But John says that Mr. McIver, with his talk of force and of starving helpless women and children, is as bad as this man Jake Vodell who has come to Millsburgh to organize a strike. It is really brother's attitude toward the workmen and their unions and his disagreement with Mr. McIver's views that make father as—as he is."

The Interpreter's voice was gentle as he asked, "Your father is not worse, is he, Helen? I have heard nothing."

"Oh, no," she returned, quickly. "That is—"

She hesitated, then continued, with careful exactness, "For a time he even seemed much better. When I went away he was really almost like his old self. But this labor situation and John's not seeing things exactly as he does worries him. The doctors all agree, you know, that father must give up everything in the nature of business and have absolute mental rest; but he insists that in the face of this expected trouble with the workmen he dares not trust the management of the Mill wholly to John, because of what he calls brother's wild and impracticable ideas. Everybody knows how father has given his life to building up the Mill. And now, he—he—It is terrible the way he is about things. Poor mother is almost beside herself." The young woman's eyes filled and her lips trembled.

The man in the wheel chair turned to the unfinished basket on the table beside him and handled his work aimlessly, as if in sorrow that he had no word of comfort for her.

When Adam Ward's daughter spoke again there was a curious note of defiance in her voice, but her eyes, when the Interpreter turned to look at her, were fixed upon her old friend with an expression of painful anxiety and fear. "Of course his condition is all due to his years of hard work and to the mental and nervous strain of his business. It—it couldn't be anything else, could it?"

The Interpreter, who seemed to be watching the intricate and constantly changing forms that the columns of smoke from the tall stacks were shaping, apparently did not hear.

"Don't—don't you think it is all because of his worry over the Mill?"

"Yes, Helen," the Interpreter answered, at last, "I am sure your father's trouble all comes from the Mill."

For a while she did not speak, but sat looking wistfully toward the clump of trees that shaded her birthplace and the white cottage where Peter Martin lived with Charlie and Mary.

Then she said, musingly, "How happy we all were in the old house, when father worked in the Mill with you and Uncle Pete, and you used to come for Sunday dinner with us. Do you know, sometimes"—she hesitated as if making a confession of which she was a little ashamed—"sometimes—that is, since brother came home from France, I—I almost hate it. I think I feel just as mother does, only neither of us dares admit it—scarcely even to ourselves."

"You almost hate what, Helen?"

"Oh, everything—the way we live, the people we know, the stupid things I am expected to do. It all seems so useless—so futile—so—so—such a waste of time."

The Interpreter was studying her with kindly interest.

"I never felt this way before brother went away. And during the war everybody was so much excited and interested, helping in every way he or she could. But now—now that it is over and John is safely home again, I can't seem to get back into the old ways at all. Life seems to have flattened out into a dull, monotonous round of nothing that really matters."

The Interpreter spoke, thoughtfully, "Many people, I find, feel that way these days, Helen."

"As for brother," she continued, "he is so changed that I simply can't understand him at all. He is like a different man—just grinds away in that dirty old Mill day after day, as if he were nothing more than a common laborer who had to work or starve. In fact," she finished with an air of triumph, "that is exactly what he says he is—simply a laborer like—like Charlie Martin and the rest of them."

The Interpreter smiled.

"It was all very well for John and Charlie Martin to be buddies, as they call it, during the war," she went on. "It was different over there in France. But now that it is all over and they are home again, and Captain Martin has gone back to his old work in the Mill where John has practically become the manager, there is no sense in brother's keeping up the intimacy. Really I don't wonder that father is worried almost to death over it all. I suppose the next thing John will be chumming with this Jake Vodell himself."

34

"I don't suppose you see much of your old friends the Martins these days, do you, Helen?" said the old basket maker, reflectively.

She retorted quickly with an air, "Certainly not."

"But I remember, in the old-house days, before you went away to school, you and Charlie Martin were—"

She interrupted him with "I was a silly child. I suppose every girl at about that age has to have her foolish little romance."

And the Interpreter saw that her cheeks were crimson.

"A young girl's first love is not in the least silly or foolish, my dear," he said.

She made an effort to speak lightly. "Well, fortunately, mine did not last long."

"I know," he returned, "but I thought perhaps because of the friendship between John and the Captain—"

"I could scarcely see much of one of the common workmen in my father's mill, could I?" she asked, warmly. "I must admit, though," she added, with an odd note in her voice, "that I admire his good sense in never accepting John's invitations to the house."

And then, suddenly, to the consternation of her companion, her eyes filled with tears.

The Interpreter looked away toward the beautiful country beyond the squalid Plats, the busy city, the smoke-clouded Mill.

There was a sound of some one knocking at the front door of the hut. Through the living room Helen saw her chauffeur.

"Yes, Tom," she called, "I am coming."

To the Interpreter she said, hurriedly, "I have really stayed longer than I should. I promised mother that I would be home early. She is so worried about father, I do not like to leave her, but I felt that I must see you. I—I haven't said at all the things I—-wanted to say. Father—" She looked at the man in the wheel chair appealingly, as she hesitated again with the manner of one who feels compelled to speak, yet fears to betray a secret. "You feel sure, don't you, that father's condition is nothing more than the natural result of his nervous breakdown and his worry over business?"

The Interpreter thought how like the look in her eyes was to the look in the eyes of timid little Maggie. And again he waited, before answering, "Yes, Helen, I am sure that your father's trouble is all caused by the Mill. Is there anything that I can do, child?"

"There is nothing that any one can do, I fear," she returned, with a little gesture of hopelessness. Then, avoiding the grave, kindly eyes of the old basket maker, she forced herself to say, in a tone that was little more than a whisper, "I sometimes think—at tines I am almost compelled to believe that there *is* something more—something that we—that no one knows about." With sudden desperate earnestness she went on with nervous haste as if she feared her momentary courage would fail. "I can't explain—but it is as if he were hiding something and dreaded every moment that it would be discovered. He is so—so afraid. Can it be possible that there is something that we do not know—some hidden thing?" And then, before the Interpreter could speak, she exclaimed, with a forced laugh of embarrassment, "How silly of me to talk like this—you will think that I am going insane."

When he was alone, the Interpreter turned again to his basket making. "Yes, Billy," he said aloud as his deaf and dumb companion appeared in the doorway a few minutes later, "yes, Billy, she will find her jewel of happiness. But it will not be easy, Billy—it will not be easy."

To which, of course, Billy made no reply. And that—the Interpreter always maintained—was one of the traits that made his companion such a delightful conversationalist. He invariably found your pet arguments and theories unanswerable, and accepted your every assertion without question.

Helen Ward could not feel that her father's condition—much as it alarmed and distressed her—was, in itself, the reason of her own unrest and discontent. She felt, rather, in a vague, instinctive way, that the source of her parent's trouble was somehow identical with the cause of her own unhappiness. But what was it that caused her father's affliction and her own dissatisfied and restless mental state? The young woman questioned herself in vain.

Pausing at one of the turns in the stairway, she stood for some time looking at the life that lay before her, as though wondering if the answer to her questions might not be found somewhere in that familiar scene.

But the Mill, with its smoking stacks and the steady song of its industry, had no meaning for her. The dingy, dust-veiled Flats spoke a language that she was not schooled to understand. The farms of the valley beyond the river, so beautiful in their productiveness, were as meaningless to her as the life on some unknown planet. To her the busy city with its varied interests was without significance. The many homes on the hillside held, for her, nothing. And yet as she looked she was possessed of a curious feeling that everything in that world before her eyes was occupied with some definite purpose—was living to some fixed end—was a part of life—belonged to life. Below her, on the road at the foot of the cliffs, an old negro with an ancient skeleton of a horse and a shaky wreck of a wagon was making slow progress toward the Flats. To Helen, even this poor creature was going

36

somewhere—to some definite place—on some definite mission. She felt strangely alone.

In those years of the war Adam Ward's daughter, like many thousands of her class, had been inevitably forced into a closer touch with life than she had ever known before. She had felt, as never before, the great oneness of humanity. She had sensed a little the thrilling power of a great human purpose. Now it was as though life ignored her, passed her by. She felt left out, overlooked, forgotten.

Slowly she went on down the zigzag stairway to her waiting automobile.

As she entered her car, the chauffeur looked at her curiously. When she gave him no instructions, he asked, quietly, "Home, Miss?"

She started. "Yes, Tom."

The man was in his place at the wheel when she added, "Did those children enjoy their ride, Tom?"

"That they did, Miss—it was the treat of their lives."

Little Maggie's princess lady smiled wistfully—almost as Maggie herself might have smiled.

As the car was moving slowly away from the foot of the old stairway, she spoke again. "Tom!"

"Yes, Miss."

"You may drive around by the old house, please."

CHAPTER IV

PETER MARTIN AT HOME

Peter Martin, with his children, Charlie and Mary, lived in the oldest part of Millsburgh, where the quiet streets are arched with great trees and the modest houses, if they seem to lack in modern smartness, more than make good the loss by their air of homelike comfort. The Martin cottage was built in the days before the success of Adam Ward and his new process had brought to Millsburgh the two extremes of the Flats and the hillside estates. The little home was equally removed from the wretched dwellings of Sam Whaley and his neighbors, on the one hand, and from the imposing residences of Adam Ward and his circle, on the other.

The house—painted white, with old-fashioned green shutters—is only a story and a half, with a low wing on the east, and a bit of porch in front, with wooden seats on either side the door. The porch step is a large uncut stone that nature shaped to the purpose, and the walk that connects the entrance with the front gate is of the same untooled flat rock. On the right of the walk, as one enters, a space of green lawn, a great tree, and rustic chairs invite one to rest in the shade; while on the left, the yard is filled with old-fashioned flowers, and a row of flowering shrubs and bushes extends the full width of the lot along the picket fence which parallels the board walk of the tree-bordered street. The fence, like the house, is painted white.

The other homes in the neighborhood are of the same modest, well kept type.

The only thing that marred the quiet domestic beauty of the scene at the time of this story was the place where Adam Ward had lived with his little family before material prosperity removed them to their estate on the hill. Joining the Martin home on the east, the old house, unpainted, with broken shutters, shattered windows, and sagging porch, in its setting of neglected, weed-grown yard and tumble-down fences, was pathetic in its contrast.

Since the death of her mother, Mary Martin had been the housekeeper for her father and her brother. She was a wholesome, clear-visioned girl, with an attractive face that glowed with the good color of health and happiness. And if at times, when the Ward automobile passed, there was a shadow of wistfulness in Mary's eyes, it did not mar for long the expression of her habitually contented and cheerful spirit. She worked at her household tasks with a song, entered into the pleasures of her friends and neighbors with hearty delight, and was known, as well, to many poverty-stricken homes in the Flats in times of need.

More than one young workman in the Mill had wanted Pete Martin's girl to help him realize his dreams of home building. But Mary had always answered "No."

Mary's brother Charlie was a strong-shouldered, athletic workman, with a fine, clean countenance and the bearing of his military experience.

38

At supper, that evening, the young woman remarked casually, "Helen Ward went by this afternoon. I was working in the roses. I thought for a moment she was going to stop—at the old house, I mean."

Captain Charlie's level gaze met his sister's look. "Did she see you?"

"She did and she didn't," replied Mary.

"Never mind, dear," returned the soldier workman, "it'll be all right."

Peter Martin—a gray-haired veteran with rather a stolid English face—looked up at his children questioningly. Presently he said, "It's a wonder Adam wouldn't fix up the old place a bit—for pride's sake if for nothing else. It's a disgrace to the neighborhood."

"I guess that's the reason he lets it go," said Captain Charlie, pushing his chair back from the table.

"What's the reason?" asked Peter.

"For his pride's sake. As it stands now, the old house advertises Adam's success. When people see it in ruins like that they always speak of the big new house on the hill. If the old house was fixed up and occupied it wouldn't cause any comment on Adam's prosperity, you see. John told me once that he had begged his father to let him do something with it, but Adam ordered him never to set foot on the place."

"Well," said Mary, "I suppose he can afford to keep the old house as a sort of monument if he wants to."

Peter Martin commented, in his slow way, "If Charlie is right about his reason for leaving it as it is, I am not so sure, daughter, that even Adam Ward can afford to do such a thing."

Captain Charlie's eyes twinkled as he addressed his sister. "Father evidently believes with the Interpreter that houses have souls or spirits or something—like human beings."

"Of course," she returned, "if the Interpreter believes it father is bound to."

The old workman smiled. "You children will believe it, too, some day; at least I hope so."

"I wonder if Helen ever goes to see the Interpreter," said Mary.

Captain Charlie returned, quickly, "I know she does."

"How do you know? Did you ever meet her there?"

The Captain answered grimly, "I hid out in the garden once with Billy Rand to keep from meeting her."

Flushed with the unparalleled adventures of the day, Bobby Whaley asked his father, "Dad, ain't the old Interpreter one of us?—ain't he?"

"Sure he is."

"Well, then, what for did old Adam Ward's daughter go to see him just like Mag an' me did?"

"I don't know nothin' about that," growled Sam Whaley, "but I can tell you kids one thing. You're a-goin' to stay out of that there automobile of hers. You let me catch you takin' up with such as Adam Ward's daughter and I'll teach you somethin' you won't fergit."

* * * * *

The cigar-store philosopher remarked casually to the chief of police, "This here savior of the people, Jake Vodell, that's recently descended upon us, is gatherin' to himself a choice bunch of disciples—I'll tell the world."

"What do you know about it?" demanded the officer of the law.

The philosopher grinned. "Oh, they most of them smoke or chew, the same as your cops. Vodell himself smokes your brand. Have one on me chief."

CHAPTER V

ADAM WARD'S ESTATE

In spite of that smile of mingled admiration, contempt and envy, with which the people always accompanied any mention of Adam Ward, Millsburgh took no little pride in the dominant Mill owner's achievements. In particular, was the Ward home, most pretentious of all the imposing estates on the hillside, an object of never-failing interest and conversational speculation. "Adam Ward's castle," the people called it, smiling. And no visiting stranger of any importance whatever could escape being driven past that glaring architectural monstrosity which stood so boldly on its most conspicuous hillside elevation and proclaimed so defiantly to all the world its owner's material prosperity.

But the sight-seers always viewed the "castle" and the "palatial grounds" (the Millsburgh *Clarion*, in a special Sunday article for which Adam paid, so described the place) through a strong, ornamental iron fence, with a more than ornamental gate guarded by massive stone columns. Only when the visiting strangers were of sufficient importance in the owner's eyes were they permitted to pass the conspicuous PRIVATE PROPERTY, NO ADMITTANCE sign at the entrance. As the cigar-stand philosopher explained, Adam Ward did not propose to give anything away.

The chief value of his possessions, in Adam's thoughts, lay in the fact that they were *his*. He always said, "*My* house—*my* grounds—*my* flowers—*my* trees—*my* fountain—*my* fence." He even extended his ownership and spoke of the very birds who dared to ignore the PRIVATE PROPERTY, No ADMITTANCE sign as *my* birds. So marked, indeed, was this characteristic habit of his speech, that no one in Millsburgh would have been surprised to hear him say, "*My* sun—*my* moonlight." And never did he so forget himself as to include his wife and children in such an expression as "our home." Why, indeed, should he? His wife and his children were as much *his* as any of the other items on the long list of the personal possessions which he had so industriously acquired.

In perfect harmony with the principles that ordered his life, the owner of the castle made great show of hospitality at times. But the recipients of his effusive welcome were invariably those from whom, or through whom, he had reason to think he might derive a definite material gain in return for his graciousness. The chief entertainment offered these occasional utilitarian guests was a verbal catalogue of the estate, with an itemized statement of the cost of everything mentioned. If the architecture of the house was noticed, Adam proudly disclaimed any knowledge of architecture, but named the architect's fee, and gave the building cost in detail, from the heating system to the window screens. If one chanced to betray an interest in a flower or shrub or tree, he boasted that he could not name a plant on the place, and told how many thousands he had paid the landscape architect, and what it cost him each year to maintain the lawns and gardens. If the visitor admired the fountain or the statuary he declared—quite unnecessarily—that he knew nothing of art, but had paid the various artists represented various definite dollars and cents. And never was there a guest of that house that poor Adam did not seek to discredit to his family and to other guests, lest by any chance any one should fail to recognize the host's superiority.

In his youth the Mill owner had received from his parents certain exaggerated religious convictions as to the desirability of gaining heaven and escaping, hell when one's years of material gains and losses should be forever past. Therefore, his spiritual life, also, was wholly a matter of personal bargain and profit. The church was an insurance corporation, of a sort, to which he paid his dues, as he paid the premiums on his policies in other less pretentious companies. As a matter of additional security—which cost nothing in the way of additional premiums—he never failed to say grace at the table.

This matter of grace, Adam found, was also a character asset of no little value when there were guests whom he, for good material reasons, wished to impress with the fine combination of business ability and sterling Christian virtue that so distinguished his simple and sincere nature. Profess yourself the disinterested friend of a man—make him believe that you value his friendship for its own sake and, on that ground, invite him to your home as your honored guest. And then, when he sits at your table, ask God to bless the food, the home, and the guest, and you have unquestionably maneuvered your friend into a position where he will contribute liberally to your business triumphs—if your contracts are cleverly drawn and you strike for the necessary signature while the glow of your generous hospitality is still warm.

And thus, with his patented process and his cleverly drawn contracts, this man had reaped from hospitality, religion and friendship the abundant gains that made him the object of his neighbors' admiration, contempt and envy.

But the end of Adam Ward's material harvest day was come. As Helen had told the Interpreter, the doctors were agreed that her father must give up everything in the nature of business and have absolute mental rest. The Mill owner must retire.

Retire! Retire to what?

The world of literature—of history and romance, of poetry and the lives of men—the world of art, with its magic of color and form—the world of music, with its power to rest the weary souls of men—the world of nature, that with its myriad interests lay about him on every side—the world of true friendships, with their inspiring sympathies and unselfish love—in these worlds there is no place for Adam Wards.

Retire! Retire to what?

* * * * *

One afternoon, a few days after her visit to the Interpreter, Helen sat with a book in a little vine-covered arbor, in a secluded part of the grounds, some distance from the house. She had been in the quiet retreat an hour, perhaps, when her attention was attracted by the sound of some one approaching. Through a tiny opening in the lattice and vine wall she saw her father.

Adam Ward apparently was on his way to the very spot his daughter had chosen, and the young woman smiled to herself as she pictured his finding her there. But a moment before the seemingly inevitable discovery, the man turned aside to a rustic seat in the shade of a great tree not far away.

Helen was about to reveal her presence by calling to him when something in her father's manner caused her to hesitate. Through the leafy screen of the arbor wall she saw him stop beside the bench and look carefully about on every side, as if to assure himself that he was alone. The young woman flushed guiltily, but, as if against her will, she remained silent. As she watched her father's face, a feeling of pity, fear and wonder held her breathless.

Helen had often seen her father suffering under an attack of nervous excitement. She had witnessed his spells of ungoverned rage that left him white and trembling with exhaustion. She had known his fears that he tried so hard to hide. She knew of his sleepless nights, of his dreams of horror, of his hours of lonely brooding. But never had she seen her father like this. It was as if Adam Ward, believing himself unobserved, let fall the mask that hid his secret self from even those who loved him most. Sinking down upon the bench, he groaned aloud, while his daughter, looking upon that huddled figure of abject misery and despair, knew that she was witnessing a mental anguish that could come only from some source deep hidden beneath the surface of her father's life. She could not move. As one under some strange spell, she was helpless.

The doctors had said—diplomatically—that Adam Ward's ill health was a nervous trouble, resulting from his lifelong devotion to his work, with no play spell or rest, and no relief through interest in other things. But Adam Ward knew the real reason for the medical men's insistent advice that he retire from the stress of the Mill to the quiet of his estate. He knew it from his wife's anxious care and untiring watchfulness. He knew it from the manner of his business associates when they asked how he felt. He knew when, at some trivial incident or word, he would be caught, helpless, in the grip of an ungovernable rage that would leave him exhausted for many weary, brooding hours. He felt it in the haunting, unconquerable fears that beset him—by the feeling of some dread presence watching him—by the convictions that unknown enemies were seeking his life—by his terrifying dreams of the hell of his inherited religion.

And the real reason for his condition Adam Ward knew. It was not the business to which he had driven himself so relentlessly. It was not that he had no other interests to take his mind from the Mill. It was a thing that he had fought, in secret, almost every hour of every year of his accumulating successes. It was a thing which his neighbors and associates and family felt in his presence but could not name—a thing which made him turn his eyes away from a frank, straightforward look and forbade him to look his fellows in the face save by an exertion of his will.

Through the vines, Helen saw her father stoop to pick from the ground a few twigs that had escaped the eyes of the caretakers. Deliberately he broke the twigs into tiny bits, and threw the pieces one by one aside. His gray face, drawn and haggard, twitched and worked with the nervous stress of his thoughts. From under his heavy brows he glanced with the quick, furtive look of a hunted thing, as though fearing some enemy that might be hidden in the near-by shrubbery. The young woman, shrinking from the look in his eyes, and not daring to make her presence known, remembered, suddenly, how the Interpreter had been reluctant to discuss her father's illness.

Casting aside the last tiny bit of the twig which he had broken so aimlessly, he found another and continued his senseless occupation.

With pity and love in her heart, Helen wanted to go to him—to help him, but she could not—some invisible presence seemed to forbid.

Suddenly Adam raised his head. A moment he listened, then cautiously he rose to his feet—listening, listening. It was no trick of his fancy this time. He could hear voices on the other side of a dense growth of shrubbery near the fence. Two people were talking. He could not distinguish the words but he could hear distinctly the low murmur of their voices.

Helen, too, heard the voices and looked in that direction. From her position in the arbor she could see the speakers. With the shadow of a quick smile, she turned her eyes again toward her father. He was looking about cautiously, as if to assure himself that he was alone. The shadow of a smile vanished from Helen's face as she watched in wondering fear.

Stooping low, Adam Ward crept swiftly to a clump of bushes near the spot from which the sound of the voices came. Crouching behind the shrubbery, he silently parted the branches and peered through. Bobby and Maggie Whaley stood on the outer side of the fence with their little faces thrust between the iron pickets, looking in.

Still in the glow of their wonderful experience at the Interpreter's hut and the magnificent climax of that day's adventure, the children had determined to go yet farther afield. It was true that their father had threatened dire results if they should continue the acquaintance begun at the foot of the Interpreter's zigzag stairway, but, sufficient unto the day.—They would visit the great castle on the hill where their beautiful princess lady lived. And, who could tell, perhaps they might see her once more. Perhaps—"But that," said tiny Maggie, "was too wonderful ever to happen again."

44

The way had been rather long for bare little feet. But excited hope had strengthened them. And so they had climbed the hill, and had come at last to the iron fence through which they could see the world of bright flowers and clean grass and shady trees, and, in the midst of it all, the big house. With their hungry little faces thrust between the strong iron pickets, Sam Whaley's children feasted their eyes on the beauties of Adam Ward's possessions. Even Bobby, in his rapture over the loveliness of the scene, forgot for the moment his desire to blow up the castle, with its owner and all.

Behind his clump of shrubbery, Adam Ward, crouching like some stealthy creature of the jungle, watched and listened.

From the shelter of the arbor, Adam Ward's daughter looked upon the scene with white-faced interest.

"Gee," said Bobby, "some place, I'd say!"

"Ain't it pretty?" murmured little Maggie. "Just like them places where the fairies live."

"Huh," returned the boy, "old Adam Ward, he ain't no fairy I'm a-tellin' yer."

To which Maggie, hurt by this suggested break in the spell of her enchantment, returned indignantly, "Well, I guess the fairies can live in all them there pretty flowers an' things just the same, if old Adam does own 'em. You can't shut fairies out with no big iron fences."

"That's so," admitted Bobby. "Gee, I wisht we was fairies, so's we could sneak in! Gee, wouldn't yer like ter take a roll on that there grass?"

"Huh," returned the little girl, "I know what I'd do if I was a fairy. I'd hide in that there bunch of flowers over there, an' I'd watch till the beautiful princess lady with the kind heart come along, an' I'd tell her where she could find them there jewels of happiness what the Interpreter told us about."

"Do yer reckon she's in the castle there, right now?" asked Bobby.

"I wonder!" murmured Maggie.

"Betcher can't guess which winder is hern."

"Bet I kin; it's that there one with all them vines around it. Princess ladies allus has vines a-growin' 'roun' their castle winders—so's when the prince comes ter rescue 'em he kin climb up."

"Wisht she'd come out."

"I wish—"

Little Maggie's wish was never expressed, for at that moment, from behind that near-by clump of shrubbery a man sprang toward them, his face distorted with passion and his arms tossing in threatening gestures.

The children, too frightened to realize the safety of their position on the other side of those iron bars, stood speechless. For the moment they could neither cry out nor run.

"Get out!" Adam Ward yelled, hoarse with rage, as he would have driven off a trespassing dog. "Get out! Go home where you belong! Don't you know this is private property? Do you think I am keeping a circus here for all the dirty brats in the country to look at? Get out, I tell you, or I'll—"

With frantic speed the two children fled down the hill.

Adam Ward laughed—laughed until he was forced to hold his sides and the tears of his ungodly mirth rolled down his cheeks.

But such laughter is a fearful thing to see. White and trembling with the shame and the horror of it, Helen crouched in her hiding place, not daring even to move. She felt, as never before, the presence of that spirit which possessed her father and haunted her home. It was as if the hidden thing of which she had forced herself to speak to the Interpreter were suddenly about to materialize before her eyes. She wanted to scream—to cry aloud her fear—to shriek her protest—but sheer terror held her motionless and dumb.

The spell was broken by Mrs. Ward who, from somewhere in the grounds, was calling, "Adam! Oh-h, Adam!"

The man heard, and Helen saw him controlling his laughter, and looking cautiously about.

Again the call came, and there was an anxious note in the voice. "Adam—father—Oh-h, father, where are you?"

With a cruel grin still twisting his gray face, Adam slunk behind a clump of bushes.

Helen Ward crept from her hiding place and, keeping the little arbor between herself and her father, stole away through the grounds. When she was beyond his hearing, she almost ran, as if to escape from a spot accursed.

46

CHAPTER VI

ON THE OLD ROAD

When Bobby and Maggie Whaley fled from the immediate vicinity of Adam Ward's estate, they were beside themselves with fear—blind, unreasoning, instinctive fear.

There is a fear that is reasonable—that is born of an intelligent comprehension of the danger that menaces, and there is a fear that is born of ignorance—of inability to understand the nature of the danger. These children of the Flats had nothing in their little lives by which they might know the owner of the Mill, or visualize the world in which the man for whom their father worked lived. To Bobby and Maggie the home of Adam Ward was a place of mystery, as far removed from the world of their actualities as any fabled castle in fairyland could possibly be.

Sam Whaley's distorted views of all employers in the industrial world, and his fanatical ideas of class loyalty, were impressed with weird exaggeration upon the fertile minds of his children. From their father's conversation with his workmen neighbors, and from the suggestive expressions and epithets which Sam had gleaned from the literature upon which he fed his mind and which he used with such gusto, Bobby and Maggie had gathered the material out of which they had created an imaginary monster, capable of destroying them with fiendish delight. They had seen angry men too often to be much disturbed by mere human wrath. But, to them, this Adam Ward who had appeared so suddenly from the shrubbery was more than a man; he was all that they had been taught to believe—a hideous thing of more dreadful power and sinister purpose than could be imagined.

With all their strength they ran down the old hill road toward the world of the Flats where they belonged. They dared not even look over their shoulders. The very ground seemed to drag at their feet to hold them back. Then little Maggie stumbled and fell. Her frantic screams reached Bobby, who was a few feet in advance, and the boy stopped instantly and faced about, with terror in his eyes but with evident determination to defend his sister at any cost.

When he had pulled Maggie to her feet, and it was certain that there was nothing pursuing them, Bobby, boylike, laughed. "Gee, but we made some git-away, that trip! Gee, I'll tell the world!"

The little girl clung to her protector, shaking with weariness and fear. "I—can't run 'nother step," she gasped. "Will he come after us here?"

"Naw," returned the boy, with reassuring boldness, "he won't come this far. Yer just lay down in the grass, under this here tree, 'til yer catch yer wind; then we'll make it on down to the Interpreter's —'tain't far to the stairs. You just take it easy. I'll watch."

The soft grass and the cool shade were very pleasant after their wild run, and they were loath to go, even when little Maggie had recovered from her exhaustion. Very soon, when no danger appeared, the boy forgot to watch and began an animated discussion of their thrilling experience.

But Maggie did not share her brother's boastful triumph. "Do you suppose," she said, wistfully, "that he is like that to the princess lady?"

Bobby shook his head doubtfully. "I don't know. Yer can't tell what he'd do to her if he took a notion. Old Adam Ward would do anything that's mean, to anybody, no matter who. I'll bet—"

The sound of some one approaching from the direction of the castle interrupted Bobby's conjectures.

Maggie would have made another frantic effort to escape, but the boy caught her roughly and drew her down beside him. "No use to run—yer can't make it," he whispered. "Best lay low. An' don't yer dast even whimper."

Lying prone, they wormed themselves into the tall grass, with the trunk of the tree between them and the road, until it would have been a keen observer, indeed, who would have noticed them in passing.

They heard the approaching danger coming nearer and nearer. Little Maggie buried her face in the grass roots to stifle a scream. Now it was on the other side of the tree. It was passing on. Suddenly they almost buried themselves in the ground in their effort to lie closer to the earth. The sound of the footsteps had ceased.

For what seemed to them hours, the frightened children lay motionless, scarcely daring to breathe. Then another sound came to their straining ears—a sound not unfamiliar to the children of the Flats. A woman was weeping.

Cautiously, the more courageous Bobby raised his head until he could peer through the tangled stems and blades of the sheltering grass. A moment he looked, then gently shook his sister's arm. Imitating her brother's caution, little Maggie raised her frightened face. Only a few steps away, their princess lady was crouching in the grass, with her face buried in her hands, crying bitterly.

"Well, what do yer know about that?" whispered Bobby.

A moment longer they kept their places, whispering in consultation. Then they rose quietly to their feet and, hand in hand, stood waiting.

Helen had not consciously followed the children. Indeed, her mind was so occupied with her own troubled thoughts that she had forgotten the little victims of her father's insane cruelty. To avoid meeting her mother, as she fled from the scene of her father's madness, she had taken a course that led her toward the entrance to the estate. With the one thought of escaping from the invisible presence of that hidden thing, she had left the grounds and followed the quiet old road.

When the storm of her grief had calmed a little, the young woman raised her head and saw Sam Whaley's dirty, ill-kept children gazing at her with wondering sympathy. It is not too much to say that Helen Ward was more embarrassed than she would have been had she found herself thus suddenly in the presence of royalty. "I am sorry you were frightened," she said, hesitatingly. "I can't believe that he really would have hurt you."

"Huh," grunted Bobby. "I'm darned glad we was outside of that there fence."

Maggie's big eyes were eloquent with compassion. "Did—did he scare yer, too?"

Helen held back her tears with an effort. "Yes, dear, he frightened me, too—dreadfully."

With shy friendliness, little Maggie drew closer. "Is he—is he sure 'nuff, yer father?"

"Yes," returned Helen, "he is my father."

"Gee!" ejaculated Bobby. "An' is he always like that?"

"Oh, no, indeed," returned Helen, quickly. "Father is really kind and good, but he—he is sick now and not wholly himself, you see."

"Huh," said Bobby. "He didn't act very sick to me. What's ailin' him?"

Helen answered slowly, "I—we don't just know what it is. The doctors say it is a nervous trouble."

"An' does he—does he ever whip yer?" asked Maggie.

In spite of the pain in her heart, Helen smiled. "No—never."

"Our dad gits mad, too, sometimes," said Bobby. "But, gee! he ain't never like that. Dad, he wouldn't care if somebody just looked into our yard. We wasn't a-hurtin' nothin'—just a-lookin'—that's all. Yer can't hurt nothin' just a-lookin', can yer?"

"I am sorry," said Helen.

"Be yer happy?" asked Maggie, suddenly, with disconcerting directness.

49

"Why!" replied Helen, "I—What makes you ask such a funny question?"

Maggie was too much embarrassed at her own boldness to answer, and Bobby came to her rescue.

"She wants to know because the Interpreter, he tole us about a princess what lived in a castle an' wasn't happy 'til the fairy told her how to find the jewel of happiness; an' Mag, here, she thinks it's you."

"And where did the princess find the jewel of happiness?" asked Helen.

Little Maggie's anxiety to help overcame her timidity and she answered precisely, "On the shores of the sea of life which was not far from the castle where the beautiful princess lived."

Helen looked toward the Flats, the Mill, and the homes in the neighborhood of the old house. "The shores of the sea of life," she repeated, thoughtfully. "I see."

"Yes," continued Maggie, with her tired little face alight, and her eyes big with excited eagerness, "but the beautiful princess, she didn't know that there jewel of happiness when she seen it."

"No?" said Helen, smiling at her little teacher.

"No—an' so she picked up all the bright, shiny stones what was no good at all, 'til the fairy showed her how the real jewel she was a-wantin' was an old, ugly, dirt-colored thing what didn't look like any jewel, no more 'n nothin'."

"Oh, I see!" said Helen again. And Bobby thought that she looked at them as though she were thinking very hard.

"Yer forgot something Mag," said the boy, suddenly.

"I ain't neither," returned his sister, with unusual boldness. "Yer shut up an' see." Then, to Helen, "Is yer heart kind, lady?"

"I—I hope so, dear," returned the disconcerted Helen. "Why?"

"Because, if it is, then the fairies will help yer find the real jewel of happiness, 'cause that was the reason, yer see, it all happened—'cause the beautiful princess's heart was kind." She turned to Bobby triumphantly, "There, ain't that like the Interpreter said?"

"Uh-huh," agreed the boy. "But yer needn't to worry—her heart's all right. Didn't she give us that there grand ride in her swell autermobile?"

Little Maggie's embarrassment suddenly returned.

"Did you really enjoy the ride?" asked Helen.

Bobby answered, "I'll say we did. Gee! but yer ought to a seen us puttin' it all over everybody in the Flats."

Something in the boy's answer brought another smile to Helen's lips, but it was not a smile of happiness.

"I really must go now," she said, rising. "Thank you for telling me about the happiness jewel. Don't you think that it is time for you to be running along home? Your mother will be wondering where you are, won't she?"

"Uh-huh," agreed Bobby.

But Maggie's mind was fixed upon more important things than the time of day. With an effort, she forced herself to say, "If the fairy comes to yer will yer tell me about it, sometime? I ain't never seen one myself an'—an'—"

"You poor little mite!" said Helen. "Yes, indeed, I will tell you about it if the fairy comes. And I will tell the fairy about you, too. But, who knows, perhaps the happiness fairy will visit you first, and you can tell her about me."

And something that shone in the beautiful face of the young woman, or something that sang in her voice, made little Maggie sure—deep down inside—that her princess lady would find the jewel of happiness, just as the Interpreter had said. But neither the child of the Flats, nor the daughter of the big house on the hill knew that the jewel of happiness was, even at that moment, within reach of the princess lady's hand.

When Helen had disappeared from their sight, the two children started on their way down the hill toward the dingy Flats.

"Gee," said Bobby, "won't we have something to tell the kids now? Gee! We'll sure make 'em sore they wasn't along. Think of us a-talkin' to old Adam Ward's daughter, herself. Gee! Some stunt—I'll tell the world."

They had reached the foot of the old stairway and were discussing whether or not they dared prolong their absence from home by paying a visit to the Interpreter, when a man appeared on the road from town. Bobby caught sight of the approaching stranger first, and the boy's freckled countenance lighted with excited interest and admiration.

"Hully Gee!" he exclaimed, catching Maggie by the arm. "Would yer look who's a-comin'!"

The man was not, in his general appearance, one to inspire a feeling of confidence. He was a little above medium height, with fat shoulders, a thick neck, and dark, heavy features with coarse lips showing through a black beard trimmed to a point, and small black eyes set close above a large nose with flaring nostrils. His clothing was good, and he carried himself with assurance. But altogether there was about him the unmistakable air of a foreigner.

Bobby continued in an excited whisper, "That there's Jake Vodell we've heard Dad an' the men talkin' so much about. He's the guy what's a-goin' to put the fear of God into the Mill bosses and rich folks. He's a-goin' to take away old Adam Ward's money an' Mill, an' autermobiles, an' house an'—everything, an' divide 'em all up 'mong us poor workin' folks. Gee, but he's a big gun, I'm tellin' yer!"

The man came on to the foot of the stairs and stopped before the children. For a long moment he looked them over with speculative interest. "Well," he said, abruptly, "and who are you? That you belong in this neighborhood it is easy to see."

"We're Bobby and Maggie Whaley," answered the boy.

The man's black eyebrows were lifted, and he nodded his head reflectively. "Oh-ho, you are Sam Whaley's kids, heh?"

"Uh-huh," returned Bobby. "An' I know who yer are, too."

"So?" said the man.

"Uh-huh, yer Jake Vodell, the feller what's a-goin' to make all the big bugs hunt their holes, and give us poor folks a chance. Gee, but I'd like to be you!"

The man showed his strong white teeth in a pleased smile. "You are all right, kid," he returned. "I think, maybe, you will play a big part in the cause sometime—when you grow up."

Bobby swelled out his chest with pride at this good word from his hero. "I'm big enough right now to put a stick o' danermite under old Adam Ward's castle, up there on the hill."

Little Maggie caught her brother's arm. "Bobby, yer ain't a-goin'—"

The man laughed. "That's the stuff, kid," he said. "But you better let jobs like that alone—until you are a bit older, heh?"

52

"Mag an' me has been up there to the castle all this afternoon," bragged the boy. "An' we talked with old Adam's daughter, too, an'—an' everything."

The man stared at him. "What is this you tell me?"

"It's so," returned Bobby, stoutly, "ain't it, Mag? An' the other day Helen Ward, she give us a ride, in her autermobile—while she was a-visitin' with the Interpreter up there."

Jake Vodell's black brows were drawn together in a frown of disapproval. "So this Adam Ward's daughter, too, calls on the Interpreter, heh! Many people, it seems, go to this Interpreter." To Bobby he said suddenly, "Look here, it will be better if you kids stay away from such people—it will get you nothing to work yourselves in with those who are not of your own class!"

"Yes, sir," returned Bobby, dutifully.

"I will tell you what you can do, though," continued the man. "You can tell your father that I want him at the meeting to-night. Think you can remember, heh?"

"Yer bet I can," replied the boy. "But where'll I tell him the meetin' is?"

"Never you mind that," returned the other. "You just tell him I want him—he will know where. And now be on your way."

To Bobby's utter amazement, Jake Vodell went quickly up the steps that led to the Interpreter's hut.

"Gee!" exclaimed the wondering urchin. "What do yer know about that, Mag? He's a-goin' to see our old Interpreter. Gee! I guess the Interpreter's one of us all right. Jake Vodell wouldn't be a-goin' to see him if he wasn't."

As they trudged away through the black dust, the boy added, "Darn it all, Mag, if the Interpreter *is* one of us what's the princess lady goin' to see him for?"

CHAPTER VII

THE HIDDEN THING

Hiding in the shrubbery, Adam Ward chuckled and grinned with strange glee as he listened to his wife calling for him. Here and there about the grounds she searched anxiously; but the man kept himself hidden and enjoyed her distress. At last, when she had come so near that discovery was certain, he suddenly stepped out from the bushes and, facing her, waited expectantly.

And now, by some miracle, Adam Ward's countenance was transformed—his eyes were gentle, his gray face calm and kindly. His smile became the affectionate greeting of a man who, past the middle years of life, is steadfast in his love for the mother of his grown-up children.

Mrs. Ward had been, in the years of her young womanhood, as beautiful as her daughter Helen. But her face was lined now with care and shadowed by sadness, as though with the success of her husband there had come, also, regrets and disappointments which she had suffered in silence and alone.

She returned Adam's smile of greeting, when she saw him standing there, but that note of anxiety was still in her voice as she said gently, "Where in the world have you been? I have looked all over the place for you."

He laughed as he went to her—a laugh of good comradeship. "I was just sitting over there under that tree," he answered. "I heard you when you called the first time, but thought I would let you hunt a while. The exercise will do you good—keep you from getting too fat in your old age."

She laughed with him, and answered, "Well, you can just come and talk to me now, while I rest."

Arm in arm, they went to the rustic seat in the shade of the tree where, a few minutes before, he had so aimlessly broken the twigs.

But when they were seated the man frowned with displeasure. "Alice, I wish to goodness there was some way to make these men about the place keep a closer watch of things."

She glanced at him quickly. "Has something gone wrong, Adam?"

"Nothing more than usual," he answered, harshly. "There are always a lot of prowlers around. But they don't stay long when I get after them." He laughed, shortly—a mirthless, shamefaced laugh.

54

"I am sorry you were annoyed," she said, gently.

"Annoyed!" he returned, with the manner of a petulant child. "I'll annoy *them*. I tell you I am not going to stand for a lot of people's coming here, sneaking and prying around to see what they can see. If anybody wants to enjoy a place like this let him work for it as I have."

She waited a while before she said, as if feeling her way toward a definite point, "It has been hard work, hasn't it, Adam? Almost too hard, I fear. Did you ever ask yourself if, after all, it is really worth the cost?"

"Worth the cost! I am not in the habit of paying more than things are worth. This place cost me exactly—"

She interrupted him, quietly, "I don't mean that, dear. I was not thinking of the money. I was thinking of what it has all cost in work and worry and—and other things."

"It has all been for you and the children, Alice," he answered, wearily; and there was that in his voice and face which brought the tears to her eyes. "You know that, so far as I am personally concerned, it doesn't mean a thing in the world to me. I don't know anything outside of the Mill myself."

She put her hand on his arm with a caressing touch. "I know—I know—and that is just what troubles me. Perhaps if you would share it more—I mean if you could enjoy it more—I might feel different about it. We were all so happy, Adam, in the old house."

When he made no reply to this but sat with his eyes fixed on the ground she said, pleadingly, "Won't you put aside all the cares and worries of the Mill now, and just be happy with us, Adam?"

The man moved uneasily.

"You know what the doctors say," she continued, gently. "You really—"

He interrupted impatiently, "The doctors are a set of fools. I'll show them!"

She persisted with gentle patience. "But even if the doctors are wrong about your health, still there is no reason why you should not rest after all your years of hard work. I am sure we have everything in the world that any one could possibly want. There is not the shadow of a necessity to make you go on wearing your life out as you have been doing."

"Much you know about what is necessary for me to do," he retorted. "A man isn't going to let the business that he has been all his life building up go to smash just because he has made money enough to keep him without work for the rest of his days."

"There are other things that can go to smash besides business, Adam," she returned, sadly. "And I am sure that the Mill will be safe enough now in John's hands."

"John!" he exclaimed, bitterly. "It's John and his crazy ideas that I am afraid of."

She returned, quickly, with a mother's pride, "Why, Adam! You have said so many times how wonderfully well John was doing, and what a splendid head he had for business details and management. It was only last week that you told me John was more capable now than some of the men that have been in the office with you for several years."

Adam Ward rose and paced uneasily up and down before her. "You don't understand at all, Alice. It is not John's business ability or his willingness to get into the harness that worries me. It is the fool notions that he picked up somewhere over there in the war—there, and from that meddlesome old socialist basket maker."

"Just what notions do you mean, Adam? Is it John's friendship with Charlie Martin that you fear?"

"His friendship with young Martin is only part of it. I am afraid of his attitude toward the whole industrial situation. Haven't you heard his wild, impracticable and dangerous theories of applying, as he says, the ideals of patriotism, and love of country, and duty to humanity, and sacrifice, and heroism, and God knows what other nonsense, to the work of the world? You know as well as I do how he talks about the comradeship of the mills and factories and workshops being like the comradeship of the trenches and camps and battlefields. His notions of the relation between an employer and his employees would be funny if they were not so dangerous. Look at his sympathy with the unions! And yet I have shown him on my books where this union business has cost me hundreds of thousands of dollars! Comradeship! Loyalty! I tell you I know what I'm talking about from experience. The only way to handle the working class is to keep them where they belong. Give them the least chance to think you are easy and they are on your neck. If I had my way I'd hold them to their jobs at the muzzle of a machine gun. McIver has the right idea. He is getting himself in shape right now for the biggest fight with labor that he has ever had. Everybody knows that agitator Jake Vodell is here to make trouble. The laboring classes have had a long spell of good times now and they're ripe for anything. All they need is a start and this anarchist is here to start them. And John, instead of lining up with McIver and getting ready to fight them to a finish, is spending his time hobnobbing with Charlie Martin and listening to that old fool Interpreter."

56

"Come, dear," she said, soothingly. "Come and sit down here with me. Don't let's worry about what may happen."

He obeyed her with the manner of a fretful child. And presently, as she talked, the cloud lifted from his gray, haggard face, and he grew calm. Soon, when she made some smiling remark, he even smiled back at her with the affectionate companionship of their years.

"You will try not to worry about things so much, won't you, Adam?" she said, at last. "For my sake, won't you?"

"But I tell you, Alice, there is serious trouble ahead."

"Perhaps that is all the more reason why you should retire now," she urged. He stirred uneasily, but she continued, "Just suppose the worst that could possibly happen should happen, suppose you even had to give up the Mill to Pete Martin and the men, suppose you lost the new process and everything, and we were obliged to give up our home here and go back to live in the old house—it would still be better than losing you, dear. Don't you know that to have you well and strong would be more to Helen and John and to me than anything else could possibly be?"

Mrs. Ward knew, as the words left her lips, that she had said the wrong thing. She had heard him rave about his ownership of the new process too many times not to know—while any mention of his old workman friend Peter Martin always threw him into a rage. But in her anxiety the forbidden words had escaped her.

She drew back with a little gasp of fear at the swift change that came over his face. As if she had touched a hidden spring in his being the man's countenance was darkened by furious hatred and desperate fear. His trembling lips were ashen; the muscles of his face twitched and worked; his eyes blazed with a vicious anger beyond all control. Springing to his feet, he faced her with a snarling exclamation, and in a voice shaking with passion, cried, "Pete Martin! What is he? Who is he? Everything he has in the world he owes to me. Haven't I kept him in work all these years? Haven't I paid him every cent of his wages? Look at his home. Not many working men have been able to own a place like that. What would he have done without the money I have given him every pay day? I could have turned him out long ago—kicked him out of a job without a cent. He's had all that's coming to him—every penny. *I* built up the Mill. That new process is mine—it's patented in my name. I have had the best lawyers I could hire to protect it on every possible point. If it hadn't been for my business brain there wouldn't be any new process. What could Pete Martin have done with it—the fool has no more business sense than a baby. I introduced it—I exploited it—I built it up and made it worth what it is, and there isn't a court in the world that wouldn't say I have a legal right to it."

In vain Mrs. Ward tried to soothe him with reassuring words, pleading with him to be calm.

57

"I know they're after me," he raved. "They have tried all sorts of tricks. There is always some sneaking spy watching for a chance to get me, but I'll fix them. I built the business up and I can tear it down. Let them try to take anything away from me if they dare. I'll burn the Mill and the whole town before I'll give up one cent of my legal rights to Pete Martin or any of his tribe."

Forgetting his companion, the man suddenly started off across the grounds, waving his arms and shaking his fists in wild gestures as he continued his tirade against his old fellow workman. Mrs. Ward knew from experience the uselessness of trying to interfere until he had exhausted himself.

* * * * *

As Helen was returning to the house after her talk with the children, she saw her mother coming slowly from that part of the grounds where the young woman had watched her father. It was evident, even at a distance, that Mrs. Ward was greatly distressed. When the young woman reached her mother's side, Mrs. Ward said, simply, "Your father, dear—he is terribly upset. Go to him, Helen, you can always do more for him than any one else—he needs you."

It was not an easy task for Helen Ward to face her father just then. As she went in search of him she tried to put from her mind all that she had seen and to remember only that he was ill. She found him in the most distant and lonely part of the grounds, sitting with his face buried in his hands—a figure of hopeless despair.

While still some distance away, she forced herself to call cheerily, "Hello, father."

As he raised his head, she turned to pick a few flowers from a near-by bed. When he had had a moment to regain, in a measure, his self-control, she went toward him, arranging her blossoms with careful attention.

Adam Ward watched his daughter as she drew near, much as a condemned man might have watched through the grating of a prison window.

"What is it, father?" she asked, gently, when she had come close to his side. "Another one of your dreadful nervous headaches?"

He put a shaking hand to his brow. "Yes," he said wearily.

"I am so sorry," she returned, sitting down beside him. "You have been thinking too hard again, haven't you?"

"Yes, I guess I have been thinking too hard."

"But you're going to stop all that now, aren't you?" she continued, cheerily. "You're just going to forget the old Mill, and do nothing but rest and play with me."

"Could I learn to play, do you think, Helen?"

"Why, of course you could, father, with me to teach you. That's the best thing I do, you know."

He watched her closely. "And you don't think that I—that I am no longer capable of managing my affairs?"

She laughed gayly. "What a silly question—*you* capable—*you*, father, the best brain—the best business executive in Millsburgh. You know that is what everybody says of you. You are just tired, and need a good rest, that is all."

The man's drooping shoulders lifted and his face brightened as he said, slowly, "I guess perhaps you are right, daughter."

"I am sure of it," she returned, eagerly. Then she added brightly, as if prompted by a sudden inspiration, "I'll tell you what you do—ask the Interpreter."

"Ask the Interpreter!"

She nodded, smiling as if she had put a puzzling conundrum to him.

"You mean for me to ask that paralyzed old basket maker's advice? You mean, ask him if I should retire from business?"

Again she nodded with a little laugh; but under her laughter there was a note of earnestness.

"And don't you know," he said, "that it is the Interpreter who is at the bottom of all my trouble?"

"Father!"

"The Interpreter, I tell you, is back of the whole thing. He is the brains of the labor organizations in Millsburgh and has been for years. Why, it was the Interpreter who organized the first union in this district. He has done more to build them up than all the others put together. Pete Martin and Charlie, the ringleaders of the Mill workers' union, are only his active lieutenants. I haven't a doubt but that he is responsible for this agitator Jake Vodell's coming to Millsburgh. That miserable shack on the cliff is the real headquarters of labor in this part of the country. Your Interpreter is a fine one for *me* to go to for advice. His hut is a fine place for your brother to spend his spare time. It would be a fine thing, right now, with this man Vodell in town, for me to resign and leave the Mill in the hands of John, who is already in the hands of the Interpreter and the Martins and their Mill workers' union!"

As Adam finished, the deep sonorous tones of the great Mill whistle sounded over the community. It was the signal for the closing of the day's work.

Obedient to the habit of years, the Mill owner looked at his watch. In his mind he saw the day force trooping from the building and the night shift coming in. Throughout the entire city, in office and shop and store and home, the people ordered their days by the sound of that whistle, and Adam Ward had been very proud of this recognition accorded him.

Wearily, as one exhausted by a day of hard labor, this man who so feared the power of the Interpreter looked up at his daughter. "I wish I could rest," he said.

CHAPTER VIII

WHILE THE PEOPLE SLEEP

The Interpreter's hands were busy with his basket weaving; his mind seemingly was occupied more with other things. Frequently he paused to look up from his work and, with his eyes fixed on the Mill, the Flats and the homes on the hillside, apparently considered the life that lay before him and of which he had been for so many years an interested observer and student. On the opposite side of the table, silent Billy was engaged with something that had to do with the manufacturing interests of their strange partnership.

When Jake Vodell reached the landing at the top of the stairway, he stopped to look about the place with curious, alert interest, noting with quick glances every object in the immediate vicinity of the hut, as if fixing them in his mind. Satisfied at last by the thoroughness of his inspection, he went toward the house, but his step on the board walk made no sound. At the outer door of the little hut the man halted again, and again he looked quickly about the premises. Apparently there was no one at home. Silently he entered the room and the next instant discovered the two men on the porch.

The Interpreter's attention at the moment was fixed upon his work and he remained unaware of the intruder's presence, while Jake Vodell, standing in the doorway, regarded the old basket maker curiously, with a contemptuous smile on his bearded lips.

But Billy Rand saw him. A moment he looked at the man in the doorway inquiringly, as he would have regarded any one of the Interpreter's many visitors; then the deaf and dumb man's expression changed. Glancing quickly at his still unobserving companion, he caught up a hatchet that lay among the tools on the table and, with a movement that was not unlike the guarding action of a huge mastiff, rose to his feet. His face was a picture of animal rage; his teeth were bared, his eyes gleamed, his every muscle was tense.

The man in the doorway was evidently no coward, but the smile vanished from his heavy face and his right hand went quickly inside his vest. "What's the matter with you?" he said, sharply, as Billy started toward him with deliberate menace in his movement.

At the sound of the man's voice the Interpreter looked up. One glance and the old basket maker caught the wheels of his chair and with a quick, strong movement rolled himself between the two men—so close to Billy that he caught his defender by the arm. Facing his enraged companion, the Interpreter talked to him rapidly in their sign language and held out his hand for the hatchet. The silent Billy reluctantly surrendered the weapon and drew back to his place on the other side of the table, where he sat glaring at the stranger in angry watchfulness.

The man in the doorway laughed harshly. "They told me I would find a helpless old cripple up here," he said. "I think you are pretty well protected at that."

Regarding the stranger gravely, the Interpreter apologized for his companion. "You can see that Billy is not wholly responsible," he explained. "He is little more than a child mentally; his actions are often apparently governed wholly by that strange instinct which seems to guide the animals. He is very devoted to me."

"He seems to be in earnest all right," said the stranger. "He is a husky brute, too."

The Interpreter, regarding the man inquiringly, almost as if he were seeking in the personality of his visitor the reason for Billy's startling conduct, replied, simply, "He would have killed you."

With a shrug of his thick shoulders, the stranger uninvited came forward and helped himself to a chair, and, with the air of one introducing a person of some importance, said, "I am Vodell—Jake Vodell. You have heard of me, I think, heh?"

"Oh, yes. Indeed, I should say that every one has heard of you, Mr. Vodell. Your work has given you even more than national prominence, I believe."

The man was at no pains to conceal his satisfaction. "I am known, yes."

"It is odd," said the Interpreter, "but your face seems familiar to me, as if I had met you before."

"You have heard me speak somewhere, maybe, heh?"

"No, it cannot be that. You have never been in Millsburgh before, have you?"

"No."

"It is strange," mused the old basket maker.

"It is the papers," returned Vodell with a shrug. "Many times the papers have my picture—you must have seen."

"Of course, that is it," exclaimed the Interpreter. "I remember now, distinctly. It was in connection with that terrible bomb outrage in—"

"Sir!" interrupted the other indignantly. "Outrage—what do you mean, outrage?"

"I was thinking of the innocent people who were killed or injured," returned the Interpreter, calmly. "I believe you were also prominent in those western strikes where so many women and children suffered, were you not?"

62

The labor agitator replied with the exact manner of a scientific lecturer. "It is unfortunate that innocent persons must sometimes be hurt in these affairs. But that is one of the penalties that society must pay for tolerating the conditions that make these industrial wars necessary."

"If I remember correctly, you were in the South, too, at the time that mill was destroyed."

"Oh, yes, they had me in jail there. But that was nothing. I have many such experiences. They are to me very commonplace. Wherever there are the poor laboring men who must fight for their rights, I go. The mines, shops, mills, factories—it is all the same to me. I go wherever I can serve the Cause. I have been in America now ten years, nearly eleven."

"You are not, then, a citizen of this country?"

Jake Vodell laughed contemptuously. "Oh, sure I am a citizen of this country—this great America of fools and cowards that talk all the time so big about freedom and equality, while the capitalist money hogs hold them in slavery and rob them of the property they create. I had to become a citizen when the war came, you see, or they would have sent me away. But for that I would make myself a citizen of some cannibal country first." The old basket maker's dark eyes blazed with quick fire and he lifted himself with sudden strength to a more erect position in his wheel chair. But when he spoke his deep voice was calm and steady. "You have been in our little city nearly a month, I understand."

"Just about. I have been looking around, getting acquainted, studying the situation. One must be very careful to know the right men, you understand. It pays, I find, to go a little slow at first. We will go fast enough later." His thick lips parted in a meaning grin.

The Interpreter's hands gripped the wheels of his chair.

"Everybody tells me I should see you," the agitator continued. "Everywhere it is the same. They all talk of the Interpreter. 'Go to the Interpreter,' they say. When they told me that this great Interpreter is an old white-headed fellow without any legs, I laughed and said, 'What can he do to help the laboring man? He is not good for anything but to sit in a wheel chair and make baskets all the day. I need *men*.' But they all answer the same thing, 'Go and see the Interpreter.' And so I am here."

When the Interpreter was silent, his guest demanded, harshly, "They are all right, heh? You are a friend to the workingman? Tell me, is it so?"

The old basket maker spoke with quiet dignity. "For twenty-five years Millsburgh has been my home, and the Millsburgh people have been my friends. You, sir, have been here less than a month; I have known you but a few minutes."

Jake Vodell laughed understandingly. "Oh-ho, so that is it? Maybe you like to see my credentials before we talk?"

The Interpreter held up a hand in protest. "Your reputation is sufficient, Mr. Vodell."

The man acknowledged the compliment—as he construed it—with a shrug and a pleased laugh. "And all that is said of you by the laboring class in your little city is sufficient," he returned. "Even the men in McIver's factory tell me you are the best friend that labor has ever had in this place." He paused expectantly.

The man in the wheel chair bowed his head.

"And then," continued Jake Vodell, with a frown of displeasure, "when I come to see you, to ask some questions about things that I should know, what do I hear? The daughter of this old slave-driver and robber—this capitalist enemy of the laboring class—Adam Ward, she comes also to see this Interpreter who is such a friend of the people."

The Interpreter laughed. "And Sam Whaley's children, they come too."

"Oh, yes, that is better. I know Sam Whaley. He is a good man who will be a great help to me. But I do not understand this woman business."

"I have known Miss Ward ever since she was born; I worked in the Mill at the same bench with her father and Peter Martin," said the man in the wheel chair, with quiet dignity.

"I see. It is not so bad sometimes to have a friend or two among these millionaires when there is no danger of it being misunderstood. But this man, who was once a workman and who deserted his class—this traitor, her father—does he also call on you, Mr. Interpreter?"

"Once in a great while," answered the Interpreter.

Jake Vodell laughed knowingly. "When he wants something, heh?" Then, with an air of taking up the real business of his visit to the little hut on the cliff, he said, "Suppose now you tell me something about this son of Adam Ward. You have known him since he was a boy too—the same as the girl?"

"Yes," said the Interpreter, "I have known John Ward all his life."

Something in the old basket maker's voice made Jake Vodell look at him sharply and the agitator's black brows were scowling as he said, "So—you are friends with him, too, I guess, heh?"

64

"I am, sir; and so is Captain Charlie Martin, who is the head of our Mill workers' union, as you may have heard."

"Exactly. That is why I ask. So many of the poor fools who slave for this son of Adam Ward in the Mill say that he is such a fine man—so kind. Oh, wonderful! Bah! When was the wolf whelped that would be kind to a rabbit? You shall tell me now about the friendship between this wolf cub of the capitalist Mill owner and this poor rabbit, son of the workman Peter Martin who has all his life been a miserable slave in the Mill. They were in the army together, heh?"

"They enlisted in the same company when the first call came and were comrades all through the worst of the fighting in France."

"And before that, they were friends, heh?"

"They had been chums as boys, when the family lived in the old house next door to the Martins. But during the years that John was away in school and college Adam moved his family to the place on the hill where they live now. When John was graduated and came home to stay, he naturally found his friends in another circle. His intimacy with Pete Martin's boy was not renewed—until the war."

"Exactly," grunted Jake Vodell. "And how did Adam Ward like it that his boy should go to war? Not much, I think. It was all right for the workman's boy to go; but the Mill owner's son—that was different, heh?"

There was a note of pride in the Interpreter's voice, as he answered, "Adam was determined that the boy should not go at all, even if he were drafted. But John said that it was bad enough to let other men work to feed and clothe him in ordinary times of peace without letting them do his fighting for him as well."

"This Adam Ward's son said that!" exclaimed the agitator. "Huh—it was for the effect—a grand-stand play."

"He enlisted," retorted the Interpreter. "And when his father would have used his influence to secure some sort of commission with an easy berth, John was more indignant than ever. He said if he ever wore shoulder straps they would be a recognition of his service to his country and not, as he put it, a pretty gift from a rich father. So he and Charlie Martin both enlisted as privates, and, as it happened, on the same day. Under such circumstances it was quite as natural that their old friendship should be reestablished as that they should have drifted apart under the influence of Adam Ward's prosperity."

Jake Vodell laughed disagreeably. "And then this wonderful son of your millionaire Mill owner comes out of the war and the army exactly as he went in, nothing but a private—not even a medal—heh? But this workman from the Mill, he comes back a captain with a distinguished service medal? I think maybe Private Ward's father and mother and sister liked that—no?"

Disregarding these comments, the Interpreter said, "Now that I have answered your questions about the friendship of John Ward and Charlie Martin, may I ask just why you are so much interested in the matter?"

The agitator gazed at the man in the wheel chair with an expression of incredulous amazement. "Is it possible you do not understand?" he demanded. "And you such a friend to the workingman! But wait—one more thing, then I will answer you. This daughter of Adam Ward—she is also good friends with her old playmate who is now Captain Martin, is she? The workman goes sometimes to the big house on the hill to see his millionaire friends, does he?"

The Interpreter answered, coldly, "I can't discuss Miss Ward with you, sir."

"Oh-ho! And now I will answer your question as to my interest. This John Ward is already a boss in the Mill. His father, everybody tells me, is not well. Any time now the old man may retire from the business and the son will have his place as general manager. He will be the owner. The friendship between these two men is not good—because Charlie Martin is the leader of the union and there can be no such friendship between a leader of the laboring class and one of the employer class without great loss to our Cause. You will see. These rich owners of the Mill, they will flatter and make much of this poor workman captain because of his influence among the people who slave for them, and so any movement to secure for the workmen their rights will be defeated. Do you understand now, Mister basket maker, heh?"

The Interpreter bowed his head.

The agitator continued. "Already I find it very hard to accomplish much with this Mill workers' union. Except for our friend, Sam Whaley, and a few others, the fools are losing their class loyalty. Their fighting spirit is breaking down. It will not do, I tell you. At the McIver factory it is all very different. It will be easy there. The workingmen show the proper spirit—they will be ready when I give the word. But I am not pleased with the situation in this Mill of Adam Ward's. This fine friendship between the son of the owner and the son of the workman must stop. Friendship—-bah!—it is a pretense, a sham, a trick."

The man's manner, when he thus passed judgment upon the comradeship of John and Charlie, was that of an absolute monarch who was righteously annoyed at some manifestation of disloyalty among his subjects. His voice was harsh with the authority of one whose mandates are not to be questioned. His countenance was dark with scowling displeasure.

"And you, too, my friend," he went on, glaring from under his black brows at the old man in the wheel chair, "you will be wise if you accept my suggestion and be a little careful yourself. It is not so bad, perhaps, this young woman coming to see you, but I am told that her brother also comes to visit with the Interpreter. And this leader of the Mill workers' union, Charlie Martin, he comes, too. Everybody says you are the best friend of the working people. But I tell you there cannot be friendship between the employer class and the laboring class—it must be between them always war. So, Mr. Interpreter, you must look out. The time is not far when the people of Millsburgh will know for sure who is a friend to the labor class and who is a friend to the employer class."

The Interpreter received this warning from Jake Vodell exactly as he had listened to Bobby Whaley's boyish talk about blowing up the castle of Adam Ward on the hill.

Rising abruptly, the agitator, without so much as a by-your-leave, went into the house where he proceeded to examine the books and periodicals on the table. Billy started from his place to follow, but the Interpreter shook his head forbiddingly, and while Jake Vodell passed on to the farther corner of the room and stood looking over the well filled shelves of the Interpreter's library, the old basket maker talked to his companion in their silent language.

When this foreign defender of the rights of the American laboring class returned to the porch he was smiling approval. "Good!" he said. "You are all right, I think. No man could read the papers and books that you have there, and not be the friend of freedom and a champion of the people against their capitalist masters. We will have a great victory for the Cause in Millsburgh, comrade. You shall see. It is too bad that you do not have your legs so that you could take an active part with me in the work that I will do."

The Interpreter smiled. "If you do not mind, I would like to know something of your plans. That is," he added, courteously, "so far as you are at liberty to tell me."

"Certainly I will tell you, comrade," returned the other, heartily. "Who can say—it may be that you will be of some small use to me after all." His eyes narrowed slyly. "It may be that for these Mill owners to come to you here in your little hut is perhaps not so bad when we think about it a little more, heh? The daughter of Adam Ward might be led to say many foolish little things that to a clever man like you would be understood. Even the brother, the manager of the Mill—well, I have known men like him to talk of themselves and their plans rather freely at times when they thought there was no harm. And what possible harm could there be in a poor crippled old basket maker like you, heh?" The man laughed as though his jest were perfectly understood and appreciated by his host—as, indeed, it was.

"But about my plans for this campaign in Millsburgh," he went on. "You know the great brotherhood that I represent and you are familiar with their teachings of course." He gestured comprehensively toward the Interpreter's library.

The man in the wheel chair silently nodded assent.

Jake Vodell continued. "I am come to Millsburgh, as I go everywhere, in the interests of our Cause. It is my experience that I can always work best through the unions."

The Interpreter interrupted. "Oh, one of our Millsburgh unions sent for you then? I did not know."

The agitator shrugged his shoulders impatiently. "No—no—I was not sent for. I was sent. I am here because it was reported that there was a good opportunity to advance the Cause. No union brings me. I come to the unions, to work with them for the freedom of the laboring class."

"And of what union are you a member, sir?" asked the Interpreter.

"Me! Ha! I am not a member of any of your silly American unions! I belong to that greater union, if you please, which embraces them all. But your unions know and receive me as a leader because of the work that I do for all. Our Cause is the cause of the working people of America, as it is the cause of the laboring classes in England, and France, and Russia, and Germany, and everywhere in the world."

Again the old basket maker bowed his silent assent.

"You have, in this place," continued the agitator, "one strong union of the Mill workers. In the other shops and factories and in the trades it is like McIver's factory, the men are not so well organized."

Again the Interpreter interrupted. "The working people of Millsburgh, generally, receive the highest wage paid anywhere in the country, do they not?"

"Ah, but surely that is not the question, comrade. Surely you understand that all the laboring people of America must be united in one brotherhood with all the other countries of the world, so that they, the producers of wealth, shall be able to take possession of, and operate, the industries of this country, and finally take this government away from the capitalist class who are now the real owners of what you call your 'land of the free and the home of the brave.' Bah! You fool Americans do not know the first meaning of the word freedom. You are a nation of slaves. If you were as brave as you sing, you very soon would be your own masters."

"And your plan for Millsburgh?" asked the Interpreter, calmly.

"It is simple. But for this John Ward and his friendship with Charlie Martin that so deceives everybody, it will be easy. The first step in my campaign here will be to call out the employees of McIver's factory on a strike. I start with McIver's workmen because his well-known position against the laboring class will make it easy for me to win the sympathy of the public for the strikers."

"But," said the Interpreter, "the factory union is working under an agreement with McIver."

The self-appointed savior of the American working people shrugged his heavy shoulders disdainfully. "That is no matter—it is always easy to find a grievance. When the factory men have walked out, then will come the sympathetic strike of your strong Mill workers' union. All the other labor organizations will be forced to join us, whether they wish to or not. I shall have all Millsburgh so that not a wheel can turn anywhere. The mills—the factories—the builders—the bakeries— everything will be in our hands and then, my comrade, then!"

The man rose to his feet and stood looking out over the life that lay within view from the Interpreter's balcony-porch, as if possessed with the magnitude of the power that would be his when this American community should be given into his hand.

Silent, watchful Billy stirred uneasily.

The Interpreter, touching his companion's arm, shook his head.

Jake Vodell, deep in his ambitious dream, did not notice. "The time is coming, comrade," he said, "and it is nearer than the fool Americans think, when the labor class will rise in their might and take what is theirs. My campaign here in Millsburgh, you must know, is only one of the hundreds of little fires that we are lighting all over this country. The American people, they are asleep. They have drugged themselves with their own talk of how safe and strong and prosperous they are. Bah! There is no people so easy to fool. They think we strike for recognition of some union, or that it is for higher wages, or some other local grievance. Bah! We use for an excuse anything that will give us a hold on the labor class. These silly unions, they are nothing in themselves. But we—*we* can use them in the Cause. And so everywhere—North, South, East, West—we light our little fires. And when we are ready—Boom! One big blaze will come so quick from all points at once that it will sweep the country before the sleeping fools wake up. And then—then, comrade, you shall see what will happen to your capitalist vultures and your employer swine, who have so long grown fat on the strength of the working class."

A moment longer he stood as if lost in the contemplation of the glory of that day, when, in the triumph of his leadership, the people of the nation he so despised and hated would rise in bloody revolution against their own government and accept in its stead the dictatorship of lawless aliens who profess allegiance to no one but their own godless selves.

Then he turned back to the Interpreter with a command, "You, comrade, shall keep me informed, heh? From these people of our enemy class who come here to your hut, you will learn the things I will want to know. I shall come to you from time to time, but not too often. But, you must see that your watchdog there has better manners for me, heh?" He laughed and was gone.

At the club that evening, Jim McIver sat with a group of men discussing the industrial situation.

"They're fixing for a fight all right," said one. "What do you think, Jim?"

The factory owner answered, "They can have a fight any time they want it. Nothing but a period of starvation will ever put the laboring class back where it belongs and the sooner we get it over the better it will be for business conditions all around."

In the twilight dust and grime of the Flats, a woman sat on the doorstep of a wretched house. Her rounded shoulders slouched wearily—her tired hands were folded in her lap. She stared with dull, listless eyes at the squalid homes of her neighbors across the street. The Interpreter had described the woman to Helen—"a girl with fine instincts for the best things of life and a capacity for great happiness."

In a room back of a pool hall of ill-repute, the man Jake Vodell sat in conference with three others of his brotherhood. A peculiar knock sounded at the door. Vodell drew the bolt. Sam Whaley entered. "My kids told me you wanted me," said the workman. Long into the night, on the balcony porch of the hut on the cliff, John Ward and Captain Charlie Martin talked with the Interpreter. As they talked, they watched the lights of the Mill, the Flats, the business streets, and the homes.

CHAPTER IX

THE MILL

It was pay day at the Mill.

No one, unless he, at some period in his life, has been absolutely dependent upon the wages of his daily toil, can appreciate a pay day. To experience properly the thrill of a pay day one must have no other source of income. The pay check must be the only barrier between one and actual hunger. Bobby and Maggie Whaley knew the full meaning of pay day. Their mother measured life itself by that event.

Throughout the great industrial hive that morning there was an electrical thrill of anticipation. Smiles were more frequent; jests were passed with greater zest; men moved with a freer step, a more joyous swing. The very machinery seemed in some incomprehensible way to be animated with the spirit of the workmen, while the droning, humming, roaring voice of the Mill was unquestionably keyed to a happier note. In the offices among the bookkeepers, clerks, stenographers and the department heads, the same brightening of the atmosphere was noticeable. Nor was the spirit of the event confined to the Mill itself; throughout the entire city—in the stores and banks, the post office, the places of amusement, in the homes on the hillside and in the Flats—pay day at the Mill was the day of days.

It was an hour, perhaps, after the whistle had started the big plant for the afternoon.

John Ward was deep in the consideration of some business of moment with the superintendent, George Parsons—a sturdy, square-jawed, steady-eyed, middle-aged man, who had come up from the ranks by the sheer force of his natural ability.

* * * * *

There is nothing at all unusual about John Ward. He is simply a good specimen of the more intelligent class of our young American manhood, with, it might be, a more than average mind for business, which he had inherited from his father. He is, in short, a fair type of the healthy, clean-living, straight-thinking, broad-gauged, big-hearted young citizen such as one may find by the hundreds of thousands in the many fields of our national activities. In our arts and industries, in our banks and commercial houses, in our factories and newspapers, on our farms and in our professions, in our educational institutions, among our writers and scientists, in our great transportation organizations, and in the business of our government, our John Wards are to be found, ready to take the places left to them by the passing of their fathers.

Since his return from the war, the young man had devoted himself with the enthusiasm of a great purpose to a practical study of his father's big industrial plant.

Adam still held the general management, but his son knew that the time must come when the responsibility of that position would fall to him.

With John's inherited executive ability and his comradeship, plus the driving force of his fixed and determined purpose, it was not strange that he so quickly gained the loyal support and cooperation of his father's long-trained assistants. His even-tempered friendliness and ready recognition of his dependence upon his fellow workers won their love. His industry, his clear-headed, open-minded consideration of the daily problems presented, with his quick grasp of essential details, commanded their admiring respect. Under the circumstance of his father's nervous trouble and the consequent enforced absence of Adam from his office for more and more frequent periods, it was inevitable that John, by common, if silent, consent of the executive heads, should be advanced more and more toward the general manager's desk.

The superintendent, gathering up his blue prints and memoranda, arose. "And will that be all, sir?" he asked, with a smile.

Nearly every one smiled when he finished an interview with Adam Ward's son; probably because John himself nearly always smiled when he ended a consultation or gave an order.

"That's all from my side, George," he said, leaning back in his chair and looking up at the superintendent in his open, straightforward way that so surely invited confidence and trust. "Have you anything else on your mind?"

"Nary a thing, John," returned the older man, and with a parting "so long" he started toward the door that opened into the Mill.

With that smile of genuine affection still lingering on his face, John watched the sturdy back of the old superintendent as if, for the moment, his thoughts had swung from George Parsons' work to George Parsons himself.

The superintendent opened the door and was about to step out when he stopped suddenly and with a quick, decided movement drew back into the room and closed the door again. To the young man in the other end of the big office it looked as though the superintendent had seen something that startled him. Another moment and George was again bending over John's desk.

"The old man is out there, John."

"What! Father! Why I had no idea that he was coming down to-day." A look of anxiety came into the frank gray eyes. "He has not been so well lately, George. I wonder why he didn't come to the office first as usual."

"He sometimes slips in back that way, you know," returned the superintendent.

"He really ought not to be here," said the young man. "I wish—" He hesitated.

"He's generally in a state of mind when he comes in like that," said George. "You're not needing a goat, are you, boy?"

John smiled. "There's not a thing wrong in the plant so far as I know, George."

"I don't know of anything either," returned the other, "but we may not know all the way. There's one thing sure, the old man ought not to be wandering through the works alone. There's some of those rough-necks would—well it's too darned easy, sometimes, for accidents to happen, do you see? I'll rustle out there and stick around convenient like. You'd better stay where you are as if you didn't know he was on the job. And remember, son, if you *should* need a goat, I'm qualified. If anything has happened—whether it has or he only thinks it has—just you blame it on to old George. I'll understand."

The work was at the height of its swing when burly Max Gardner paused a second to straighten his back and wipe the sweat from his sooty face. As he stooped again to his heavy task, he said to his mates in a voice that rumbled up from the depths of his naked, hairy chest, "Get a gate on y'—get a gate on y'—y' rough-necks. 'Tis th' boss that's a-lookin' 'round to see who he'll be tyin' th' can to next."

The men laughed.

"There's one thing sure," said Bill Connley, who looked as though his body were built of rawhide stretched over a framework of steel, "when John Ward ties the can to a man, that man knows what 'tis for. When he give Jim Billings his time last week, he says to him, says he, 'Jim, I'm sorry for y'. Not because I'm fir'in' y',' says he, 'but because y're such a loafer that y're no good to yerself nor to anybody else—y're a disgrace to the Mill,' says he, 'and to every honest working man in it.' An' Jim, he never give a word back—just hung his head an' got out of sight like a dog with his tail between his legs after a good swift kick."

"An' th' young boss was right at that," commented sturdy Soot Walters. "Jim was a good man when he was new on the job, but since he got the wrinkles out of his belly, he's been killin' more time than any three men in the works."

"Pass me that pinch bar, Bill," called Dick Grant from the other side. As he reached for the tool, his glance took in the figure that had caught the eye of big Max. "Holy Mike!" he exclaimed, "'tis the old man himself."

Every man in the group except Max turned his face toward Adam Ward, who stood some distance away, and a very different tone marked the voice of Bill Connley as he said, "Now what d'ye think brings that danged old pirate here to look us over this day?"

"Who the devil cares?" growled Scot, as, with an air of sullen indifference, they turned again to their work.

* * * * *

No one seeing the Mill owner as he viewed his possessions that day could have believed that this was the wretched creature that Helen had watched from the arbor. Away from the scenes of his business life Adam Ward was like some poor, nervous, half-insane victim of the drug habit. At the Mill, he was that same drug fiend under the influence of his "dope."

His manner was calm and steady, with no sign of nervousness or lack of control. His gray face—which, in a way, was the face of a student—gave no hint of the thoughts and emotions that stirred within him. As he looked about the great industrial institution to which he had given himself, body, mind and soul, all the best years of his life, his countenance was as expressionless as the very machines of iron and steel and wood among which he moved—a silent, lonely, brooding spirit. No glow of worthy pride in the work of his manhood, no gleam of friendly comradeship for his fellow workmen, no joy of his kinship with the great humanity that was here personified shone in his eyes or animated his presence. Cold and calculating, he looked upon the human element in the Mill exactly as he looked upon the machinery. Men cost him a certain definite sum of dollars; they must be made to return to him a certain increase in definite dollars on that cost. The living bodies, minds, and souls that, moving here and there in the haze of smoke and steam and dust, vitalized the inanimate machinery and gave life and intelligent purpose to the whole, were no more to him than one of his adding machines in the office that, mechanically obedient to his touch, footed up long columns of dollars and cents. It is not strange that the humanity of the Mill should respond to the spirit of its owner with the spirit of his adding machines and give to him his totals of dollars and cents—with nothing more.

Quickly the feeling of Adam Ward's presence spread throughout the busy plant. Smiling faces grew grim and sullen. In the place of good-natured jest and cheerful laugh there were muttered curses and contemptuous epithets. The very atmosphere seemed charged with antagonism and rebellious hatred.

"Wad ye look at it?" said one. "And they tell me that white-faced old devil used to work along side of Pete and the Interpreter at that same bench where Pete's a-workin' yet."

"He did that," said another. "I was a kid in the Mill at the time; 'twas before he got hold of his new process."

"Pete Martin is a better man than Adam Ward ever was or will be at that—process or no process," said a third, while every man within hearing endorsed the sentiment with a hearty word, an oath or a pointed comment.

74

"But the young boss is a different sort, though," came from the first speaker.

"He is that!"

"The boy's all right."

"John's a good man."

A workman with a weak face and shifty eyes paused in passing to say, "You'll find out how different the boy is onct he's put to the test. He's the same breed, an' it's just like Jake Vodell said last night, there ain't one of the greedy capitalist class that wouldn't nail a laboring man to the cross of their damnable system of slavery if they dast."

A silence fell over the group.

Then a dry voice drawled, "Jake Vodell ain't never overworked himself as anybody knows of, has he? As for you, Sam Whaley, I'm thinkin' it would take somethin' more than a crucifyin' to get much profit out of you, the way you mooch around."

There was a general laugh at this and Sam Whaley went on his weak way to do whatever it was that he was supposed to be doing.

"Sam's all right, Bob," said one who had laughed. "His heart is in the right place."

"Sure he is," agreed Bob. "But I sometimes can't help thinkin', just the same, that if I was a-ownin' and a-workin' slaves, I'd consider him a mighty poor piece of property."

When Adam Ward entered the office, some time later, he walked straight to his son's desk, without so much as a glance or a nod of recognition toward any other soul in the big room.

"I want to talk with you, John," he said, grimly, and passed on into his private office.

The closing of the door of that sacred inner room behind John was the signal for a buzz of excited comments.

"Lordy," gasped a stenographer to her nearest neighbor, "but I'm sorry for poor young Mr. Ward—did you see the old man's face?"

The half-whispered remark expressed, with fair accuracy, the general sentiment of the entire force.

Adam Ward did not sit down at his desk, but going to a window he stood looking out as though deep in thought.

"Father," said John, at last, "what is it? Has anything happened?"

Adam turned slowly, and it was evident that he was holding his self-control by a supreme effort of will. "I have made up my mind to quit," he said. "From to-day on you will take my place and assume my responsibilities in the Mill."

"I am glad, father," said John, simply, "You really should be free from all business cares. As for my taking your place in the Mill," he smiled, "no one could ever do that, father."

"You have full control and absolute authority from to-day on," returned Adam. "I shall never put my foot inside the doors of the plant or the office again."

"But, father!" cried John. "There is no need for you to—"

Adam interrupted him with an imperious gesture. "There is no use arguing about it," he said, coldly. "But there are two or three things that I want to tell you—that I think you ought to know. You can take them from me or not, as you please. My ideas and policies that made this institution what it is to-day will probably be thrown aside as so much worthless junk, but I am going to give you a word or two of warning just the same."

John knew that when his father was in this mood there was nothing to do but to keep silent. But the expression of the old Mill owner's face filled his son's heart with pity, and the boy could not refrain from saying, "I am sorry you feel that way about it, father, because really you are all wrong. Can't we sit down and talk it over comfortably?"

"I prefer to stand," returned Adam. "I can say all I have to say in a few words. I am retiring because I know, now, after"—he hesitated—"after the last two nights, that I must. I am turning the Mill over to you because I would rather burn it to the ground than see it in the hands of any one outside the family. I believe, too, that the only way to get the wild, idiotic ideas of that old fool basket maker out of your head is to make you personally responsible for the success or failure of this business. I have watched you long enough to know that you have the ability to handle it, and I am convinced that once you realize how much money you can make, you will drop all your sentimental nonsense and get your feet on solid ground."

John Ward's cheeks flushed, but he made no reply to his father's pointed observations.

"I had those same romantic notions about work and business myself when I was your age," continued Adam, "but experience taught me better. Experience will teach you." He paused and went to stand at the window again.

John waited.

Presently Adam faced about once more. "I suppose you have noticed that McIver is greatly interested in your sister Helen?"

"I imagined so," returned John, soberly. "Well, he is. He wants to marry her. If she will only be sensible and see it right, it is a wonderful opportunity for us. McIver made over a million out of the war. His factory is next to this in size and importance and it is so closely related to the Mill that a combination of the two industries, with the control of the new process, would give you a tremendous advantage. You could practically put all competitors out of business. McIver has approached me several times on the proposition but I have been holding off, hoping that Helen would accept him, so that their marriage would tie the thing up that much tighter. You and McIver, with the family relation established by Helen, would make a great team." He hesitated and his face worked with nervous emotion as he added, "There is something about the new process that perhaps—you should know—I—" He stopped abruptly to pace up and down the room in nervous excitement, as if fighting for the mastery of the emotions aroused by this mention of his patented property.

As John Ward watched his father and felt the struggle within the man's secret self, the room seemed suddenly filled with the invisible presence of that hidden thing. The younger man's eyes filled with tears and he cried in protest, "Father—father—please don't—"

For a moment Adam Ward faced his son in silence. Then, with a sigh of relief, he muttered, "It's all right, John; just one of my nervous attacks. It's gone now."

Changing the subject abruptly, he said, "I must warn you, my boy—keep away from the Interpreter. Have nothing to do with him; he is dangerous. And watch out for Pete Martin and Charlie, too. They are all three together. This agitator, Jake Vodell, is going to make trouble. He is already getting a start with McIver's men. You have some radicals right here on your pay roll, but if you stick with McIver and follow his lead you will come through easily and put these unions where they belong. That's all, I guess," he finished, wearily. "Call in your superintendent."

"Just a moment, father," said John Ward, steadily. "It is not fair to either of us for me to accept the management of the Mill without telling you that I can't do all that you have suggested."

Adam looked at his son sharply. "And what can't you do?" he demanded.

"I shall never work with McIver in any way," answered John slowly. "You know what I think of him and his business principles. Helen's interest in him is her own affair, but I have too great a sense of loyalty to my country and too much self-respect ever to think of McIver as anything but a traitor and an enemy."

"And what else?" asked Adam.

"I will not promise to keep away from the Interpreter. I reserve the right to choose my own friends and business associates, and I will deal with the employees of the Mill and with the unions without regard to McIver's policies or any consideration of his interest in any way whatever."

For a long moment Adam Ward looked at his son who stood so straight and uncompromisingly soldier-like before him. Suddenly, to John's amazement, his father laughed. And there was not a little admiration and pride in the old Mill owner's voice as he said, "I see! In other words, if you are going to be the boss, you don't propose to have any strings tied to you."

"Would you, sir?" asked John.

"No, I wouldn't," returned Adam and laughed again. "Well, go ahead. Have it your own way. I am not afraid for you in the long run. You are too much like me not to find out where your own interests lie, once you come squarely up against the situation. I only wanted to help you, but it looks as though you would have to go through the experience for yourself. It's all right, son, go to it! Now call George."

When the superintendent entered the private office, Adam Ward said, briefly, "George, I am turning the Mill over to John here. From to-day on he is the manager without any strings on him in any way. He has the entire responsibility and is the only authority. He accounts to no one but himself. That is all."

Abruptly Adam Ward left the private office. Without even a look toward the men in the big outer room who had served with him for years, he passed on out to the street.

When the whistle sounded, John went out into the Mill to stand near the window where the workmen passing in line received their envelopes.

From every part of the great main building, from the yards and the several outer sheds and structures they came. From furnace and engine and bench and machine they made their way toward that given point as scattered particles of steel filings are drawn toward a magnet. The converging paths of individuals touched, and two walked side by side. Other individuals joined the two and as quickly trios and quartets came together to form groups that united with other similar groups; while from the mass thus assembled, the thin line was formed that extended past the pay clerk's window and linked the Mill to the outer world.

In that eager throng of toilers Adam Ward's son saw men of almost every race: Scotchmen greeted Norwegians; men from Ireland exchanged friendly jests with men from Italy; sons of England laughed with the sons of France; Danes touched elbows with Dutchmen; and men from Poland stood shoulder to shoulder with men whose fathers fought with Washington. And every man was marked alike with the emblems of a common brotherhood—the brotherhood of work. Their faces were colored with the good color of their toil—with the smoke of their furnaces, and the grime of their engines, and the oil from their machines mixed with the sweat of their own bodies. Their clothing was uniform with the insignia of their united endeavor. And to the newly appointed manager of the Mill, these men of every nation were comrades in a common cause, spending the strength of their manhood for common human needs. He saw that only in the work of the world could the brotherhood of man be realized; only in the Mill of life's essential industries could the nations of the earth become as one.

In that gathering of workmen the son of Adam Ward saw men of many religions, sects and creeds: Christians and pagans; Catholics and Protestants; men who worshiped the God of Abraham and men who worshiped no God; followers of strange fanatical spiritualism and followers of a stranger materialism. And he saw those many shades of human beliefs blended and harmonized—brought into one comprehensive whole by the power of the common necessities of human life.

He saw that the unity of the warring religions of the world would not be accomplished in seminaries of speculative theological thought, but that in the Mill of life the spiritual brotherhood of all mankind would be realized. In work, he saw the true worship of a common God whose vice-regent on earth is humanity itself.

In that pay-day assembly John saw men of middle age to whom the work into which they daily put the strength of their lives meant nothing less than the lives of their families. In the families dependent upon the Mill he saw the life of the nation dependent upon the nation's industries. As he saw in the line men old and gray and bent with the toil of many years, he realized how the generation of this day is indebted for every blessing of life—for life itself, indeed—to these veterans of the Mill who have given, their years in work that the nation might, through its industries, live and, in the building up of its industries, grow strong.

As he watched the men of his own age, he thought how they, too, must receive the torch from the failing hands of their passing fathers, and in the Mill prove their manhood's right to carry the fire of their country's industrial need.

And there were boys on the edge of manhood, who must be, by the Mill, trained in work for the coming needs of their country; who must indeed find their very manhood itself in work, or through all their years remain wards of the people—a burden upon humanity—the weakness of the nation. For as surely as work is health and strength and honor and happiness and life, so surely is idleness disease and weakness and shame and misery and death.

The home builder, the waster, the gambler, the loyal citizen, the slacker, the honest and dishonest—they were all there at the pay window of the Mill. And to each the pay envelope meant a different thing. To big Max the envelope meant an education for his son. To Bill Connley it meant food and clothing for his brood of children. To young Scot it meant books for his study. To others it meant medicine or doctors for sick ones at home. To others it meant dissipation and dishonor. To all alike those pay envelopes meant Life.

As these men of the Mill passed the son of Adam Ward, there were many smiling nods and hearty words of greeting. Now and then one would speak a few words about his work. Others passed a laughing jest. Many who were his comrades in France gave him the salute of their military days—half in fun, but with a hint of underlying seriousness that made the act a recognition of his rank in the industrial army.

And John returned these greetings in the same good spirit of fellowship. To one it was, "Hello, Tony, how is that new baby at your house?" To another, whose hand was swathed in a dirty bandage, "Take care of that hand, Mack; don't get funny with it just because it's well enough to use again." To another, "How is the wife, Frank, better? Good, that's fine." Again it was, "You fellows on number six machine made a record this week." Again, "Who's the hoodoo on number seven furnace?—four accidents in six days is going some—better look around for your Jonah." And again, "I heard about that stunt of yours, Bill; the kid would have been killed sure if you hadn't kept your head and nerve. It was great work, old man." And to a lad farther down the line, "You'll know better next time, won't you, son?" But there were some who passed John Ward with averted faces or downcast eyes. Here and there there were sneering, vicious glances and low muttered oaths and curses and threats. Not infrequently the name of Jake Vodell was mentioned with approved quotations from the agitator's speeches of hatred against the employer class.

The last of the long line of workmen was approaching the window when Pete Martin greeted the son of his old bench mate with a smile of fatherly affection and pride.

"Hello, Uncle Pete," returned John. "Where is Charlie?"

"I'm sure I don't know, John," the old man answered, looking about. "I supposed he had gone on, I was a little slow myself."

"There he is," said John, as the soldier workman came running from a distant part of the building.

When Captain Charlie came up to them, his father moved on to the window so that for a moment the two friends were alone.

"It's come, Charlie," said John, in a low tone. "Father told me and gave it out to the superintendent to-day."

80

"Hurrah!" said Charlie Martin, and he would have said more but his comrade interrupted him.

"Shut up, will you? We must go out to the hill to-morrow for a talk. I'll come for you early."

"Right!" said Charlie with a grin, "but may I be permitted to say congratulations?"

"Congratulations your foot!" returned the new general manager. "It's going to be one whale of a job, old man."

The last of the stragglers came near and Charlie Martin moved on, in his turn, to the pay window.

When John arrived home in the late afternoon, his sister met him with many joyful exclamations. "Is father in earnest? Are you really to take his place, John?"

John laughed. "You would have thought he was in earnest if you had heard him." Then he asked, soberly, "Where is father, Helen; is he all right?"

"He has been shut up in his room all alone ever since he told us," she returned, sadly. "I do hope he will be better now that he is to have complete rest."

As if determined to permit no cloud to mar the joy of the occasion, she continued, with eager interest, "Do tell me about it, brother. Were the men in the office glad? Aren't you happy and proud? And how did the workmen take it?"

"The people in the office were very nice," he answered, smiling back at her. "Good old George looked a little like he wanted to laugh and cry at the same time. The men in the plant don't know yet, except Charlie—I told him."

A little shadow fell over Helen's happy face and she looked away. "I suppose of course you would tell Charlie Martin the first thing," she said, slowly. Then, throwing her arm suddenly about his neck, she kissed him. "You are a dear, silly, sentimental old thing, but I am as proud as I can be of you."

"As for that," returned John, "I guess it must run in the family somehow. I notice little things now and then that make me think my sister may not always be exactly a staid, matter-of-fact old lady owl."

When he had laughed at her blushes, and had teased her as a brother is in duty bound, he said, seriously, "Will you tell me something, Helen? Something that I want very much to know—straight from you."

"What is it, John?"

"Are you going to marry Jim McIver?"

"How do you know that he wants me?"

"Father told me to-day. Don't fence please, dear. Either tell me straight out or tell me to mind my own business."

She replied with straightforward honesty, "Mr. McIver has asked me, John, but I can't tell you what my answer will be. I don't know myself."

CHAPTER X

CONCERNING THE NEW MANAGER

When the Mill whistle sounded at the close of that pay day, Mary was sitting under the tree in the yard with her sewing basket—a gift from the Interpreter—on the grass beside her chair. The sunlight lay warm and bright on the garden where the ever industrious bees were filling their golden bags with the sweet wealth of the old-fashioned flowers. Bright-winged butterflies zigzagged here and there above the shrubbery along the fence and over her head; in the leafy shadows of the trees her bird friends were cheerfully busy with their small duties. Now and then a passing neighbor paused to exchange a word or two of their common interests. Presently workmen from the Mill went by—men of her father's class who lived in that vicinity of well-kept cottage homes; and each one called a greeting to the daughter of his friend.

And so, at last, Peter Martin himself and Captain Charlie turned in at the little white gate and came to sit down on the grass at her feet.

"You are late to-day," said Mary, smiling. "I suppose you both have forgotten that the vegetable garden is to be hoed this afternoon and that you, Charlie, promised to beat the rugs for me."

Captain Charlie stretched himself lazily on the cool grass. "We should worry about gardens and rugs and things," he returned. "This is the day we celebrate."

The father laughed quietly at his daughter's look of puzzled inquiry.

"The day you celebrate?" said Mary. "Celebrate what?"

Charlie answered with a fair imitation of a soapbox orator, "This, my beloved sister, is the day of our emancipation from the iron rule of that cruel capitalist, who has for so many years crushed the lives of his toiling slaves in his Mill of hell, and coined our heart's blood into dollars to fill his selfish coffers of princely luxury. Down through the ringing ages of the future this day will be forever celebrated as the day that signals the dawning of a new era in the industrial world of—uh-wow! Stop it!"

Captain Charlie was ticklish and the toe of Mary's slippered foot had found a vital spot among his ribs.

"You sound like that Jake Vodell," she said. "Stop your nonsense this minute and tell me what you mean or—" Her foot advanced again threateningly.

Captain Charlie rolled over to a safe distance and sat up to grin at her with teasing impudence.

"What's the matter with him, father?" she demanded.

But Pete only laughed and answered, "I guess maybe he thinks he's going to get promoted to some higher-up position in the Mill."

"No such luck for me!" said Charlie quickly. "John will need me too much right where I am."

A bright color swept into Mary's cheeks and her eyes shone with glad excitement. "Do you mean that John—that his father has—" She looked from her father's face to her brother and back to her father again.

Pete nodded silently.

"You've guessed it, sister," said Charlie. "Old Adam walked out for good to-day, turned the whole works over to John—troubles, triumphs, opportunities, disasters and all. And it's a man's sized job the boy has drawn, believe me—especially right now, with Jake Vodell as busy as he is."

"The men in the Mill were all pleased with the change, weren't they?" asked Mary.

"They will be, when they hear of it," answered Captain Charlie, getting to his feet. "That is," he added, as he met his father's look, "most of them will be."

"There's some in the Mill that it won't make any difference to, I'm afraid," said Peter Martin, soberly.

Then the two men went into the house to, as they said, "clean up"—an operation that required a goodly supply of water with plenty of soap and a no little physical effort in the way of vigorous rubbing.

When her father and brother were gone, Mary Martin sat very still. So still was she that a butterfly paused in its zigzag flight about the yard to rest on the edge of the work basket at her side. At last the young woman rose slowly to her feet, dropping the sewing she had held on the other things in the basket. The startled butterfly spread its gorgeous wings and zigzagged away unnoticed. Crossing the little lawn, Mary made her way among the flowers in the garden until she stood half hidden in the tall bushes which grew along the fence that separated the Martin home from the neglected grounds about the old house. When her father and brother went to their pleasant task in the vegetable garden she was still standing there, but the men did not notice.

* * * * *

Later, when Mary called the men to supper, the change in the management of the Mill was again mentioned. And all during the evening meal it was the topic of their conversation. It was natural that the older man should recall the days when he and Adam and the Interpreter had worked together.

"The men generally showed a different spirit toward their work in those days," said the veteran. "They seemed to have a feeling of pride and a love for it that I don't see much of now. Of late years, it looks as though everybody hates his job and is ashamed of what he is doing. They all seem to think of nothing but their pay, and busy their minds with scheming how they can get the most and give the least. It's the regular thing to work with one eye on the foreman and the other on the clock, and to count it a great joke when a job is spoiled or a breakdown causes trouble." All of which was a speech of unusual length for Pete Martin. Captain Charlie asked, thoughtfully, "And don't you think, father, that Adam looks on the work of the Mill in exactly that spirit of 'get the most for the least' without regard to the meaning and purpose of the work itself?"

"There's no reason to doubt it, son, that I can see," returned the old workman.

"I have often wondered," said Charlie, "how much the attitude of the employees toward their work is due to the attitude of their employers toward that same work."

The old workman returned, heartily, "We'll be seeing a different feeling in the Mill under John, I am thinkin'—he's different."

"I should say he is different," agreed Charlie, quickly. "John would rather work at his job for nothing than do anything else for ten times the salary he draws. But was Adam always as he is now?"

"About his work do you mean?"

"Yes."

Adam Ward's old comrade answered, slowly, "I've often wondered that myself. I can't say for sure. As I look back now, I think sometimes that he used to have an interest in the work itself at first. Takin' his development of the new process and all—it almost seems that he must have had. And yet, there's some things that make me think that all the time it meant nothing to him but just what he could get out of it for himself."

"Helen will be happy over the change, won't she?" remarked Mary.

"Helen!" ejaculated Captain Charlie, with more emphasis perhaps than the occasion demanded.

"She won't give it so much as a thought. Why should she? She can go on with her dinners and card parties and balls and country club affairs with the silk-hatted slackers of her set, just the same as if nothing had happened."

Mary laughed. "Seems to me I have heard something like that before—'silk-hatted slackers'—it sounds familiar."

Captain Charlie watched her suspiciously.

The father laughed quietly.

"Oh, yes," she exclaimed, with an air of triumph. "It was Bobby Whaley who said it. I remember thinking at the time that it probably came to him from his father, who of course got it from Jake Vodell. Silk-hatted slackers—sounds like Jake, doesn't it, father?"

Captain Charlie grinned sheepishly. "I know it was a rotten thing to say," he admitted. "Some of the best and bravest men in our army were silk-hatters at home. They were in the ranks, too, a lot of them—just like John Ward. And some of the worst cowards and shirkers and slackers that ever lived belonged to our ancient and noble order of the horny-handed sons of toil, that Jake Vodell orates about. But what gets me, is the way some of those fellows who were everything but slackers in France act, now that they are back home. Over there they were on the job with everything they had, to the last drop of their blood. But now that they are back in their own home country again, they have simply thrown up their hands and quit—-that is, a lot of them have. They seem to think that the signing of the Armistice ended it all and that they can do nothing now for the rest of their lives. Who was it said, 'Peace hath her victories,' or something like that? Well, peace hath her defeats, too. I'll be hanged if I can understand how a man who has it in him to be a one hundred per cent American hero in war can be a Simon-pure slacker in times of peace."

As he finished, Captain Charlie pushed his chair back from the table and, finding his pipe, proceeded to fill it with the grim determination of an old-time minuteman ramming home a charge in his Bunker Hill musket.

Later the two men went out to enjoy their pipes on the lawn in the cool of the evening. They were discussing the industrial situation when Mary, having finished her household work for the night, joined them.

"I forgot to tell you," she said, "that Jake Vodell called to-day."

"Again!" exclaimed Charlie.

"If Vodell wants to talk with us he'll have to come when we are at home," said Pete Martin, slowly, looking at his daughter.

86

With a laugh, the young woman returned, "But I don't think that it was you or Charlie that he wanted to see this time, father."

"What did he want?" demanded her brother quickly.

"He wanted me to go with him to a dance next Tuesday," she answered demurely.

"Huh," came in a tone of disgust from Charlie.

The father asked, quietly, "And what did you say to him, Mary?"

"I told him that I went to dances only with my friends."

"Good!" said Captain Charlie.

"And what then?" asked Pete.

"Then," she hesitated, "then he said something about my being careful that I had the right sort of friends and referred to Charlie and John."

"Yes?" said Mary's father.

"He said that the only use John Ward had for Charlie was to get a line on the union and the plans of the men—that his friendship was only a the union men wouldn't stand for it."

Captain Charlie muttered something under his breath that he could not speak aloud in the presence of his sister.

Pete Martin deliberately knocked the ashes from his pipe.

"Then," continued Mary, "he talked about how everybody knew that John was nothing but a"—she laughed mockingly at her brother—"a silk-hatted swell who couldn't hold his job an hour if it wasn't that his father owned the Mill, and that Charlie was a hundred times more competent to manage the business. He said that anybody could see how Charlie's promotion in the army proved him superior to John, who was never anything but a common private."

Captain Charlie laughed aloud. "John and I understand all about that superiority business. I was lucky, that's all—our captain just happened to be looking in my direction. Believe me, good old John was just as busy as I ever dared to be, only it was his luck to be busy at some other point that the captain didn't see."

"Is that all Jake had to say, daughter?"

"No," answered the young woman, slowly. "I—I am afraid I was angry at what he called John—I mean at what he said about Charlie and John's friendship—and so I told him what I thought about him and Sam Whaley and their crowd, and asked him to go and not come back again except to see you or Charlie."

"Good for you, Mary!" exclaimed her brother.

But the old workman said nothing.

"And how did Jake take his dismissal?" asked Charlie, presently.

"He went, of course," she answered. "But he said that he would show me what the friendship of a man of John Ward's class meant to a working man; that the union men would find out who the loyal members were and when the time came they would know whom to reward and whom to treat as traitors to the Cause."

For a little while after this the three sat in silence. At last Peter Martin rose heavily to his feet. "Come, Charlie, it is time we were on our way to the meeting; we mustn't be late, you know."

When her father and brother were gone to the meeting of the Mill workers' union, Mary Martin locked the door of the cottage and walked swiftly away.

It was not far to the Interpreter's hut, and presently the young woman was climbing the old zigzag stairway to the little house on the edge of the cliff above. There was no light but the light of the stars—the faint breath of the night breeze scarcely stirred the leaves of the bushes or moved the tall weeds that grew on the hillside. At the top of the stairs Mary paused to look at the many lights of the Flats, the Mill, the business houses, the streets and the homes, that shone in the shadowy world below.

She was about to move toward the door of the hut when the sound of voices coming from the balcony-porch halted her. The Interpreter was speaking. She could not distinguish his words, but the deep tones of the old basket maker's voice were not to be mistaken. Then the young woman heard some one reply, and the laughing voice that answered the Interpreter was as familiar to Mary Martin as the laugh of her own brother. The evening visitor to the little hut on the cliff was the son of Adam Ward.

Very softly Mary Martin stole back down the zigzag steps to the road below. Slowly she went back through the deep shadows of the night to her little home, with its garden of old-fashioned flowers, next door to the deserted house where John Ward was born.

Late that night, while John was still at the Interpreter's hut, Adam Ward crept alone like some hunted thing about the beautiful grounds of his great estate. Like a haunted soul of wretchedness, the Mill owner had left his bed to escape the horror of his dreams and to find, if possible, a little rest from his torturing fears in the calm solitude of the night.

* * * * *

When Pete Martin, with Captain Charlie and their many industrial comrades, had returned to their homes after the meeting of their union, five men gathered in that dirty, poorly lighted room in the rear of Dago Bill's pool hall.

The five men had entered the place one at a time. They spoke together in low, guarded tones of John Ward and his management of the Mill, of Pete Martin and Captain Charlie, of the Interpreter and McIver.

And three of those five men had come to that secret place at Jake Vodell's call, directly from the meeting of the Mill workers' union.

CHAPTER XI

COMRADES

Mary was in the flower garden that Sunday forenoon when John Ward stopped his big roadster in front of the Martin cottage.

It was not at all unusual for the one-time private, John, to call that way for his former superior officer. Nearly every Sunday when the weather was fine the comrades would go for a long ride in John's car somewhere into the country. And always they carried a lunch prepared by Captain Charlie's sister.

Sometimes there might have been a touch of envy in Mary's generous heart, as she watched the automobile with her brother and his friend glide away up the green arched street. After all, Mary was young and loved the country, and John Ward's roadster was a wonderful machine, and the boy who had lived in the old house next door had been, in her girlhood days, a most delightful comrade and playfellow.

The young woman could no more remember her first meeting with John or his sister Helen than she could recall the exact beginning of her acquaintance with Charlie. From her cradle days she had known the neighbor children as well as she had known her own brother. Then the inevitable separation of the playmates had come with Adam Ward's increasing material prosperity. The school and college days of John and Helen and the removal of the family from the old house to the new home on the hill had brought to them new friends and new interests—friends and interests that knew nothing of Pete Martin's son and daughter. But in Mary's heart, because it was a woman's heart, the memories of the old house lived. The old house itself, indeed, served to keep those memories alive.

John did not see her at first, but called a cheery greeting to her father, who with his pipe and paper was sitting under the tree on the lawn side of the walk.

Mary drew a little back among the flowers and quietly went on with her work.

"Is Charlie here, Uncle Pete?" asked John, as he came through the gate.

"He's in the house, I think, John, or out in the back yard, maybe," answered the old workman. And, then, in his quiet kindly way, Peter Martin spoke a few words to Adam Ward's son about the change in the management of the Mill—wishing John success, expressing his own gratification and confidence, and assuring him of the hearty good will that prevailed, generally, among the employees.

Presently, as the two men talked together, Mary went to express her pleasure in the promotion of her old playmate to a position of such responsibility and honor in the industrial world. And John Ward, when he saw her coming toward him with an armful of flowers, must at least have noticed the charming picture she made against that background of the garden, with its bright-colored blossoms in the flood of morning sunlight.

Certainly the days of their childhood companionship must have stirred in his memory, for he said, presently, "Do you know, Mary, you make me think of mother and the way she used to go among her flowers every Sunday morning when we lived in the old house there." He looked thoughtfully toward the neighboring place.

"How is your mother these days, John?" asked Mary's father.

"She is well, thank you, Uncle Pete," returned John. "Except of course," he added, soberly, "she worries a good deal about father's ill health."

"Your father will surely be much better, now that he is relieved from all his business care," said Mary.

"We are all hoping so," returned John.

There was an awkward moment of silence.

As if the mention of his father's condition had in some way suggested the thought, or, perhaps, because he wished to change the subject, John said, "The old house looks pretty bad, doesn't it? It is a shame that we have permitted it to go to ruin that way."

Neither Peter Martin nor his daughter made reply to this. There was really nothing they could say.

John was about to speak again when Captain Charlie, coming from the house with their lunch basket in his hand, announced that he was ready, and the two men started on their way.

Standing at the gate, Mary waved good-by as her brother turned to look back. Even when the automobile had finally passed from sight she stood there, still looking in the direction it had gone.

Peter Martin watched his daughter thoughtfully.

Without speaking, Mary went slowly into the house.

Her father sat for some minutes looking toward the door through which she had passed. At last with deliberate care he refilled his pipe. But the old workman did not, for an hour or more, resume the reading of his Sunday morning paper.

Beyond a few casual words, the two friends in the automobile seemed occupied, each with his own thoughts. Neither asked, "Where shall we go?" or offered any suggestion for the day's outing. As if it were understood between them, John turned toward the hill country and sent the powerful machine up the long, winding grade, as if on a very definite mission. An hour's driving along the ridges and the hillsides, and they turned from the main thoroughfare into a narrow lane between two thinly wooded pastures. A mile of this seldom traveled road and John stopped his car beside the way. Here they left the automobile, and, taking the lunch basket, climbed the fence and made their way up the steep side of the hill to a clump of trees that overlooked the many miles of winding river and broad valley and shaded hills. The place was a favorite spot to which they often came for those hours of comradeship that are so necessary to all well-grounded and enduring friendships.

"Well, *Mister* Ward," said Captain Charlie, when they were comfortably seated and their pipes were going well, "how does it feel to be one of the cruel capitalist class a-grindin' the faces off us poor?"

The workman spoke lightly, but there was something in his voice that made John look at him sharply. It was a little as though Captain Charlie were nerving himself to say good-by to his old comrade.

The new general manager smiled, but it was a rather serious smile. "Do you remember how you felt when you received your captain's commission?" he asked.

"I do that," returned Charlie. "I felt that I had been handed a mighty big job and was scared stiff for fear I wouldn't be able to make good at it."

"Exactly," returned John. "And I'll never forget how *I* felt when they stepped you up the first time and left me out. And when you had climbed on up and Captain Wheeler was killed and you received your commission, with me still stuck in the ranks—well—I never told you before but I'll say now that I was the lonesomest, grouchiest, sorest man in the whole A.E.F. It seemed to me about then that being a private was the meanest, lowest, most no-account job on earth, and I was darned near deserting and letting the Germans win the war and be hanged. I thought it would serve the Allies right if I was to let 'em get licked good and plenty just for failing to appreciate me."

Captain Charlie laughed.

"Oh, yes, you can laugh," said the new general manager of the Mill. "It's darned funny *now*, but I can tell you that there wasn't much humor in it for me *then*. We had lived too close together from that first moment when we found ourselves in the same company for me to feel comfortable as a common buck private, watchin' you strut around in the gentleman officer class, and not daring even to tell you to go to——"

"You poor old fool," said Charlie, affectionately. "You knew my promotion was all an accident."

"Exactly," returned John dryly. "We've settled all that a hundred times."

"And you ought to have known," continued Captain Charlie, warmly, "that my feeling toward you would have been no different if they had made me a general."

"Sure, I ought to have known," retorted John, with an air of triumph.

And then it appeared that John Ward had a very definite purpose in thus turning his comrade's mind to their army life in France. "And you should have sense enough to understand that my promotion in the Mill is not going to make any difference in our friendship. Your promotion was the result of an accident, Charlie, exactly as my position in the Mill to-day is the result of an accident. Your superior officer happened to see you. I happen to be the son of Adam Ward. If I should have known *then* that your rank would make no difference in your feeling toward me, you have got to understand *now* that my position can make no difference in my feeling toward you."

Charlie Martin's silence revealed how accurately John had guessed his Mill comrade's hidden thoughts.

The new manager continued, "The thing that straightened me out on the question of our different ranks was that scrap where Captain Charlie and Private John found themselves caught in the same shell hole with no one else anywhere near except friend enemy, and somebody had to do something darned quick. Do you remember our argument?"

"Do I remember!" exclaimed Charlie. "I remember how you said it was your job to take the chance because I, being an officer, was worth more to the cause and because the loss of a private didn't matter so much anyhow."

John retorted quickly, "And you said that it was up to you to take the chance because it was an officer's duty to take care of his men."

"And then," said Charlie, "you told me to go to hell, commission and all. And I swore that I'd break you for insolence and insubordination if we ever got out of the scrape alive."

"And so," grinned John, "we compromised by pulling it off together. And from that time on I felt different and was as proud of you and your officer's swank as if I had been the lucky guy myself."

"Yes," said Captain Charlie, smiling affectionately, "and I could see the grin in your eyes every time you saluted."

"No one else ever saw it, though," returned Private Ward, proudly.

"Don't think for a minute that I overlooked that either," said Captain Martin. "If any one else had seen it, I would have disciplined you for sure."

"And don't you think for a minute that I didn't know that, too," retorted John. "I could feel you laying for me, and every man in the company knew it just as be knew our friendship. That's what made us all love you so. We used to say that if Captain Charlie would just take a notion to start for Berlin and invite us to go along the war would be over right there."

Charlie Martin laughed appreciatively. Then he said, earnestly, "After all, old man, it wasn't an officers' war and it wasn't a privates' war, was it? Any more than it was the war of America, or England, or France, or Australia, or Canada—it was *our* war. And that, I guess, is the main reason why it all came out as it did."

"Now," said John, with hearty enthusiasm, "you are talking sense."

"But it is all very different now, John," said Charlie, slowly. "Millsburgh is not France and the Mill is not the United States Army."

"No," returned John, "and yet there is not such a lot of difference, when you come to think it out."

"We can't disguise the facts," said Captain Martin stubbornly.

"We are not going to disguise anything," retorted John. "I had an idea how you would feel over my promotion, and that is why I wanted you out here to-day. You've got to get this 'it's all very different now' stuff out of your system. So go ahead and shoot your facts."

"All right," said Charlie. "Let's look at things as they are. It was all very well for us to moon over what we would do if we ever got back home when we knew darned well our chances were a hundred to one against our ever seeing the old U.S. again. We spilled a lot of sentiment about comradeship and loyalty and citizenship and equality and all that, but—"

"Can your chatter!" snapped John. "Drag out these facts that you are so anxious to have recognized. Let's have a good look at whatever it is that makes you rough-neck sons of toil so superior to us lily-fingered employers. Go to the bat."

"Well," offered Charlie, reluctantly, "to begin with, you are a millionaire, a university man, member of select clubs; I am nothing but a common workman."

John returned, quickly, "We are both citizens of the United States. In the duties and privileges of our citizenship we stand on exactly the same footing, just as in the army we stood on the common ground of loyalty. And we are both equally dependent upon the industries of our country—upon the Mill, and upon each other. Exactly as we were both dependent upon the army and upon each other in France."

"You are the general manager of the Mill, practically the owner," said Charlie. "I am only one of your employees."

The son of Adam Ward answered scornfully, "Yes, over there it was Captain Charlie Martin and Private John Ward of the United States Army. I suppose it is a lot different now that it is Captain John Ward and Private Charlie Martin of the United States Industries."

Charlie continued, "You live in a mansion in a select district on the hill, I live in a little cottage on the edge of the Flats!"

"Over there it was officers' quarters and barracks," said John, shortly.

Charlie tried again, "You wear white collars and tailored clothes at your work—I wear dirty overalls."

"We used to call 'em uniforms," barked John.

Captain Charlie hesitated a little before he offered his next fact, and when he spoke it was with a little more feeling. "There are our families to take into account too, John. Your sister—well—isn't it a fact that your sister would no more think of calling on Mary than she would think of putting on overalls and going to work in the Mill?"

It was John's turn now to hesitate.

"Don't you see?" continued Charlie, "we belong to different worlds, I tell you, John."

Deliberately Helen's brother knocked the ashes from his pipe and refilled it with thoughtful care.

Then he said, gravely, "Helen doesn't realize, as we do, old man. How could she? The girl has not had a chance to learn what the war taught us. She is exactly like thousands of other good women, and men, too, for that matter. They simply don't understand. Good Lord!" he exploded, suddenly "when I think what a worthless snob I was before I enlisted I want to kick my fool self to death. But we are drifting away from the main thought," he finished.

"Oh, I don't know," returned the other.

"I thought we were discussing the question of rank," said John.

"Well," retorted Charlie, dryly, "isn't that exactly the whole question as your sister sees it?"

"You give me a pain!" growled John. "I'll admit that Helen, right now, attaches a great deal of importance to some things that—well, that are not so very important after all. But she is no worse than I was before I learned better. And you take my word she'll learn, too. Sister visits the old Interpreter too often not to absorb a few ideas that she failed to acquire at school. He will help her to see the light, just as he helped me. But for him, I would have been nothing but a gentleman slacker myself—if there is any such animal. But what under heaven has all this to do with our relation as employer and employee in the Mill? What effect would Mary have had on you over there if she had gone to you with 'Oh, Charlie dear, you mustn't go out in that dreadful No Man's Land to-night. It is so dirty and wet and cold. Remember that you are an officer, Charlie dear, and let Private John go.'"

Captain Charlie laughed—this new general manager of the Mill was so like the buddie he had loved in France. "Do you remember that night—" he began, but his comrade interrupted him rudely.

"Shut up! I've got to get this thing off my chest and you've got to hear me out. This country of ours started out all right with the proposition that all men are created free and equal. But ninety per cent of our troubles are caused by our crazy notions as to what that equality really means. The rest of our grief comes from our fool claims to superiority of one sort or another. It looks to me as though you and Helen agreed exactly on this question of rank and I am here to tell you that you are both wrong."

Captain Charlie Martin sat up at this, but before he could speak John shot a question at him. "Tell me, when Private Ward saluted Captain Martin as the regulations provide, was the action held by either the officer or the private to be a recognition of the superiority of Captain Martin or the inferiority of Private Ward—was it?"

"Not that any one could notice," answered Charlie with a grin.

"You bet your life it wasn't," said John. "Well, then," he continued, "what was it that the salute recognized?"

"Why, it was the captain's *rank*."

"Exactly; and what determined that rank?"

"The number of men he commanded."

96

"That's it!" cried John. "The rank of the captain represented the—the"—he searched for a word—"the *oneness* of all the men in his command. And so you see the thing that the individual private really saluted as superior to himself was the *oneness* of all his comrades, both privates and officers in the company."

"Sure," said Charlie, looking a little puzzled, as if he did not quite see what the manager of the Mill was driving at. "The salute was merely a sign of the individual's surrender of his own personal will to the authority of the rank that represented all his fellow individuals."

"Yes," said John, "and when Jack Pershing stood up there with the rest of the kings and we paraded past, were we humiliated because we were not dressed exactly like the reviewing generals? We were not. We stuck out our chests and pulled in our chins as if the whole show was framed to honor us. And that is exactly what it was, Charlie, because we were all included in Pershing's rank. The army was not honoring Pershing the man, it was honoring *itself*."

"Yes," said Charlie, as if he still did not quite grasp his comrade's purpose.

"Here," said John, "this is the idea. You remember how when we were kids we used to get hold of an old magnifying glass and use it as a burning glass?"

"I remember we darned near set fire to Hank Webster's barn once," smiled Charlie.

"Well," returned John, "think of the army as a sun, and of every loyal individual soldier, officer and private alike, as a ray of that sun and *there* is your true equality. Pershing's rank was simply the burning glass that focused our two million individual rays to a point of such equality that they could move as one. And I noticed another thing in that review, too," continued John, earnestly, "even if I was supposed to have my eyes front, I noticed that General Pershing saluted the colors. And that meant simply this, that as each individual soldier honored the whole army in his recognition of the general's rank, the army itself, through its commander, honored the greater *oneness* of the nation. And so Foch's rank was a burning glass that focused the different allied nations into a still greater *oneness*, and drew their strength to such a point of equality that it lighted a fire under old Kaiser Bill."

"But what has all this to do with you and me now?" demanded Charlie. "It looks to me as though you are the one that is getting away from the main thought."

"I am not," returned John. "It has this to do with you and me: Our little part as a nation in that world job in France is finished all right, and the national job that we have to tackle now, here at home, is a little different, but the principle of unity involved is exactly the same. Our everyday work can no more be done by those who work with their hands alone than the Germans could have been whipped by privates alone. Nor can our industries be carried on by those who do the planning and managing alone any more than the army could have carried out a campaign with nothing but officers."

"Oh, I see now what you are getting at," said Charlie.

"It's about time that you woke up," retorted John.

"You mean," continued Charlie, carefully, "that just as the unity of the army was in the different ranks that focused the individual soldier rays upon one common purpose, so the true equality of our industries is possible only through the difference in rank, such as—well, such as yours and mine—manager and workman or employer and employee."

"Now you're getting wise," cried John. "Really at times you show signs of almost human intelligence."

Charlie returned, doubtfully, "How do you suppose Sam Whaley and a few others I could name in our union would take to this equality stuff of yours?"

"And how do you suppose McIver and others like him would take to it?" retorted John. "All the men in your union are not Sam Whaleys by a long shot, neither are all employers like McIver. As I remember, you had to discipline a man now and then in Company K. And you have heard of officers being cashiered, haven't you?"

"That's all right," returned the captain, "but how will the rank and file of our industrial army as a whole ever get it?"

For some time John Ward did not reply to this, but sat brooding over the question, while his former superior officer waited expectantly.

Then the manager said, earnestly, "Charlie, what was it that drew over four million American citizens of almost every known parentage from every walk of life, and made them an army with one purpose? And what was it that inspired one hundred million more to back them?

"I'll tell you what it was," he continued, when his companion did not answer, "it was the Big Idea.

"Oh, yes, I know there were all kinds of graft and incompetency and jealousy and mutiny and outrages. And there were traitors and profiteers and slackers of every sort. But the Big Idea that focused the strength of the nation as a whole, Charlie, was so much bigger than any individual or group that it absorbed all. It took possession of us all—inspired us all—dominated and drove us all, into every conceivable effort and sacrifice, until it made heroism a common thing. And this Big Idea was so big that it not only absorbed disloyalty and selfishness as a great living river takes in a few drops of poison, but it assimilated, as well, every brand of class and caste. It

98

made no distinction between officer and private, it ruled General Pershing and Private Jones alike. It recognized no difference between educated and uneducated and sent university professors and bootblacks over the top side by side. And this Big Idea that so focused the individual rays of our nation against German imperialism was nothing more or less than *the idea of the oneness of all humanity.* It may be lost in a scramble for the spoils of victory, it is true, but it was the Big Idea that won the victory just the same."

John Ward was on his feet now, pacing back and forth. His face was flushed and eager, his eyes were glowing, as he himself was possessed of the Big Idea which he strove to put into words.

And Captain Charlie's pipe was forgotten as he watched his friend and listened. This John Ward was a John Ward that few people in Millsburgh knew. But Captain Charlie knew him. Captain Charlie had seen him tested in all the ways that war tests men. In cold and hunger and the unspeakable discomforts of mud and filth and vermin—in the waiting darkness when an impatient whisper or a careless move to ease overstrained nerves meant a deluge of fire and death—in the wild frenzy of actual conflict—in the madness of victory—in the delirium of defeat—in the dreary marking time—in the tense readiness for the charge—in those many moments when death was near enough to strip the outward husks from these two men and leave their naked souls face to face—Captain Charlie had learned to know John Ward.

"Do you remember what the Interpreter said to us the first time we went to see him after we got home?" demanded John.

Charlie nodded. "He said for us not to make the mistake of thinking that the war was over just because the Armistice was signed and we were at home in Millsburgh again. I'm afraid a good many people, though, are making just that mistake."

"I didn't understand what our old friend meant then, Charlie," continued John, "but I know now. He meant that the same old fight between the spirit of imperialism that seeks the selfish dominion of an individual or class and the spirit of democracy that upholds the oneness of all for all, is still on, right here at home. The President said that the war was to make the world safe for democracy, and there are some wild enthusiasts who say that we Americans won it."

"That 'we won the war' stuff is all bunk," interrupted Charlie, in a tone of disgust.

"'Bunk' is right," agreed John. "The old A.E.F. did have a hand, though, in putting a crimp in the Kaiser's little plan for acquiring title to the whole human race for himself and family. But if the American people don't wake up to the fact that the same identical principles of human right and human liberty that sent us to France are involved in our industrial controversies here at home, we might as well have saved ourselves the trouble of going over there at all."

"That is all true enough," agreed Captain Charlie, "but what is going to wake us up? What is going to send us as a nation against the Kaiser Bills of capital and the Kaiser Bills of labor, or, if you like it better, the imperialistic employers and the equally imperialistic employees?"

John Ward fairly shouted his answer, "The Big Idea, my boy—the same Big Idea that sent us to war against imperialism over there will wake us up to drive the spirit of imperialism out of our American industries here at home."

Charlie shook his head doubtfully. "It was different during the World War, John. Then the Big Idea was held up before the people to the exclusion of everything else. When we think of the speeches and parades and rallies and sermons and books and newspapers and pictures and songs that were used in the appeal to our patriotism and our common humanity, it was no wonder that we all felt the pull of it all. But no one now is saying anything about the Big Idea, except for an occasional paragraph here and there. And certainly no one is making much noise about applying it in our industries."

"Yes, I know we can't expect any such hurrah as we had when men were needed to die for the cause in a foreign land. You go to France and get shot for humanity and you are a hero. Stay at home and sweat for the same cause and you are a nobody. From the publicity point of view" there seems to be a lot of difference between a starving baby in Belgium and a starving kid in our Millsburgh Flats. But just the same it is the Big Idea that will save us from the dangers that are threatening our industries and, through our industries, menacing the very life of out nation."

"But how will the people get it, John?"

"I don't know how it will come; but, somehow, the appeal must be made to the loyal citizens of this nation in behalf of the humanity that is dependent for life itself upon our industries, exactly as the appeal was made in behalf of the humanity that looked to us for help in time of war. We must, as a nation, learn, somehow, to feel our work as we felt our war. The same ideals of patriotism and sacrifice and heroism that were so exalted in the war must be held up in our everyday work. We must learn to see our individual jobs in the industrial organizations of our country as we saw our places in the nation's army. As a people we must grasp the mighty fact that humanity is the issue of our mills and shops and factories and mines, exactly as it was the issue of our campaigns in France. America, Charlie, has not only to face in her industries the same spirit of imperialism that we fought in France, but she has to contend with the same breed of disloyal grafters, profiteers and slackers that would have betrayed us during the war. And these traitors to our industries must be branded wherever they are found—among the business forces or in the ranks of labor, in our schools and churches or on our farms.

"The individual's attitude toward the industries of this nation must be a test of his loyal citizenship just as a man's attitude toward our army was a test. And Americans dare not continue to ignore the danger that lies in the work of those emissaries who are seeking to weaken the loyalty of our workmen and who by breeding class hatred and strife in our industries are trying to bring about the downfall of our government and replace the stars and stripes with the flag that is as foreign to our American independence as the flag of the German Kaiser himself."

Captain Charlie said, slowly, "That is all true, John, but at the same time you and I know that there is no finer body of loyal citizens anywhere in the world than the great army of our American workmen. And we know, too, that the great army of our American business men are just as fine and true and loyal."

"Exactly," cried John, "but if these loyal American citizens who work with their hands in the Mill and these loyal citizens who work in the office of the Mill don't hold together, in the same spirit of comradeship that united them in the war, to defend our industries against both the imperialism of capital and the equally dangerous imperialism of labor, we may as well run up a new flag at Washington and be done with it."

"You are right, of course, John," said Captain Charlie, "but how?"

"You and I may not know how," retorted the other, "any more than we knew how the war was going to be won when we enlisted. But we do know our little parts right here in Millsburgh clear enough. As I see it, it is up to us to carry the torch of Flanders fields into the field of our industries right here in our own home town."

He paced to and fro without speaking for a little while, the other watching him, waited.

"Of course," said John at last, "a lot of people will call us fanatics and cranks and idealists for saying that the Big Idea, of the war must dominate us in our industrial life. And, of course, it is going to be a darned sight harder in some ways to stand for the principles of our comradeship here at home than it was over there. 'Don't go out into No Man's Land to-night, Captain Charlie, it is so dirty and dark and wet and cold and dangerous; let Private John go.' But the darned fool, Captain Charlie, went into the cold and the wet and the danger because he and Private John were comrades in the oneness of the Big Idea."

His voice grew a little bitter as he finished. "Don't go into that awful Mill, Captain John, it is so dirty and dangerous and you will get so tired; let Private Charlie do the work while you stay at home and play tennis or bridge or attend to the social duties of your superior class."

With ringing earnestness Charlie Martin added, "But the darned fool fanatic and idealist Captain John will go just the same because he and Private Charlie are comrades in the oneness of the Big Idea of the Mill here at home."

For a few moments John stood looking into the distance as one who sees a vision, then he said, slowly, "And the Big Idea will win again, old man, as it has always won; and the traitors and slackers and yellow dogs will be saved with the rest, I suppose, just as they always have been saved from themselves."

He turned to see his comrade standing at attention. Gravely Captain Charlie saluted.

* * * * *

Perhaps Jake Vodell was right in believing that the friendship of John Ward and Charlie Martin was dangerous to his cause in Millsburgh.

The Vodells, who with their insidious propaganda, menace America through her industrial troubles, will be powerless, indeed, when American employers and employees can think in terms of industrial comradeship.

CHAPTER XII

TWO SIDES OF A QUESTION

That evening the new manager of the Mill stayed for supper at the Martin cottage. It was the first time since he had left the old house next door for his school in a distant city that he had eaten a meal with these friends of his boyhood.

Perhaps because their minds were so filled with things they could not speak, their talk was a little restrained. Captain Charlie attempted a jest or two; John did his best, and Mary helped them all she could. The old workman, save for a kindly word now and then to make the son of Adam Ward feel at home, was silent.

But when the supper was over and the twilight was come and they had carried their chairs out on the lawn where, in their boy and girl days they had romped away so many twilight hours, the weight of the present was lifted. While Peter Martin smoked his pipe and listened, the three made merry over the adventures of their childhood, until the old house next door, so deserted and forlorn, must have felt that the days so long past were come again.

It was rather late when John finally said goodnight. As he drove homeward he told himself many times that it had been one of the happiest evenings he had ever spent. He wondered why.

The big house on the hill, as he approached the iron gates, seemed strangely grim and forbidding. The soft darkness of the starlit night invited him to stay out of doors. Reluctantly, half in mind to turn back, he drove slowly up the long driveway. The sight of McIver's big car waiting decided him. He did not wish to meet the factory owner that evening. He would wait a while before going indoors. Finding a comfortable lawn chair not far from the front of the house, he filled his pipe.

As he sat there, many things unbidden and apparently without purpose passed in leisurely succession through his mind. Bits of boyhood experiences, long forgotten and called up now, no doubt, by his evening at the cottage that had once been as much his home as the old house itself. How inseparable the four children had been! Fragments of his army life—what an awakening it had all been for him! The coming struggle with the followers of Jake Vodell—his new responsibilities. He had feared that his comradeship with Charlie might be weakened—well, that was settled now. He was glad they had had their talk.

The door of the house opened and McIver came down the steps to his automobile. For a moment Helen stood framed against the bright light of the interior, then the car rolled away. The door was closed.

John recalled what his father had said. Would his sister finally accept McIver? For a long time the factory owner had been pressing his suit. Would she marry him at last? A combination of the Ward Mill and the McIver factory would be a mighty power in the manufacturing world. He dismissed the thought. He wished that Helen were more like Mary. His sister was a wonderful woman in his eyes—he was proud of her; but again his mind went back to the workman's home and to his happy evening there. His own home was so different. His mother! What a splendid old man Uncle Peter was!

John Ward's musings were suddenly disturbed by a faint sound. Turning his head, he saw the form of a man, dark and shadowy in the faint light of the stars, moving toward the house. John held his place silently, alert and ready. Cautiously the dark form crept forward with frequent pauses as if to look about. Then, as the figure stood for a moment silhouetted against a lighted window of the house, John recognized his father.

At the involuntary exclamation which escaped the younger man Adam whirled as if to run.

John spoke, quietly, "That you, father?"

The man came quickly to his son. With an odd nervous laugh, he said, "Lord, boy, but you startled me! What are you doing out here at this time of the night?"

"Just enjoying a quiet smoke and looking at the stars," John answered, easily.

It was evident that Adam Ward was intensely excited. His voice shook with nervous agitation and he looked over his shoulder and peered into the surrounding darkness as if dreading some lurking danger.

"I couldn't sleep," he muttered, in a low cautious tone. "Dreams—nothing in them of course—all foolishness—nerves are all shot to pieces."

He dropped down on the seat beside his son, then sprang to his feet again. "Did you hear that?" he whispered, and stooping low, he tried to see into the shadows of the shrubbery behind John.

The younger man spoke soothingly. "There is nothing here, father, sit down and take it easy."

"You don't know what you're talking about," retorted Adam Ward. "I tell you they are after me—there's no telling what they will do—poison—a gun—infernal machines through the mail—bomb. No one has any sympathy with me, not even my family. All these years I have worked for what I have and now nobody cares. All they want is what they can get out of me. And you—you'll find out! I saw your car in front of Martin's again this evening. You'd better keep away from there. Peter Martin is dangerous. He would take everything I have away from me if he could."

John tried in vain to calm his father, but in a voice harsh with passion he continued, and as he spoke, he moved his hands and arms constantly with excited and vehement gestures.

"That process is mine, I tell you. The best lawyers I could get have fixed up the patents. Pete Martin is an old fool. I'll see him in his grave before—" he checked himself as if fearing his own anger would betray him. As he paced up and he muttered to himself, "I built up the business and I can tear it down. I'll blow up the Mill. I—" his voice trailed off into hoarse unintelligible sounds.

John Ward could not speak. He believed that his father's strange fears for the loss of his property were due to nothing more than his nervous trouble. Peter Martin's name, which Adam in his most excited moments nearly always mentioned in this manner, meant nothing more to John than the old workman's well-known leadership in the Mill workers' union.

Suddenly Adam turned again to his son, and coming close asked in a whisper, "John—I—is there really a hell, John? I mean such as the preachers used to tell about. Does a man go from this life to the horrors of eternal punishment? Does he, son?"

"Why, father, I—" John started to reply, but Adam interrupted him with, "Never mind; you wouldn't know any more than any one else about it. The preachers ought to know, though. Seems like there must be some way of finding out. I dreamed—"

As if he had forgotten the presence of his son, he suddenly started away toward the house.

Not until John Ward had assured himself that his father was safely in his room and apparently sleeping at last, did he go to his own apartment.

But the new manager of the Mill did not at once retire. He did not even turn on the lights. For a long time he stood at the darkened window, looking out into the night. "What was it?" he asked himself again and again. "What was it his father feared?"

In the distance he could see a tiny spot of light shining high against the shadowy hillside above the darkness of the Flats. It was a lighted window in the Interpreter's hut.

* * * * *

As they sat in the night on the balcony porch, Jake Vodell said harshly to the old basket maker, "You shall tell me about this Adam Ward, comrade. I hear many things. From what you say of your friendship with him in the years when he was a workman in the Mill and from your friendship with his son and daughter you must know better than any one else. Is it true that it was his new patented process that made him so rich?"

"The new process was undoubtedly the foundation of his success," answered the Interpreter, "but it was the man's peculiar genius that enabled him to recognize the real value of the process and to foresee how it would revolutionize the industry. And it was his ability as an organizer and manager, together with his capacity for hard work, that enabled him to realize his vision. It is easily probable that not one of his fellow workmen could have developed and made use of the discovery as he has."

Jake Vodell's black brows were raised with quickened interest. "This new process was a discovery then? It was not the result of research and experiment?"

The Interpreter seemed to answer reluctantly. "It was an accidental discovery, as many such things are."

The agitator must have noticed that the old basket maker did not wish to talk of Adam Ward's patented process, but he continued his questions.

"Peter Martin was working in the Mill at the time of this wonderful discovery, was he?"

"Yes."

"Oh! and Peter and Adam were friends, too?"

"Yes."

The Interpreter's guest shrugged his shoulders and scowled his righteous indignation. "And all these years that Adam Ward has been building up this Mill that grinds the bodies and souls of his fellow men into riches for himself and makes from the life blood of his employees the dollars that his son and daughter spend in wicked luxury—all these years his old friend Peter Martin has toiled for him exactly as the rest of his slaves have toiled. Bah! And still the priests and preachers make the people believe there is a God of Justice."

The Interpreter replied, slowly, "It may be after all, sir, that Peter Martin is richer than Adam Ward."

"How richer?" demanded the other. "When he lives in a poor little house, with no servants, no automobiles, no luxuries of any kind, and must work every day in the Mill with his son, while his daughter Mary slaves at the housekeeping for her father and brother! Look at Adam Ward and his great castle of a home—look at his possessions—at the fortune he will leave his children. Bah! Mr. Interpreter, do not talk to me such foolishness."

"Is it foolishness to count happiness as wealth?" asked the Interpreter.

"Happiness?" growled the other. "Is there such a thing? What does the laboring man know of happiness?"

And the Interpreter answered, "Peter Martin, in the honorable peace and contentment of his useful years, and in the love of his family and friends, is the happiest man I have ever known. While Adam Ward—"

Jake Vodell sprang to his feet as if the Interpreter's words exhausted his patience, while he spoke as one moved by a spirit of contemptuous intolerance. "You talk like a sentimental old woman. How is it possible that there should be happiness and contentment anywhere when all is injustice and slavery under this abominable capitalist system? First we shall have liberty—freedom—equality—then perhaps we may begin to talk of happiness. Is Sam Whaley and his friends who live down there in their miserable hovels—is Sam Whaley happy?"

"Sam Whaley has had exactly the same opportunity for happiness that Peter Martin has had," answered the Interpreter. "Opportunity, yes," snarled the other "Opportunity to cringe and whine and beg his master for a chance to live like a dog in a kennel, while he slaves to make his owners rich. Do you know what this man McIver says? I will tell you, Mr. Interpreter—you who prattle about a working man's happiness. McIver says that the laboring classes should be driven to their work with bayonets—that if his factory employees strike they will be forced to submission by the starvation of their women and children. Happiness! You shall see what we will do to this man McIver before we talk of happiness. And you shall see what will happen to this castle of Adam Ward's and to this Mill that he says is his."

"I think I should tell you, sir," said the Interpreter, calmly, "that in your Millsburgh campaign, at least, you are already defeated."

"Defeated! Hah! That is good! And who do you say has defeated me, before I have commenced even to fight, heh?"

"You are defeated by Adam Ward's retirement from business," came the strange reply.

BOOK II

THE TWO HELENS

"O Guns, fall silent till the dead men hear
Above their heads the legions pressing on:

* * * *

Bid them be patient, and some day, anon,
They shall feel earth enwrapt in silence deep;
Shall greet, in wonderment, the quiet dawn,
And in content may turn them to their sleep."

CHAPTER XIII

THE AWAKENING

Immediately following that day when she had watched her father from the arbor and had talked with Bobby and Maggie Whaley on the old road, Helen Ward had thrown herself into the social activities of her circle as if determined to find, in those interests, a cure for her discontent and unhappiness.

Several times she called for a few minutes at the little hut on the cliff. But she did not again talk of herself or of her father to the old basket maker as she had talked that day when she first met the children from the Flats. Two or three times she saw the children. But she passed them quickly by with scarcely a nod of greeting. And yet, the daughter of Adam Ward felt with increasing certainty that she could never be content with the busy nothingness which absorbed the lives of so many of her friends. Her father, since his retirement, seemed a little better. But she could not put out of her mind the memory of what she had seen. For her, the dreadful presence of the hidden thing always attended him. Because she could not banish the feeling and because there was nothing she could do, she sought relief by escaping from the house as often as possible on the plea of social duties.

There were times when the young woman thought that her mother knew. At times she fancied that her brother half guessed the secret that so overshadowed their home. But Mrs. Ward and her children alike shrank from anything approaching frankness in mentioning the Mill owner's condition. And so they went on, feeling the hidden thing, dreading they knew not what—deceiving themselves and each other with hopes that in their hearts they knew were false.

The mother, brave, loyal soul, seeing her daughter's unhappiness and wishing to protect her from the thing that had so saddened her own life, encouraged Helen to find what relief she could in the pleasures that kept her so many hours from home. John, occupied by the exacting duties of his new position, needed apparently nothing more. Indeed, to Helen, her brother's attitude toward his work, his views of life and his increasing neglect of what she called the obligations of their position in Millsburgh, were more and more puzzling. She had thought that with John's advancement to the general managership of the Mill his peculiar ideas would be modified. But his promotion seemed to have made no sign of a change in his conception of the relationship between employer and employee, or in his attitude toward the unions or toward the industrial situation as a whole.

Of one thing Helen was certain—her brother had found that which she, in her own life, was somehow missing. And so the young woman observed her brother with increasing interest and a growing feeling that approached envy. At every opportunity she led him to talk of his work or rather of his attitude toward his work, and encouraged him to express the convictions that had so changed his own life and that were so foreign to the tenets of Helen and her class. And always their talks ended with John's advice: "Go ask the Interpreter; he knows; he will make it so much clearer than I can."

But with all John's absorbing interest in his work and in the general industrial situation of Millsburgh, which under the growing influence of Jake Vodell was becoming every day more difficult and dangerous, the general manager could not escape the memories of that happy evening at the Martin cottage. The atmosphere of this workman's home was so different from the atmosphere of his own home in the big house on the hill. There was a peace, a contentment, a feeling of security in the little cottage that was sadly wanting in the more pretentious residence. Following, as it did, his father's retirement from the Mill with his own promotion to the rank of virtual ownership and his immediate talk with Captain Charlie, that evening had restablished for him, as it were, the relationship and charm of his boyhood days. It was as though, having been submitted to a final test, he was now admitted once more, without reserve, to the innermost circle of their friendship.

On his way to and from his office he nearly always, now, drove past the Martin cottage. The distance was greater, it is true, but John thought that the road was enough better to more than make up for that. Besides, he really did enjoy the drive down the tree-arched street and past the old house. It was all so rich in memories of his happy boyhood, and sometimes—nearly always, in fact—he would catch a glimpse of Mary among her flowers or on the porch or perhaps at the gate.

Occasionally this young manager of the Mill, with his strange ideas of industrial comradeship, found it necessary to spend an evening with these workmen who were leaders in the union that was held by his father and by McIver to be a menace to the employer class. It in no way detracted from the value of these consultations with Captain Charlie and his father that Mary was always present. In fact, Mary herself was in a position materially to help John Ward in his study of the industrial problems that were of such vital interest to him. No one knew better than did Pete Martin's daughter the actual living conditions of the class of laboring people who dwelt in the Flats. Certainly, as he watched the progress of Jake Vodell's missionary work among them, John could not ignore these Sam Whaleys of the industries as an important factor in his problem.

So it happened, curiously enough, that Helen herself was led to call at the little home next door to the old house where she had lived in those years of her happy girlhood.

* * * * *

Helen was downtown that afternoon on an unimportant shopping errand. She had left the store after making her purchases and was about to enter her automobile, when McIver, who chanced to be passing, stopped to greet her.

There was no doubting the genuineness of the man's pleasure in the incident, nor was Helen herself at all displeased at this break in what had been, so far, a rather dull day.

110

"And what brings you down here at this unreasonable hour?" he asked; "on Saturday, too? Don't you know that there is a tennis match on at the club?"

"I didn't seem to care for the tennis to-day somehow," she returned. "Mother wanted some things from Harrison's, so I came downtown to get them for her."

He caught a note in her voice that made him ask with grave concern, "How is your father, Helen?"

She answered, quickly, "Oh, father is doing nicely, thank you." Then, with a cheerfulness that was a little forced, she asked in turn, "And why have you deserted the club yourself this afternoon?"

"Business," he returned. "There will be no more Saturday afternoons off for me for some time to come, I fear." Then he added, quickly, "But look here, Helen, there is no need of our losing the day altogether. Send your man on, and come with me for a little spin. The roadster is in the next block. I'll take you home in an hour and get on back to my office."

Helen hesitated.

"The ride will do you good."

"Sure you can spare the time?"

"Sure. It will do me good, too."

"And you're not asking me just to be nice—you really want me?"

"Don't you know by this time whether I want you or not?" he returned, in a tone that brought the color to her cheeks. "Please come!"

"All right," she agreed.

When they were seated in McIver's roadster, she added, "I really can't deny myself the thrilling triumph of taking a business man away from his work during office hours."

"You take my thoughts away from my work a great many times during office hours, Helen," he retorted, as the car moved away. "Must I wait much longer for my answer, dear?"

She replied, hurriedly, "Please, Jim, not that to-day. Let's not think about it even."

"All right," he returned, grimly. "I just want you to know, though, that I am waiting."

"I know, Jim—and—and you are perfectly wonderful but—Oh, can't we forget it just for an hour?"

As if giving himself to her mood, McIver's voice and manner changed. "Do you mind if we stop at the factory just a second? I want to leave some papers. Then we can go on up the river drive."

* * * * *

An hour later they were returning, and because it was the prettiest street in that part of Millsburgh, McIver chose the way that would take them past the old house.

John Ward's machine was standing in front of the Martin cottage.

McIver saw it and looked quickly at his companion. There was no need to ask if Helen had recognized her brother's car.

The factory owner considered the new manager of the Mill a troublesome obstacle in his own plans for making war on the unions. He felt, too, that with John now in control of the business, his chances of bringing about the combination of the two industries were materially lessened. He had wondered, at times, if it was not her brother's influence that caused Helen to put off giving him her final answer to his suit.

When he saw that Helen had recognized John's car, he remarked, with an insinuating laugh, "Evidently I am not the only business man who can be lured from his office during working hours."

"Jim, how can you?" she protested. "You know John is there on business to see Charlie or his father."

"It is a full hour yet before quitting time at the Mill," he returned.

She had no reply to this, and the man continued with a touch of malicious satisfaction, "After all, Helen, John is human, you know, and old Pete Martin's daughter is a mighty attractive girl."

Helen Ward's cheeks were red, but she managed to control her voice, as she said, "Just what do you mean by that, Jim?"

"Is it possible that you really do not know?" he countered.

112

"I know that my brother, foolish as he may be about some things, would never think of paying serious attention to the daughter of one of his employees," she retorted, warmly.

"That is exactly the situation," he returned. "No one believes for a moment that the affair is serious on John's part."

The color was gone from Helen's face now. "I think you have said too much not to go on now, Jim. Do you mean that people are saying that John is amusing himself with Mary Martin?"

"Well," he returned, coolly, "what else can the people think when they see him going there so often; when they see the two together, wandering about the Flats; when they hear his car tearing down the street late in the evening; when they see her every morning at the gate watching for him to pass on his way to work? Your brother is not a saint, Helen. He is no different, in some ways, from other men. I always did feel that there was something back of all this comrade stuff between him and Charlie Martin. As for the girl, I don't think you need to worry about her. She probably understands it all right enough."

"Jim, you must not say such things to me about Mary! She is not at all that kind of girl. The whole thing is impossible."

"What do you know about Mary Martin?" he retorted. "I'll bet you have never even spoken to her since you moved from the old house."

Helen did not speak after this until they were passing the great stone columns at the entrance to the Ward estate, then she said, quietly, "Jim, do you always believe the worst possible things about every one?"

"That's an odd thing for you to ask," he returned, doubtfully, as they drove slowly up the long curving driveway. "Why?"

"Because," she answered, "it sometimes seems to me as if no one believed the best things about people these days. I know there is a world of wickedness among us, Jim, but are we all going wholly to the bad together?"

McIver laughed. "We are all alike in one thing, Helen. No matter what he professes, you will find that at the last every man holds to the good old law of 'look out for number one.' Business or pleasure, it's all the same. A man looks after his own interests first and takes what he wants, or can get, when and where and how he can."

"But, Jim, the war—"

He laughed cynically. "The war was pure selfishness from start to finish. We fed the fool public a lot of patriotic bunk, of course—we had to—we needed them. And the dear people fell for the sentimental hero business as they always do." With the last word he stopped the car in front of the house.

When Helen was on the ground she turned and faced him squarely. "Jim McIver, your words are an insult to my brother and to ninety-nine out of every hundred men who served under our flag, and you insult my intelligence if you expect me to accept them in earnest. If I thought for a minute that you were capable of really believing such abominable stuff I would never speak to you again. Good-by, Jim. Thank you so much for the ride."

Before the man could answer, she ran up the steps and disappeared through the front door.

But McIver's car was no more than past the entrance when Helen appeared again on the porch. For a moment she stood, as if debating some question in her mind. Then apparently, she reached a decision. Ten minutes later she was walking hurriedly down the hill road—the way Bobby and Maggie had fled that day when Adam Ward drove them from the iron fence that guarded his estate. It was scarcely a mile by this road to the old house and the Martin cottage.

CHAPTER XIV

THE WAY BACK

That walk from her home to the little white cottage next door to the old house was the most eventful journey that Helen Ward ever made. She felt this in a way at the time, but she could not know to what end her sudden impulse to visit again the place of her girlhood would eventually lead.

As she made her way down the hill toward that tree-arched street, she realized a little how far the years had carried her from the old house. She had many vivid and delightful memories of that world of her childhood, it is true, but the world to which her father's material success had removed her in the years of her ripening womanhood had come to claim her so wholly that she had never once gone back. She had looked back at first with troubled longing. But Adam Ward's determined efforts to make the separation of the two families final and complete, together with the ever-increasing bitterness of his strange hatred for his old workman friend, had effectually prevented her from any attempt at a continuation of the old relationship. In time, even the thought of taking so much as a single step toward the intimacies from which she had come so far, had ceased to occur to her. And now, suddenly, without plan or premeditation, she was on her way actually to touch again, if only for a few moments, the lives that had been so large a part of the simple, joyous life which she had known once, but which was so foreign to her now.

Nor was it at all clear to her why she was going or what she would do. As she had observed with increasing interest the change in her brother's attitude toward the pleasures that had claimed him so wholly before the war, she had wondered often at his happy contentment in contrast to her own restless and dissatisfied spirit. McIver's words had suddenly forced one fact upon her with startling clearness: John, through his work in the Mill, his association with Captain Charlie and his visits to the Martin home, was actually living again in the atmosphere of that world which she felt they had left so far behind. It was as though her brother had already gone back.

And McIver's challenging question, "What do you know about Mary Martin?" had raised in her mind a doubt, not of her brother and his relationship to these old friends of their childhood, but of herself and all the relationships that made her present life such a contrast to her life in the old house.

With her mind and heart so full of doubts and questionings, she turned into the familiar street and saw her brother's car still before the Martin home.

As she went on, a feeling of strange eagerness possessed her. Her face glowed with warm color, her eyes shone with glad anticipation, her heart beat more quickly. As one returning to well loved home scenes after many years in a foreign land, the daughter of Adam Ward went down the street toward the place where she was born.

In front of the old house she stopped. The color went from her cheeks—the brightness from her eyes.

In her swiftly moving automobile, nearly always with gay companions, Helen had sometimes passed the old house and had noticed with momentary concern its neglected appearance. But these fleeting glimpses had been so quickly forgotten that the place was most real to her as she saw it in her memories. But now, as she stood there alone, in the mood that had brought her to the spot, the real significance of the ruin struck her with appalling force.

Those rooms with their shattered windowpanes, their bare, rotting casements and sagging, broken shutters appealed to her in the mute eloquence of their empty loneliness for the joyous life that once had filled them. The weed-grown yard, the tumbledown fence, the dilapidated porch, and even the chimneys that were crumbling and ragged against the sky, cried out to her in sorrowful reproach. A rushing flood of home memories filled her eyes with hot tears. With the empty loneliness of the old house in her heart, she went blindly on to the little cottage next door. There was no thought as to how she would explain her unusual presence there. She did not, herself, really know clearly why she had come.

Timidly she paused at the white gate. There was no one in the yard to bid her welcome. As one in a dream, she passed softly into the yard. She was trembling now as one on the threshold of a great adventure. What was it? What did it mean—-her coming there?

Wonderingly she looked about the little yard with its bit of lawn—at the big shade tree—the flowers—it was all just as she had always known it. Where were they?—- John and Mary and Charlie? Why was there no sound of their voices? Her cheeks were suddenly hot with color. What if Charlie Martin should suddenly appear! As one awakened from strange dreams to a familiar home scene, Helen Ward was all at once back in those days of her girlhood. She had come as she had come so many, many times from the old house next door, to find her brother and their friends. Her heart was eager with the shy eagerness of a maid for the expected presence of her first boyish lover.

* * * * *

Then Peter Martin, coming around the house from the garden, saw her standing there.

The old workman stopped, as if at the sight of an apparition. Mechanically he placed the garden tool he was carrying against the corner of the house; deliberately he knocked the ashes from his pipe and placed it methodically in his pocket.

With a little cry, Helen ran to him, her hands outstretched, "Uncle Pete!"

116

The old workman caught her and for a few moments she clung to him, half laughing, half crying, while they both, in the genuineness of their affection, forgot the years.

"Is it really you, Helen?" he said, at last, and she saw a suspicious moisture in the kindly eyes. "Have you really come back to see the old man after all these years?"

Then, with quick anxiety, he asked, "But what is the matter, child? Your father—your mother—are they all right? Is there anything wrong at your home up on the hill yonder?"

His very natural inquiry broke the spell and placed her instantly back in the world to which she now belonged. Drawing away from him, she returned, with characteristic calmness, "Oh, no, Uncle Pete, father and mother are both very well indeed. But why should you think there must be something wrong, simply because I chanced to call?"

The old workman was clearly confused at this sudden change in her manner. He had welcomed the girl—the Helen of the old house—this self-possessed young woman was quite a different person. She was the princess lady of little Maggie and Bobby Whaley's acquaintance, who sometimes condescended to recognize him with a cool little nod as her big automobile passed him swiftly by.

Pete Martin could not know, as the Interpreter would have known, how at that very moment the Helen of the old house and the princess lady were struggling for supremacy.

Removing his hat and handling it awkwardly, he said, with a touch of dignity in his tone and manner in spite of his embarrassment, "I'm glad the folks are well, Helen. Won't you take a seat and rest yourself?"

As they went toward the chairs in the shade of the tree, he added, "It is a long time since we have seen you in this part of town—walking, I mean."

The Helen of the old house wanted to answer—she longed to cry out in the fullness of her heart some of the things that were demanding expression, but it was the princess lady who answered, "I saw my brother's car here and thought perhaps he would let me ride home with him."

The old workman was studying her now with kind but frankly understanding eyes. "John and Mary have gone to see some of the folks that she is looking after in the Flats," he said, slowly. "They'll be back any minute now, I should think."

She did not know what to reply to this. There were so many things she wanted to know—so many things that she felt she must know. But she felt herself forced to answer with the mere commonplace, "You are all well, I suppose, Uncle Pete?"

"Fine, thank you," he answered. "Mary is always busy with her housework and her flowers and the poor sick folks she's always a-looking after—just like her mother, if you remember. Charlie, he's working late to-day—some breakdown or something that's keeping him overtime. That brother of yours is a fine manager, Miss Helen, and," he added, with a faint note of something in his voice that brought a touch of color to her cheeks, "a finer man."

Again she felt the crowding rush of those questions she wanted to ask, but she only said, with an air of calm indifference, "John has changed so since his return from France—in many ways he seems like a different man."

"As for that," he replied, "the war has changed most people in one way or another. It was bound to. Everybody talks about getting back to normal again, but as I see it there'll be no getting back ever to what used to be normal before the war started."

She looked at him with sudden, intense interest. "How has it so changed every one, Uncle Pete? Why can't people be just as they were before it happened? The change in business conditions and all that, I can understand, but why should it make any difference to—well, to me, for example?"

The old workman answered, slowly, "The people are thinking deeper and feeling deeper. They're more human, as you might say. And I've noticed generally that the way the people think and feel is at the bottom of everything. It's just like the Interpreter says, 'You can't change the minds and hearts of folks without changing what they do.' Everybody ain't changed, of course, but so many of them have that the rest will be bound to take some notice or feel mighty lonesome from now on."

Helen was about to reply when the old workman interrupted her with, "There come John and Mary now."

The two coming along the street walk to the gate did not at first notice those who were watching them with such interest. John was carrying a market basket and talking earnestly to his companion, whose face was upturned to his with eager interest. At the gate they paused a moment while the man, with his hand on the latch, finished whatever it was that he was saying. And Helen, with a little throb of something very much like envy in her heart, saw the light of happiness in the eyes of the young woman who through all the years of their girlhood had been her inseparable playmate and loyal friend.

When John finally opened the gate for her to pass, Mary was laughing, and the clear ringing gladness in her voice brought a faint smile of sympathy even to the face of the now coolly conventional daughter of Adam Ward.

Mary's laughter was suddenly checked; the happiness fled from her face. With a little gesture of almost appealing fear she put her hand on her companion's arm.

In the same instant John saw and stood motionless, his face blank with amazement. Then, "Helen! What in the world are you doing here?"

John Ward never realized all that those simple words carried to the three who heard him. Peter Martin's face was grave and thoughtful. Mary blushed in painful embarrassment. His sister, calm and self-possessed, came toward them, smiling graciously.

"I saw your roadster and thought I might ride home with you. Uncle Pete and I have been having a lovely little visit. It is perfectly charming to see you again like this, Mary. Your flowers are beautiful as ever, aren't they?"

"But, Helen, how do you happen to be wandering about in this neighborhood alone and without your car?" demanded the still bewildered John.

"Don't be silly," she laughed. "I was out for a walk—that is all. I do walk sometimes, you know." She turned to Mary. "Really, to hear this brother of mine, one would think me a helpless invalid and this part of Millsburgh a very dangerous community."

Mary forced a smile, but the light in her eyes was not the light of happiness and her cheeks were still a burning red.

"Don't you think we should go now, John?" suggested Helen.

The helpless John looked from Mary to her father appealingly.

"Better sit down awhile," Pete offered, awkwardly.

John looked at his watch. "I suppose we really ought to go." To Mary he added, "Will you please tell Charlie that I will see him to-morrow?"

She bowed gravely.

Then the formal parting words were spoken, and Helen and John were seated in the car. Mary had moved aside from the gate and stood now very still among her flowers.

* * * * *

Before John had shifted the gears of his machine to high, he heard a sound that caused him to look quickly at his sister. Little Maggie's princess lady was sobbing like a child.

"Why, Helen, what in the world—"

She interrupted him. "Please, John—please, don't—don't take me home now. I—-I—Let us stop here at the old house for a few minutes. I—I can't go just yet."

Without a word John Ward turned into the curb. Tenderly he helped her to the ground. Reverently he lifted aside the broken-down gate and led her through the tangle of tall grass and weeds that had almost obliterated the walk to the front porch. Over the rotting steps and across the trembling porch he helped her with gentle care. Very softly he pushed open the sagging door.

CHAPTER XV

AT THE OLD HOUSE

From room to room in the empty old house the brother and sister went silently or with low, half-whispered words. They moved softly, as if fearing to disturb some unseen tenant of those bare and dingy rooms. Often they paused, and, drawing close to each other, stood as if in the very presence of some spirit that was not of their material world. At last they came to the back porch, which was hidden from the curious eyes of any chance observer in the neighborhood by a rank growth of weeds and bushes and untrimmed trees.

As John Ward looked at his sister now, that expression of wondering amazement with which he had greeted her was gone. In its place there was gentle understanding.

With a little smile, Helen sat down on the top step of the porch and motioned him to a seat beside her. "Won't you tell me about it, John?" she said, softly.

"Tell you about what, Helen?"

"About everything—your life, your work, your friends." She made a little gesture toward the cottage next door.

They could see the white gable through the screen of tangled boughs.

"What is it that has changed you so?" she went on. "Your interests are so different now. You are so happy and contented—so—so alive—and I"—her voice broke—"I feel as if you were going away off somewhere and leaving me behind. I am so miserable. John, won't you tell me about things?"

"You poor old girl!" exclaimed John with true brotherly affection. "I've been a blind fool. I ought to have seen. That's nearly always the way, though, I guess," he went on, reflectively. "A fellow gets so darned interested trying to make things go right outside his own home that he forgets to notice how the people that he really loves most of all are getting along. It looks as though I have not been doing so much better than poor old Sam Whaley, after all."

He paused and seemed to be following his thoughts into fields where only he could go. Helen moved a little closer, and he came back to her.

"I never dreamed that you were feeling anything like this, sister. I knew that you were worried about father, of course, as we all are, but aside from that you seemed to be so occupied with your various interests and with McIver—" He paused, then finished, abruptly, "Look here, Helen, what about you and McIver anyway; have you given him his answer yet?"

"Has that anything to do with it?" she answered, doubtfully. "There is nothing that I can tell you about McIver. I don't seem to be able to make up my mind, that is all. But McIver is only a part of the whole trouble, John. Oh, can't you understand! How am I to know whether or not I want to marry him or any one else until—until I have found myself—until I know where I really belong."

He looked at her blankly for a second, then a smile broke over his face. "By George!" he exclaimed "that is exactly what I had to do—find myself and find where I belonged. I never dreamed that my sister might be compelled to go through the same experience."

"Was it your army life that helped you to know?"

His face was serious now. "It was the things I saw and experienced while in France."

"Tell me," she demanded. "I mean, tell me some of the things that you men never talk about—the things you were forced to think and feel and believe—that showed you your own real self—that changed you into what you are to-day."

And because John Ward was able that afternoon to understand his sister's need, he did as she asked. It may have been the influence of the old house that enabled him to lay bare for her those experiences of his innermost self—those soul adventures about which, as she had so truly said, men never talk. Certainly he could never have spoken in their home on the hill as he spoke in that atmosphere from which their father and his material prosperity had so far removed them. And Helen, as she listened, knew that she had found at last the key to all in her brother's life that had so puzzled her.

But after all, she reflected, when he had finished, John's experience could not solve her problem. She could not find herself in the things that he had thought and felt.

"If only I could have been with you over there." she murmured.

"But, Helen," he cried, eagerly, "it is all right here at home. The same things are happening all about us every day—don't you understand? The one biggest thing that came to me out of the war is the realization that, great and terrible though it was, it was in reality only a part of the greater war that is being fought all the time."

She shook her head with a doubtful smile at his earnestness.

And then he tried to tell her of the Mill as he saw it in its relation to human life—of the danger that threatened the nation through the industrial situation—of the menace to humanity that lay in the efforts of those who were setting class against class in a deadly hatred that would result in revolution with all its horrors. He tried to make her feel the call of humanity's need in the world's work, as it was felt in the need of

122

the world's war. He sought to apply for her the principles of heroism and comradeship and patriotism and service to this war that was still being waged against the imperialistic enemies of the nation and the race.

But when he paused at last, she only smiled again, doubtfully. "You are wonderful in your enthusiasm, John dear," she said, "and I love you for it. I think I understand you now, and for yourself it is right, of course, but for me—it is all so visionary—so unreal."

"And yet," he returned, "you were very active during the war—you made bandages and lint and sweaters, and raised funds for the Red Cross. Was it all real to you?"

"Yes," she answered, honestly, "it was very real John; it was so real that in contrast nothing that I do now seems of any importance."

"But you never saw a wounded soldier—you never witnessed the horrors—you never came in actual touch with the suffering, did you?"

"No."

"And yet you say the war was real to you."

"Very real," she replied.

"Do you think, Helen," he said, slowly, "that the Interpreter's suffering would have been more real if he had lost his legs by a German machine gun instead of by a machine in father's mill?"

"John!" she exclaimed, in a shocked tone.

"You say the suffering away over there in France was real to you," he continued. "Well, less than a mile from this spot, I called this afternoon on a man who is dying by inches of consumption, contracted while working in our office. For eight years he was absent from his desk scarcely a day. The force nicknamed him 'Old Faithful.' When he dropped in his tracks at last they carried him out and stopped his pay. He has no care—nothing to eat, even, except the help that the Martins give him. Another case: A widow and four helpless children—the man was killed in McIver's factory last week. He died in agony too horrible to describe. The mother is prostrated, the children are hungry. God knows what will become of them this next winter. Another: A workman who was terribly burned in the Mill two years ago. He is blind and crippled in the bargain—"

She interrupted him with a protesting cry, "John, John, for pity's sake, stop!"

123

"Well, why are not these things right here at home as real to you as you say the same things were when they happened in France?" he demanded.

She did not attempt to answer his question but instead asked, gently, "Is that why you have been going to the Flats with Mary?"

If he noticed any special significance in her words he ignored it. "Mary visits the people in the Flats as her mother did—as our mother used to do. She told me about some of the cases, and I have been going with her now and then to see for myself—that is all."

Then they left the old house and drove back to their pretentious home on the hill, where Adam Ward suffered his days of mental torture and was racked by his nightly dreams of hell. And the dread shadow of that hidden thing was over them all.

* * * * *

That night when John told the Interpreter of his afternoon with his sister the old basket maker listened silently. His face was turned toward the scene that, save for the twinkling lights, lay wrapped in darkness before them. And he seemed to be listening to the voice of the Mill. When John had finished, the man in the wheel chair said very little.

But when John was leaving, the Interpreter asked, as an afterthought, "And where was Captain Charlie this afternoon, John?"

"At the Mill," John answered. "I'm glad he wasn't at home, too; it was bad enough as it was."

"Perhaps it was just as well," said the old basket maker. And John Ward, in the darkness, could not see that the Interpreter was smiling.

CHAPTER XVI

HER OWN PEOPLE

"A lady to see you, sir."

John did not take his eyes from the work on his desk. "All right, Jimmy, show her in."

The general manager read on to the bottom of the typewritten page, signed his name to the sheet, placed it in the proper basket and turned in his chair.

"Helen!"

Little Maggie's princess lady was so lovely that afternoon, as she stood there framed in the doorway of the manager's office that even her brother noticed.

She was laughing at his surprise, and there was a half teasing, half serious look in her eyes that was irresistible.

"By George, you are a picture, Helen!" John exclaimed, with not a little brotherly pride in his face and voice. "But what is the idea? What are you down here for—all dolled up like this?"

She blushed with pleasure at his compliment. "That is very nice of you, John; you are a dear to notice it. Are you going to ask me to sit down, or must you put me out for interrupting?"

He was on his feet instantly. "Forgive me; I am so stunned by the unexpected honor of your visit that I forget my manners."

When she was seated, he continued, "And now what is it? what can I do for you, sister?"

She looked about the office—at his desk and through the open door into the busy outer room. "Are you quite sure that you have time for me?"

"Surest thing in the world," he returned, with a reassuring smile. Then to a man who at that moment appeared in the doorway, "All right, Tom." And to Helen, "Excuse me just a second, dear."

She watched him curiously as he turned sheet after sheet of the papers the man handed him, seeming to absorb the pages at a glance, while a running fire of quick questions, short answers, terse comments and clear-cut instructions accompanied the examination.

Helen had never before been inside the doors of the industrial plant to which her father had literally given his life. In those old-house days, when Adam worked with Pete and the Interpreter, she had gone sometimes to the outer gate to meet her father when his day's work was done. On rare occasions her automobile had stopped in front of the office. That was all.

In a vague, indefinite way the young woman realized that her education, her pleasures, the dresses she wore, her home on the hill, everything that she had, in fact, came to her somehow from those great dingy, unsightly buildings. She knew that people who were not of her world worked there for her father. Sometimes there were accidents—men were killed. There had been strikes that annoyed her father. But no part of it all had ever actually touched her. She accepted it as a matter of course—without a thought—as she accepted all of the established facts in nature. The Mill existed for her as the sun existed. It never occurred to her to ask why. There was for her no personal note in the droning, moaning voice of its industry. There was nothing of personal significance in the forest of tall stacks with their overhanging cloud of smoke. Indeed, there had been, rather, something sinister and forbidding about the place. The threatening aspect of the present industrial situation was in no way personal to her except, perhaps, as it excited her father and disturbed John.

"You've got it all there, Tom," said the manager, finishing his examination of the papers. "Good work, too. Baird will have those specifications on that Miller and Wilson job in to-morrow, will he?"

"Yes, sir."

"Good, that's the stuff!"

The man was smiling as he moved toward the door.

"Oh, Tom, just a moment."

Still smiling, the man turned back.

"I want you to meet my sister. Helen, may I present Mr. Conway? Tom is one of our Mill family, you know, mighty important member, too—regular shark at figuring all sorts of complicated calculations that I couldn't work out in a month of Sundays." He laughed with boyish happiness and pride in Tom's superior accomplishments.

It was a simple little incident, but there was something in it somewhere that moved Helen Ward strangely. A spirit that was new to her seemed to fill the room. She felt it as one may feel the bigness of the mountains or sense the vast reaches of the ocean. These two men, employer and employee, were in no way conscious of their relationship as she understood it. Tom did not appear to realize that he was working *for* John—he seemed rather to feel that he was working *with* John.

When the man was gone, she asked again, timidly, "Are you sure, brother, that I am not in the way?"

"Forget it!" he cried. "Tell me what I can do for you."

"I want to see the Mill," she answered.

John did not apparently quite understand her request. "You want to see the Mill?" he repeated.

She nodded eagerly. "I want to see it all—not just the office but where the men work—everything."

She laughed at his bewildered expression as the sincerity of her wish dawned upon him.

"But what in the world"—he began—"why this sudden interest in the Mill, Helen?"

Half teasing, half laughing, she answered, "You didn't really think, did you, John, that I would forget everything you said to me at the old house?"

"No," he said, doubtfully. "At least, I suppose I didn't. But, honestly, I didn't think that I had made much of an impression."

She made a little gesture of helpless resignation. "Here I am just the same and so much interested already that I can't tear myself away. Come on, let's start—that is, if you really have the time to take me."

Time to take her! John Ward would have lost the largest contract he had ever dreamed of securing rather than miss taking Helen through the Mill.

* * * * *

With an old linen duster, which had hung in the office closet since Adam Ward's day, to cover her from chin to shoes, and a cap that John himself often wore about the plant, to replace her hat, they set out.

Helen's first impression, as she stood just inside the door to the big main room of the plant, was fear. To her gentle eyes the scene was one of terrifying confusion and unspeakable dangers.

127

Those great machines were grim and threatening monsters with ponderous jaws and arms and chains that seemed all too light to control their sullen strength. The noise—roaring, crashing, clanking, moaning, shrieking, hissing—was overpowering in its suggestion of the ungoverned tumult that belonged to some strange, unearthly realm. Everywhere, amid this fearful din and these maddening terrors, flitting through the murky haze of steam and smoke and dust, were men with sooty faces and grimy arms. Never had the daughter of Adam Ward seen men at work like this. She drew closer to John's side and held to his arm as though half expecting him to vanish suddenly and leave her alone in this monstrous nightmare.

Looking down at her, John laughed aloud and put his arm about her reassuringly. "Great game, old girl!" he said, with a wholesome pride in his voice. "This is the life!"

And all at once she remembered that this *was*, indeed, life—life as she had never seen it, never felt it before. And this life game—this greatest of all games—was the game that John played with such absorbing interest day after day.

"I can understand now why you are not so devoted to tennis and teas as you used to be," she returned, laughing back at him with a new admiration in her face.

Then John led her into the very midst of the noisy scene. Carefully he guided her steps through the seeming hurry and confusion of machinery and men. Now they paused before one of those grim monsters to watch its mighty work. Now they stopped to witness the terrific power displayed by another giant that lifted, with its great arms of steel, a weight of many tons as easily as a child would handle a toy. Again, they stepped aside from the path of an engine on its way to some distant part of the plant, or stood before a roaring furnace, or paused to watch a group of men, or halted while John exchanged a few brief words with a superintendent or foreman. And always with boyish enthusiasm John talked to her of what they saw, explaining, illustrating, making the purpose and meaning of every detail clear.

Gradually, as she thus went closer to this life that was at first so terrifying to her, the young woman was conscious of a change within herself. The grim monsters became kind and friendly as she saw how their mighty strength was obedient always to the directing eye and hand of the workmen who controlled them. The many noises, as she learned to distinguish them, came to blend into one harmonious whole, like the instruments in a great orchestra. The confusion, as she came to view it understandingly, resolved itself into orderly movement. As she recalled some of the things that her brother had said to her as they sat on the back porch of the old house, her mind reached out for the larger truth, and she thrilled to the feeling that she was standing, as it were, in the living, beating heart of the nation. The things that she had been schooled to hold as of the highest value she saw now for the first time in their just relation to the mighty underlying life of the Mill. The petty refinements that had so largely ruled her every thought and deed were no more than frothy bubbles on the surface of the industrial ocean's awful tidal power. The male idlers of her set were suddenly contemptible in her eyes, as she saw them in comparison with her brother or with his grimy, sweating comrades.

Presently John was saying, "This is where father used to work—before the days of the new process, I mean. That bench there is the very one he used, side by side with Uncle Pete and the Interpreter."

Helen stared at the old workbench that stood against the wall and at the backs of the men, as though under a spell. Her father working there!

Her brain all at once was crowded with questions to which there were no answers. What if Adam Ward were still a workman at that bench? What if it had been the Interpreter who had discovered the new process? What if her father had lost his legs? What if John, instead of being the manager, were one of those men who worked with their hands? What if they had never left the old house next door to Mary and Charlie? What if—

"Uncle Pete," said John, "look here and see who's with us this afternoon."

Mary's father turned from his work and they laughed at the expression on his face when he saw her standing there.

And it was the Helen of the old house who greeted him, and who was so interested in what he was doing and asked so many really intelligent questions that he was proud of her.

They had left Uncle Pete at his bench, and Helen's mind was again busy with those unanswerable questions—so busy, in fact, that she scarcely heard John saying, "I want to show you a lathe over here, Helen, that is really worth seeing. It is, on the whole, the finest and most intricate piece of machinery in the whole plant." And, he added, as they drew near the subject of his remarks, "You may believe me, it takes an exceptional workman to handle it. There are only three men in our entire force who are ever permitted to touch it. They are experts in their line and naturally are the best paid men we have."

As he finished speaking they paused beside a huge affair of black iron and gray steel, that to Helen seemed an incomprehensible tangle of wheels and levers.

A workman was bending over the machine, so absorbed apparently in the complications of his valuable charge that he was unaware of their presence.

Helen spoke close to her brother's ear, "Is he one of your three experts?"

John nodded. "He is the chief. The other two are really assistants—sort of understudies, you know."

At that moment the man straightened up, stood for an instant with his eyes still on his work, then, as he was turning to another part of the intricate mechanism, he saw them.

"Hello, Charlie!" said the grinning manager, and to his sister, "Surely you haven't forgotten Captain Martin, Helen?"

In the brief moments that followed Helen Ward knew that she had reached the point toward which she had felt herself moving for several months—impelled by strange forces beyond her comprehension.

Her brother's renewed and firmly established friendship with this playmate of their childhood years, together with the many stirring tales that John had told of his comrade captain's life in France, could not but awaken her interest in the boy lover whom she had, as she believed, so successfully forgotten. The puzzling change in her brother's life interests, has neglect of so many of his pre-war associates and his persistent comradeship with his fellow workman, had kept alive that interest; while Captain Martin's repeated refusals to accept John's invitations to the big home on the hill had curiously touched her woman's pride and at the same time had compelled her respect.

The clash between John's new industrial and social convictions and the class consciousness to which she had been so carefully schooled, with its background of her father's wretched mental condition, the unhappiness of her home and her own repeated failures to find contentment in the privileges of material wealth, raised in her mind questions which she had never before faced.

Her talks with the Interpreter, the slow forming of the lines of the approaching industrial struggle, with the sharpening of the contrast between McIver and John, her acquaintance with Bobby and Maggie, even—all tended to drive her on in her search for the answer to her problem.

And so she had been carried to the Martin cottage—to her talk with John at the old house—to the Mill—to this.

As one may intuitively sense the crisis in a great struggle between life and death, this woman knew that in this man all her disturbing life questions were centered. Deep beneath the many changes that her father's material success in life had brought to her, one unalterable life fact asserted itself with startling power: It was this man who had first awakened in her the consciousness of her womanhood. Face to face with this workman in her father's Mill, she fought to control the situation.

To all outward appearances she did control it. Her brother saw only a reserved interest in his workman comrade. Captain Martin saw only the daughter of his employer who had so coldly preferred her newer friends to the less pretentious companions of her girlhood.

But beneath the commonplace remarks demanded by the occasion, the Helen of the old house was struggling for supremacy. The spirit that she had felt in the office when John talked with his fellow workmen, she felt now in the presence of this workman. The power, the strength, the bigness, the meaning of the Mill, as it had come to her, were all personified in him. A strange exultation of possession lifted her up. She was hungry for her own; she wanted to cry out: "This work is my work—these people are my people—this man is my man!"

It was Captain Charlie who ended the interview with the excuse that the big machine needed his immediate attention. He had stood as they talked with a hand on one of the controls and several times he had turned a watchful eye on his charge. It was almost, Helen thought with a little thrill of triumph, as though the man sought in the familiar touch of his iron and steel a calmness and self-control that he needed. But now, when he turned to give his attention wholly to his work, with the effect of politely dismissing her, she felt as though he had suddenly, if ever so politely, closed a door in her face.

John must have felt it a little, too, for he became rather quiet as they went on and soon concluded their inspection of the plant.

At the office door, Helen paused and turned to look back, as if reluctant to leave the scene that had now such meaning for her, while her brother stood silently watching her. Not until they were back in the manager's office and Helen was ready to return to the outside world did John Ward speak.

Facing her with his straightforward soldierly manner, he said, inquiringly, "Well?"

She returned his look with steady frankness. "I can't tell you what I think about it all now, John dear. Sometime, perhaps, I may try. It is too big—too vital—too close. I am glad I came. I am sorry, too."

So he took her to her waiting car.

For a moment he stood looking thoughtfully after the departing machine and then, with an odd little smile, went back to his work.

CHAPTER XVII

IN THE NIGHT

Helen knew, even as she told the chauffeur to drive her home, that she did not wish to return just then to the big house on the hill. Her mind was too crowded with thoughts she could not entertain in the atmosphere of her home; her heart was too deeply moved by emotions that she scarcely dared acknowledge even to herself.

She thought of the country club, but that, in her present mood, was impossible. The Interpreter—she was about to tell Tom that she wished to call at the hut on the cliff, but decided against it. She feared that she might reveal to the old basket maker things that she wished to hide. She might go for a drive in the country, but she shrank from being alone. She wanted some one who could take her out of herself—some one to whom she could talk without betraying herself.

Not far from the Mill a number of children were playing in the dusty road.

Helen did not notice the youngsters, but Tom, being a careful driver, slowed down, even though they were already scurrying aside for the automobile to pass. Suddenly she was startled by a shrill yell. "Hello, there! Hello, Miss!"

Bobby Whaley, in his frantic efforts to attract her attention, was jumping up and down, waving his cap and screeching like a wild boy, while his companions looked on in wide-eyed wonder, half in awe at his daring, half in fear of the possible consequence.

To the everlasting honor and glory of Sam Whaley's son, the automobile stopped. The lady, looking back, called, "Hello, Bobby!" and waited expectantly for him to approach.

With a look of haughty triumph at Skinny and Chuck, the lad swaggered forward, a grin of overpowering delight at his achievement on his dirty, freckled countenance.

"I am so glad you called to me," Helen said, when he was close. "I was just wishing for some one to go with me for a ride in the country. Would you like to come?"

"Gee," returned the urchin, "I'll say I would."

"Do you think your mother would be willing for you to go?"

"Lord, yes—ma, she ain't a-carin' where we kids are jest so's we ain't under her feet when she's a-workin'."

"And could you find Maggie, do you think? Perhaps she would enjoy the ride, too."

132

Bobby lifted up his voice in a shrill yell, "Mag! Oh—oh—Mag!"

The excited cry was caught up by the watching children, and the neighborhood echoed their calls. "Mag! Oh, Mag! Somebody wants yer, Mag! Come a-runnin'. Hurry up!"

Their united efforts were not in vain. From the rear of a near-by house little Maggie appeared. A dirty, faded old shawl was wrapped about her tiny waist, hiding her bare feet and trailing behind. A sorry wreck of a hat trimmed with three chicken feathers crowned her uncombed hair, and the ragged remnants of a pair of black cotton gloves completed her elegant costume. In her thin little arms she held, with tender mother care, a doll so battered and worn by its long service that one wondered at the imaginative power of the child who could make of it anything but a shapeless bundle of dirty rags.

"Get a move on yer, Mag!" yelled the masterful Bobby, with frantic gestures. "The princess lady is a-goin' t' take us fer a ride in her swell limerseen with her driver 'n' everything."

For one unbelieving moment, little Maggie turned to the two miniature ladies who, in costumes that rivaled her own, had come to ask the cause of this unseemly disturbance of their social affair. Then, at another shout from her brother, she discarded her finery and, holding fast to her doll with true mother instinct, hurried timidly to the waiting automobile.

On that day when Helen had sent her servant to take them for a ride, these children of the Flats had thought that no greater happiness was possible to mere human beings. But now, as they sat with their beautiful princess lady between them on the deep-cushioned seat, and watched the familiar houses glide swiftly past, even Bobby was silent. It was all so unreal—so like a dream. Their former experience was so far surpassed that they would not have been surprised had the automobile been suddenly transformed into a magic ship of the air, with Tom a fairy pilot to carry them away up among the clouds to some wonderful sunshine castle in the sky.

It is true that Bobby's conscience stirred uneasily when he felt an arm steal gently about him and he was drawn a little closer to the princess lady's side. A feller with a proper pride does not readily permit such familiarities. It had been a long time since any one had put an arm around Bobby—he did not quite understand.

But as for that, the princess lady herself did not quite understand either. Perhaps the sight of little Maggie and her play lady friends so elegantly costumed for their social function had suddenly convinced her that these children of the Flats were of her world after all. Perhaps the shouting children had awakened memories that banished for the moment the sadness of her grown-up years. Or it may have been simply the way that wee Maggie held her battered doll. It may have been that the mother instinct of this wistful mite of humanity quickened in the heart of the young woman something that was deeper, more vital, more real to her womanhood than the things to which she had so far given herself. As the Helen of the old house had longed to cry aloud in the Mill her recognition of her man, she hungered now with a strange woman hunger for the feel of a child in her arms.

And so, with no care for her gown, which was sure to be ruined by this contact with the grime of the Flats, with no question as to what people might think, with no thought for class standards or industrial problems, the daughter of Adam Ward took the children of Sam Whaley in her arms and carried them away from the shadow of that dark cloud that hung always above the Mill. From the smoke and dust and filth of their heritage, she took them into the clean, sunny air of the hillside fields and woods. From the hovels and shanties of their familiar haunts she took them where birds made their nests and the golden bees and bright-winged butterflies were busy among their flowers. From the squalid want and cruel neglect of their poverty she took them into a fairyland that was overflowing with the riches that belong to childhood.

And then, when the sun was red above the bluff where the curving line of cliffs end at the river's edge, she brought them back.

For some reason that has never been made satisfactorily clear by the wise ones who lead the world's thinking, Bobby and Maggie must always be brought back to their home in the Flats, the princess lady must always return to her castle on the hill.

* * * * *

Charlie Martin was unusually quiet when he returned home from his work that day. The father mentioned Helen's visit to the Mill, and Mary had many questions to ask, but the soldier workman, usually so ready to talk and laugh with his sister, answered only in monosyllables or silently permitted the older man to carry the burden of the conversation.

When supper was over and it was dark, Charlie, saying that he thought he ought to attend Jake Vodell's street meeting that evening, left the house.

But Captain Charlie did not go to hear the agitator's soap-box oration that night. For an hour or more, under cover of the darkness, the workman sat on the porch of the old house next door to his home.

He had pushed aside the broken gate and made his way up the weed-tangled walk so quietly that neither his sister nor his father, who were on the porch of the cottage, heard a sound. So still was he that two neighborhood lovers, who paused in their slow walk, as if tempted by the friendly shadow of the lonely old place, did not know that he was there. Then at something her father said, Mary's laugh rang out, and the lovers moved on.

A little later Captain Charlie stole softly out of the yard and up the street in the direction from which Helen had come the day of her visit to the old house. When the sound of his feet on the walk could not be heard at the cottage, the workman walked briskly, taking the way that led toward the Interpreter's hut.

One who knew him would have thought that he was going for an evening call on the old basket maker. He saw the light of the little house on the cliff presently, and for a moment walked slowly, as if debating whether or not he should go on as he had intended. Then he turned off from the way to the Interpreter's and took that seldom used road that led up the hill toward the home of Adam Ward. With a strong, easy stride he swung up the grade until he came to the corner of the iron fence. Slowly and quietly he moved on now in the deeper shadows of the trees. When he could see the gloomy mass of the house unobstructed against the sky, he stopped.

The lower floor was brightly lighted. The windows above were dark. With his back against the trunk of a tree Captain Charlie waited.

An automobile came out between the stone columns of the big gate and thundered away down the street with reckless speed. Adam Ward, thought the man under the tree—even John never drove like that. And he wondered where the old Mill owner could be going at such an hour of the night.

Still he waited.

Suddenly a light flashed out from the windows of an upper room. A moment, and the watcher saw the form of a woman framed in the casement against the bright background. For some time she stood there, her face, shaded by her hands, pressed close to the glass, as if she were trying to see into the darkness of the night. Then she drew back. The shade was drawn.

Very slowly Captain Charlie went back down the hill.

BOOK III

THE STRIKE

"O flashing muzzles, pause, and let them see The coming dawn that streaks the sky afar; Then let your mighty chorus witness be To them, and Cæsar, that we still make war."

CHAPTER XVIII

THE GATHERING STORM

In the weeks immediately following her visit to the Mill, Helen Ward met the demands of her world apparently as usual. If any one noticed that she failed to enter into the affairs of her associates with the same lively interest which had made her a leader among those who do nothing strenuously, they attributed it to her father's ill health. And in this they were partially right. Ever since the day when she half revealed her fears to the Interpreter, the young woman's feeling that her father's ill health and the unhappiness of her home were the result of some hidden thing, had gamed in strength. Since her meeting with Captain Charlie there had been in her heart a deepening conviction that, but for this same hidden thing, she would have known in all its fullness a happiness of which she could now only dream.

More frequently than ever before, she went now to sit with the Interpreter on the balcony porch of that little hut on the cliff. But Bobby and Maggie wished in vain for their princess lady to come and take them again into the land of trees and birds and flowers and sunshiny hills and clean blue sky. Often, now, she went to meet her brother when his day's work was done, and, sending Tom home with her big car, she would go with John in his roadster. And always while he told her of the Mill and led her deeper into the meaning of the industry and its relation to the life of the people, she listened with eager interest. But she did not go again to the Martin cottage or visit the old house.

Once at the foot of the Interpreter's zigzag stairway she met Captain Martin and greeted him in passing. Two or three times she caught a glimpse of him among the men coming from the Mill as she waited for John in front of the office. That was all. But always she was conscious of him. When from the Interpreter's hut she watched the twisting columns of smoke rising from the tall stacks, her thoughts were with the workman who somewhere under that cloud was doing his full share in the industrial army of his people. When John talked to her of the Mill and its meaning, her heart was glad for her brother's loyal comradeship with this man who had been his captain over there. The very sound of the deep-toned whistle that carried to Adam Ward the proud realization of his material possessions carried to his daughter thoughts of what, but for those same material possessions, might have been.

For relief she turned to McIver. There was a rocklike quality in the factory owner that had always appealed to her. His convictions were so unwavering—his judgments so final. McIver never doubted McIver. He never, in his own mind, questioned what he did by the standards of right and justice. The only question he ever asked himself was, Would McIver win or lose? Any suggestion of a difference of opinion on the part of another was taken as a personal insult that was not to be tolerated. Therefore, because the man was what he was, his class convictions were deeply grounded, fixed and certain. In the turmoil of her warring thoughts and disturbed emotions Helen felt her own balance so shaken that she instinctively reached out to steady herself by him. The man, feeling her turn to him, pressed his suit with all the ardor she would permit, for he saw in his success not only possession of the woman he wanted, but the overthrow of John's opposition to his business plans and the consequent triumph of his personal material interests and the interests of his class. But, in spite of the relief she gained from the strength of McIver's convictions, some strange influence within herself prevented her from yielding. She probably would yield at last, she told herself drearily—because there seemed to be nothing else for her to do.

* * * * *

Meanwhile, from his hut on the cliff, the Interpreter watched the approach of the industrial storm.

The cloud that had appeared on the Millsburgh horizon with the coming of Jake Vodell had steadily assumed more threatening proportions until now it hung dark with gloomy menace above the work and the homes of the people. To the man in the wheel chair, looking out upon the scene that lay with all its varied human interests before him, there was no bit of life anywhere that was not in the shadow of the gathering storm. The mills and factories along the river, the stores and banks and interests of the business section, the farms in the valley, the wretched Flats, the cottage homes of the workmen and the homes on the hillside, were all alike in the path of the swiftly approaching danger.

The people with anxious eyes watched for the storm to break and made such hurried preparations as they could. They heard the dull, muttering sound of its heavy voice and looked at one another in silent dread or talked, neighbor to neighbor, in low tones. A strange hush was over this community of American citizens. In their work, in their pleasures, in their home life, in their love and happiness, in their very sorrows, they felt the deadening presence of this dread thing that was sweeping upon them from somewhere beyond the borders of their native land. And against this death that filled the air they seemingly knew not how to defend themselves.

This, to the Interpreter, was the almost unbelievable tragedy—that the people should not know what to do; that they should not have given more thought to making the structure of their citizenship stormproof.

"The great trouble is that the people don't line up right," said Captain Charlie to John and the Interpreter one evening as the workman and the general manager were sitting with the old basket maker on the balcony porch.

"Just what do you mean by that, Charlie?" asked John. The man in the wheel chair was nodding his assent to the union man's remark.

"I mean," Charlie explained, "that the people consider only capital and labor, or workmen and business men. They put loyal American workmen and imperialist

138

workmen all together on one side and loyal American business men and imperialist business men all together on the other. They line up *all* employees against *all* employers. For example, as the people see it, you and I are enemies and the Mill is our battle ground. The fact is that the imperialist manual workman is as much my enemy as he is yours. The imperialist business man is as much your enemy as he is mine."

"You are exactly right, Charlie," said the Interpreter. "And that is the first thing that the Big Idea applied to our industries will do—it will line up the great body of loyal American workmen that you represent with the great body of loyal American business men that John represents against the McIvers of capital and the Jake Vodells of labor. And that new line-up alone would practically insure victory. Nine tenths of our industrial troubles are due to the fact that employers and employees alike fail to recognize their real enemies and so fight their friends as often as they fight their foes.

"The people must learn to call an industrial slacker a slacker, whether he loafs on a park bench or loafs on the veranda of the country club house. They have to recognize that a traitor to the industries is a traitor to the nation and that he is a traitor whether he works at a bench or runs a bank. They have to say to the imperialist of business and to the imperialist of labor alike, 'The industries of this country are not for you or your class alone, they are for all because the very life of the nation is in them and is dependent upon them.' When the people of this country learn to draw the lines of class where they really belong there will be an end to our industrial wars and to all the suffering that they cause."

"If only the people could be lined up and made to declare themselves openly," said John, "Jake Vodell would have about as much chance to make trouble among us as the German Crown Prince would have had among the French Blue Devils."

Charlie laughed.

"Which means, I suppose," said the Interpreter, "that there would be a riot to see who could lay hands on him first."

* * * * *

The storm broke at McIver's factory. It was as Jake Vodell had told the Interpreter it would be—"easy to find a grievance."

McIver declared that before he would yield to the demands of his workmen, his factory should stand idle until the buildings rotted to the ground.

The agitator answered that before his men would yield they would make Millsburgh as a city of the dead.

Two or three of the other smaller unions supported McIver's employees with sympathetic strikes. But the success or failure of Jake Vodell's campaign quickly turned on the action of the powerful Mill workers' union. The commander-in-chief of the striking forces must win John Ward's employees to his cause or suffer defeat. He bent every effort to that end.

Sam Whaley and a few like him walked out. But that was expected by everybody, for Sam Whaley had identified himself from the day of Vodell's arrival in Millsburgh as the agitator's devoted follower and right-hand man. But this unstable, whining weakling and his fellows from the Flats carried little influence with the majority of the sturdy, clearer-visioned workmen.

At a meeting of the Millsburgh Manufacturing Association, McIver endeavored to pledge the organization to a concerted effort against the various unions of their workmen.

John Ward refused to enter into any such alliance against the workmen, and branded McIver's plan as being in spirit and purpose identical with the schemes of Jake Vodell. John argued that while the heads of the various related mills and factories possessed the legal right to maintain their organization for the purpose of furthering such business interests as were common to them all, they could not, as loyal citizens, attempt to deprive their fellow workmen citizens of that same right. Any such effort to array class against class, he declared, was nothing less than sheer imperialism, and antagonistic to every principle of American citizenship.

When McIver characterized Vodell as an anarchist and stated that the unions were back of him and his schemes against the government, John retorted warmly that the statement was false and an insult to many of the most loyal citizens in Millsburgh. There were individual members of the unions who were followers of Jake Vodell, certainly. But comparatively few of the union men who were led by the agitator to strike realized the larger plans of their leader, while the unions as a whole no more endorsed anarchy than did the Manufacturing Association.

McIver then drew for his fellow manufacturers a very true picture of the industrial troubles throughout the country, and pointed out clearly and convincingly the national dangers that lay in the threatening conditions. Millsburgh was in no way different from thousands of other communities. If the employers could not defend themselves by an organized effort against their employees, he would like Mr. Ward to explain who would defend them.

To all of which John answered that it was not a question of employers defending themselves against their employees. The owners had no more at stake in the situation than did their workmen, for the lives of all were equally dependent upon the industries that were threatened with destruction. In the revolution that Jake Vodell's brotherhood was fomenting the American employers could lose no more than would the American employees. The question was, How could American industries be protected against both the imperialistic employer and the imperialistic employee?

140

The answer was, By the united strength of the loyal American employers and employees, openly arrayed against the teachings and leadership of Jake Vodell, on the one hand, and equally against all such principles and actions as had been proposed by Mr. McIver, on the other.

When the meeting closed, McIver had failed to gain the support of the association.

Realizing that without the Mill he could never succeed in his plans, the factory owner appealed to Adam Ward himself.

The old Mill owner, in full accord with McIver, attempted to force John into line. But the younger man refused to enlist in any class war against his loyal fellow workmen.

Adam stormed and threatened and predicted utter ruin. John calmly offered to resign. The father refused to listen to this, on the ground that his ill health did not permit him to assume again the management of the business, and that he would never consent to the Mill's being operated by any one outside the family.

When Helen returned to her home in the early evening, she found her father in a state of mind bordering on insanity.

Striding here and there about the rooms with uncontrollable nervous energy, he roared, as he always did on such occasions, about his sole ownership of the Mill— the legality of the patents that gave him possession of the new process—how it was his genius and hard work alone that had built up the Mill—that no one should take his possessions from him—waving his arms and shaking his fists in violent, meaningless gestures. With his face twitching and working and his eyes blazing with excitement and rage, his voice rose almost to a scream: "Let them try to take anything away from me! I know what they are going to do, but they can't do it. I've had the best lawyers that I could hire and I've got it all tied up so tight that no one can touch it.

"I could have thrown Pete Martin out of the Mill any time I wanted. He has no claim on me that any court in the world would recognize. Let him try anything he dares. I'll starve him to death—I'll turn him into the streets—he hasn't a thing in the world that he didn't get by working for me. I made him—I will ruin him. You all think that I am sick—you think that I am crazy—that I don't know what I am talking about. I'll show you—you'll see what will happen if they start any thing—"

The piteous exhibition ended as usual. As if driven by some invisible fiend, the man rushed from the presence of those whom he most loved to the dreadful company of his own fearful and monstrous thoughts.

And the room where the wife and children of Adam Ward sat was filled with the presence of that hidden thing of which they dared not speak.

* * * * *

Everywhere throughout the city the people were discussing John Ward's opposition to McIver.

The community, tense with feeling, waited for an answer to the vital question, What would the Mill workers' union do? Upon the answer of John Ward's employees to the demands of the agitator for a sympathetic strike depended the success or failure of Jake Vodell's Millsburgh campaign.

CHAPTER XIX

ADAM WARD'S WORK

It was evening. The Interpreter was sitting in his wheel chair on the balcony porch with silent Billy not far away. Beyond the hills on the west the sky was faintly glowing in the last of the sun's light. The Flats were deep in gloomy shadows out of which the grim stacks of the Mill rose toward the smoky darkness of their overhanging cloud. Here and there among the poor homes of the workers a lighted window or a lonely street lamp shone in the murky dusk. But the lights of the business section of the city gleamed and sparkled like clusters and strings of jewels, while the residence districts on the hillside were marked by hundreds of twinkling, starlike points.

The quiet was rudely broken by a voice at the outer doorway of the hut. The tone was that of boisterous familiarity. "Hello! hello there! Anybody home?"

"Here," answered the Interpreter. "Come in. Or, I should say, come out," he added, as his visitor found his way through the darkness of the living room. "A night like this is altogether too fine to spend under a roof."

"Why in thunder don't you have a light?" said the visitor, with a loud freedom carefully calculated to give the effect of old and privileged comradeship. But the laugh of hearty good fellowship which followed his next remark was a trifle overdone "Ain't afraid of bombs, are you? Don't you know that the war is over yet?"

The Interpreter obligingly laughed at the merry witticism, as he answered, "There is light enough out here under the stars to think by. How are you, Adam Ward?"

From where he stood in the doorway, Adam could see the dim figure of the Interpreter's companion at the farther end of the porch. "Who is that with you?" demanded the Mill owner suspiciously.

"Only Billy Rand," replied the man in the wheel chair reassuringly. "Won't you sit down?"

Before accepting the invitation to be seated, Adam advanced upon the man in the wheel chair with outstretched hands, as if eagerly meeting a most intimate friend whose regard he prized above all other relationships of life. Seizing the Interpreter's hand, he clung to it in an excess of cordiality, all the while pouring out between short laughs of pretended gladness, a hurried volume of excuses for having so long delayed calling upon his dear old friend. To any one at all acquainted with the man, it would have been very clear that he wanted something.

"It seems ages since I saw you," he declared, as he seated himself at last. "It's a shame for a man to neglect an old friend as I have neglected you."

The Interpreter returned, calmly, "The last time you called was just before your son enlisted. You wanted me to help you keep him at home."

It was too dark to see Adam's face. "So it was, I remember now." There was a suggestion of nervousness in the laugh which followed his words.

"The time before that," said the Interpreter evenly, "was when Tom Blair was killed in the Mill. You wanted me to persuade Tom's widow that you were in no way liable for the accident."

The barometer of Adam's friendliness dropped another degree. "That affair was finally settled at five thousand," he said, and this time he did not laugh.

"The time before that," said the Interpreter, "was when your old friend Peter Martin's wife died. You wanted me to explain to the workmen who attended the funeral how necessary it was for you to take that hour out of their pay checks."

"You have a good memory," said the visitor, coldly, as he stirred uneasily in the dusk.

"I have," agreed the man in the wheel chair; "I find it a great blessing at times. It is the only thing that preserves my sense of humor. It is not always easy to preserve one's sense of humor, is it, Adam Ward?"

When the Mill owner answered, his voice, more than his words, told how determined he was to hold his ground of pleasant, friendly comradeship, at least until he had gained the object of his visit.

"Don't you ever get lonesome up here? Sort of gloomy, ain't it—especially at nights?"

"Oh, no," returned the Interpreter; "I have many interesting callers; there are always my work and my books and always, night and day, I have our Mill over there."

"Heh! What! *Our* Mill! Where? Oh, I see—yes—*our* Mill—that's good! *Our* Mill!"

"Surely you will admit that I have some small interest in the Mill where we once worked side by side, will you not, Adam?"

"Oh, yes," laughed Adam, helping on the jest. "But let me see—I don't exactly recall the amount of your investment—what was it you put in?"

144

"Two good legs, Adam Ward, two good legs," returned the old basket maker.

Again Adam Ward was at a loss for an answer. In the shadowy presence of that old man in the wheel chair the Mill owner was as a wayward child embarrassed before a kindly master.

When the Interpreter spoke again his deep voice was colored with gentle patience.

"Why have you come to me like this, Adam Ward? What is it that you want?"

Adam moved uneasily. "Why—nothing particular—I just thought I would call— happened to be going by and saw your light."

There had been no light in the hut that evening. The Interpreter waited. The surrounding darkness of the night seemed filled with warring spirits from the gloomy Flats, the mighty Mill, the glittering streets and stores and the cheerfully lighted homes.

Adam tried to make his voice sound casual, but he could not altogether cover the nervous intensity of his interest, as he asked the question that was so vital to the entire community. "Will the Mill workers' union go out on a sympathetic strike?"

"No."

The Mill owner drew a long breath of relief. "I judged you would know."

The Interpreter did not answer.

Adam spoke with more confidence. "I suppose you know this agitator Jake Vodell?"

"I know who he is," replied the Interpreter. "He is a well-known representative of a foreign society that is seeking, through the working people of this country, to extend its influence and strengthen its power."

"The unions are going too far," said Adam. "The people won't stand for their bringing in a man like Vodell to preach anarchy and stir up all kinds of trouble."

The Interpreter spoke strongly. "Jake Vodell no more represents the great body of American union men than you, Adam Ward, represent the great body of American employers."

"He works with the unions, doesn't he?"

"Yes, but that does not make him a representative of the union men as a whole, any more than the fact that your work with the great body of American business men makes you their representative."

"I should like to know why I am not a representative American business man." It was evident from the tone of his voice that the Mill owner controlled himself with an effort.

The Interpreter answered, without a trace of personal feeling, "You do not represent them, Adam Ward, because the spirit and purpose of your personal business career is not the spirit and purpose of our business men as a whole—just as the spirit and purpose of such men as Jake Vodell is not the spirit and purpose of our union men as a whole."

"But," asserted the Mill owner, "it is men like me who have built up this country. Look at our railroads, our great manufacturing plants, our industries of all kinds! Look what I have done for Millsburgh! You know what the town was when you first came here. Look at it now!"

"The new process has indeed wrought great changes in Millsburgh," suggested the Interpreter.

"The new process! You mean that *I* have wrought great changes in Millsburgh. What would the new process have amounted to if it had not been for me? Why, even the poor old fools who owned the Mill at that time couldn't have done anything with it. I had to force it on them. And then when I had managed to get it installed and had proved what it would do, I made them increase their capitalization and give me a half interest—told them if they didn't I would take my process to their competitors and put them out of business. Later I managed to gain the control and after that it was easy." His voice changed to a tone of arrogant, triumphant boasting. "I may not be a representative business man in *your* estimation, but my work stands just the same. No man who knows anything about business will deny that I built up the Mill to what it is to-day."

"And that," returned the Interpreter, "is exactly what Vodell says for the men who work with their hands in coperation with men like you who work with their brains. You say that you built the Mill because you thought and planned and directed its building. Jake Vodell says the men whose physical strength materialized your thoughts, the men who carried out your plans and toiled under your direction built the Mill. And you and Jake are both right to exactly the same degree. The truth is that you have *all together* built the Mill. You have no more right to think or to say that you did it than Pete Martin has to think or to say that he did it."

When Adam Ward found no answer to this the Interpreter continued. "Consider a great building: The idea of the structure has come down through the ages from the first habitation of primitive man. The mental strength represented in the structure in its every detail is the composite thought of every generation of man since the days

146

when human beings dwelt in rocky caves and in huts of mud. But listen: The capitalist who furnished the money says he did it; the architect says he did it; the stone mason says he did it; the carpenter says he did it; the mountains that gave the stone say they did it; the forests that grew the timber say they did it; the hills that gave the metal say they did it.

"The truth is that all did it—that each individual worker, whether he toiled with his hands or with his brain, was dependent upon all the others as all were dependent upon those who lived and labored in the ages that have gone before, as all are dependent at the last upon the forces of nature that through the ages have labored for all. And this also is true, sir, whether you like to admit it or not; just as we—you and I and Pete Martin and the others—all together built the Mill, so we all together built it for all. You, Adam Ward, can no more keep for yourself alone the fruits of your labor than you alone and single-handed could have built the Mill."

The Interpreter paused as if for an answer.

Adam Ward did not speak.

A flare of light from, the stacks of the Mill, where the night shift was sweating at its work, drew their eyes. Through the darkness came the steady song of industry—a song that was charged with the life of millions. And they saw the lights of the business district, where Jake Vodell was preaching to a throng of idle workmen his doctrine of class hatred and destruction.

The Interpreter's manner was in no way aggressive when he broke the silence. There was, indeed, in his deep voice an undertone of sorrow, and yet he spoke as with authority. "You were driven here to-night by your fear, Adam Ward. You recognize the menace to this community and to our nation in the influence and teaching of men like Jake Vodell. Most of all, you fear for yourself and your material possessions. And you have reason to be afraid of this danger that you yourself have brought upon Millsburgh."

"What!" cried the Mill owner. "You say that I am responsible?—that I brought this anarchist agitator here?"

The Interpreter answered, solemnly, "I say that but for you and such men as you, Adam Ward, Jake Vodell could never gain a hearing in any American city."

Adam Ward laughed harshly.

But the old basket maker continued as if he had not heard. "Every act of your business career, sir, has been a refusal to recognize those who have worked with you. Your whole life has been an over assertion of your personal independence and a denial of the greatest of all laws—the law of *dependence*, which is the vital principle of life itself. And so you have, through these years, upheld and exemplified to the working people the very selfishness to which Jake Vodell appeals now with such sad effectiveness. It is the class pride and intolerance which you have fostered in yourself and family that have begotten the class hatred which makes Vodell's plans against our government a dangerous possibility. Your fathers fought in a great war for independence, Adam Ward. Your son must now fight for a recognition of that *dependence* without which the *independence* won by your father will surely perish from the earth."

At the mention of his son, the Mill owner moved impatiently and spoke with bitter resentment. "A fine mess you are making of things with your 'dependence.'"

"It is a fine mess that you have made of things, Adam Ward, with your '*in*dependence,'" returned the Interpreter, sternly.

"I can tell you one thing," said Adam. "Your unions will never straighten anything out with the help of Jake Vodell and his gang of murdering anarchists."

"You are exactly right," agreed the Interpreter. "And I can tell you a thing to match the truth of your statement. Your combinations of employers will never straighten anything out with the help of such men as McIver and his hired gunmen and his talk about driving men to work at the point of the bayonet. But McIver and his principles are not endorsed by our American employers," continued the Interpreter, "any more than Jake Vodell and his methods are endorsed by our American union employees. The fact is that the great body of loyal American employers and employees, which is, indeed, the body of our nation itself, is fast coming to recognize the truth that our industries must somehow be saved from the destruction that is threatened by both the McIvers of capital and the Vodells of labor. Our Mill, Adam Ward, that you and Pete Martin and I built together and that, whether you admit it or not, we built for all mankind, our Mill must be protected against both employers and employees. It must be protected, not because the ownership, under our laws, happens to be vested in you as an individual citizen, but because of that larger ownership which, under the universal laws of humanity, is vested in the people whose lives are dependent upon that Mill as an essential industry. The Mill must be saved, indeed, for the very people who would destroy it."

"Very fine!" sneered Adam; "and perhaps you will tell me who is to save my Mill that is not my Mill for the very people who own it and who would destroy it?"

The voice of the Interpreter was colored with the fire of prophecy as he answered, "In the name of humanity, the sons of the men who built the Mill will save it for humanity. Your boy John, Adam Ward, and Pete Martin's boy Charlie represent the united armies of American employers and employees that stand in common loyalty against the forces that are, through the destruction of our industries, seeking to bring about the downfall of our nation."

Adam Ward laughed. "Tell that to your partner Billy Rand over there; he will hear it as quick as the American people will."

148

But the man in the wheel chair was not disturbed by Adam Ward's laughing.

"The great war taught the American people some mighty lessons, Adam Ward," he said. "It taught us that patriotism is not of one class or rank, but is common to every level of our national social life. It taught us that heroism is the birthright of both office and shop. Most of all did the war teach us the lesson of comradeship—that men of every rank and class and occupation could stand together, live together and die together, united in the bonds of a common, loyal citizenship for a common, human cause. And out of that war and its lessons our own national saviors are come. The loyal patriot employers and the loyal patriot employees, who on the fields of war were brother members of that great union of sacrifice and death, will together free the industries of their own country from the two equally menacing terrors—imperialistic capital and imperialistic labor.

"The comradeship of your son with the workman Charlie Martin, the stand that John has taken against McIver, and the refusal of the Mill workers' union to accept Vodell's leadership—is the answer to your question, 'Who is to save the Mill?'"

"Rot!" exclaimed Adam Ward. "You talk as though every man who went to that war was inspired by the highest motives. They were not all heroes by a good deal."

"True," returned the Interpreter, "they were not all heroes. But there was the leaven that leavened the lump, and so the army itself was heroic."

"What about the moral degeneracy and the crime wave that have followed the return of your heroic army?" demanded Adam.

"True, again," returned the Interpreter; "it is inevitable that men whose inherited instincts and tendencies are toward crime should acquire in the school of war a bolder spirit—a more reckless daring in their criminal living. But again there is the saving leaven that leavens the lump. If the war training makes criminals more bold, it as surely makes the leaven of nobility more powerful. One splendid example of noble heroism is ten thousand times more potent in the world than a thousand revolting deeds of crime. No—no, Adam Ward, the world will not forget the lessons it learned over there. The torch of Flanders fields has not fallen. The world will carry on."

There was such a quality of reverent conviction in the concluding words of the man in the wheel chair that Adam Ward was silenced.

For some time they sat, looking into the night where the huge bulk of the Mill with its towering stacks and overhanging clouds seemed to dominate not only the neighboring shops and factories and the immediate Flats, but in some mysterious way to extend itself over the business district and the homes of the city, and, like a ruling spirit, to pervade the entire valley, even unto the distant line of hills.

When the old basket maker spoke again, that note of strange and solemn authority was in his voice. "Listen, Adam Ward! In the ideals, the heroism, the suffering, the sacrifice of the war—in shell hole and trench and bloody No Man's Land, the sons of men have found again the God that you and men like you had banished from the Mill. Your boy and Pete Martin's boy, with more thousands of their comrades than men of your mind realize, have come back from the war fields of France to enthrone God once more in the industrial world. And it shall come that every forge and furnace and anvil and machine shall be an organ to His praise—that every suit of overalls shall be a priestly robe of ministering service. And this God that you banished from the Mill and that is to be by your son restored to His throne and served by a priesthood of united employers and employees, shall bear a new name, Adam Ward, and that name shall be WORK."

Awed by the strange majesty of the Interpreter's voice, Adam Ward could only whisper fearfully, "Work—the name of God shall be Work!" "Ay, Adam Ward, WORK—and why not? Does not the work of the world express the ideals, the purpose, the needs, the life, the *oneness* of the world's humanity, even as a flower expresses the plant that puts it forth? And is not God the ultimate flowering of the human plant?"

The Mill owner spoke with timid hesitation, "Could I—do you think—could I, perhaps, help to, as you say, put God back into the Mill?"

"Your part in the building of the Mill is finished, Adam Ward," came the solemn answer. "You have made many contracts with men, sir; you should now make a contract with your God."

The owner of the new process sprang to his feet with an exclamation of fear. As one who sees a thing of horror in the dark, he drew back, trembling.

That deep, inexorable voice of sorrowful authority went on, "Make a contract with your God, Adam Ward; make a contract with your God."

With a wild cry of terror Adam Ward fled into the night.

The Interpreter in his wheel chair looked up at the stars.

* * * * *

It seems scarcely possible that the old basket maker could have foreseen the tragic effect of his words—and yet—

CHAPTER XX

THE PEOPLE'S AMERICA

At his evening meetings on the street, Jake Vodell with stirring oratory kindled the fire of his cause. In the councils of the unions, through individuals and groups, with clever arguments and inflaming literature, he sought recruits. With stinging sarcasm and withering scorn he taunted the laboring people—told them they were fools and cowards to submit to the degrading slavery of their capitalist owners. With biting invective and blistering epithet he pictured their employer enemies as the brutal and ruthless destroyers of their homes. With thrilling eloquence he fanned the flames of class hatred, inspired the loyalty of his followers to himself and held out to them golden promises of reward if they would prove themselves men and take that which belonged to them.

But the Mill workers' union, as an organization, was steadfast in its refusal to be dominated by this agitator who was so clearly antagonistic to every principle of American citizenship. Jake Vodell could neither lead nor drive them into a strike that was so evidently called in the interests of his cause. And more and more the agitator was compelled to recognize the powerful influence of the Interpreter. It was not long before he went to the hut on the cliff with a positive demand for the old basket maker's open support.

"I do not know why it is," he said, "that a poor old cripple like you should have such power among men, but I know it is so. You shall tell this Captain Charlie and his crowd of fools that they must help me to win for the laboring people their freedom. You shall, for me, enlist these Mill men in the cause."

The Interpreter asked, gravely, "And when you have accomplished this that you call freedom—when you have gained this equality that you talk about—how will your brotherhood be governed?"

Jake Vodell scowled as he gazed at the man in the wheel chair with quick suspicion. "Governed?"

"Yes," returned the Interpreter. "Without organization of some sort nothing can be done. No industries can be carried on without the concerted effort which is organization. Without the industry that is necessary to human life the free people you picture cannot exist. Without government—which means law and the enforcement of law—organization of any kind is impossible."

"There will have to be organization, certainly," answered Vodell.

"Then, there will be leaders, directors, managers with authority to whom the people must surrender themselves as individuals," said the Interpreter, quietly. "An organization without leadership is impossible."

The agitator's voice was triumphant, as he said, "Certainly there will be leaders. And their authority will be unquestioned. And these leaders will be those who have led the people out of the miserable bondage of their present condition."

The Interpreter's voice had a new note in it now, as he said, "In other words, sir, what you propose is simply to substitute *yourself* for McIver. You propose to the people that they overthrow their present leaders in the industries of their nation in order that you and your fellow agitators may become their masters. You demand that the citizens of America abolish their national government and in its place accept you and your fellows as their rulers? What assurance can you give the people, sir, that under your rule they will have more freedom for self-government, more opportunities for self-advancement and prosperity and happiness than they have at present?"

"Assurance?" muttered the other, startled by the Interpreter's manner.

The old basket maker continued, "Are you and your self-constituted leaders of the American working people, gods? Are you not as human as any McIver or Adam Ward of the very class you condemn? Would you not be subject to the same temptations of power—the same human passions? Would you not, given the same opportunity, be all that you say they are—or worse?"

Jake Vodell's countenance was black with rage. He started to rise, but a movement of Billy Rand made him hesitate. His voice was harsh with menacing passion. "And you call yourself a friend of the laboring class?"

"It is because I am a friend of my fellow American citizens that I ask you what freedom your brotherhood can insure to us that we have not now," the Interpreter answered, solemnly. "Look there, sir." He swept, in a gesture, the scene that lay within view of his balcony porch. "*That* is America—*my* America—the America of the *people*. From the wretched hovels of the incompetent and unfortunate Sam Whaleys in the Flats down there to Adam Ward's castle on the hill yonder, it is *our* America. From the happy little home of that sterling workman, Peter Martin, to the homes of the business workers on the hillside over there, it is *ours*. From the business district to the beautiful farms across the river, it belongs to *us all*. And the Mill there— representing as it does the industries of our nation and standing for the very life of our people—is *our* Mill. The troubles that disturb us—the problems of injustice—the wrongs of selfishness that arise through such employers as McIver and such employees as Sam Whaley, are *our* troubles, and we will settle our own difficulties in our own way as loyal American citizens."

The self-appointed apostle of the new freedom had by this time regained his self-control. His only answer to the Interpreter was a shrug of his thick shoulders and a flash of white teeth in his black beard.

The old basket maker with his eyes still on the scene that lay before them continued. "Because I love my countrymen, sir, I protest the destructive teachings of your

152

brotherhood. Your ambitious schemes would plunge my country into a bloody revolution the horrors of which defy the imagination. America will find a better way. The loyal American citizens who labor in our industries and the equally loyal American operators of these industries will never consent to the ruthless murder by hundreds and thousands of our best brains and our best manhood in support of your visionary theories. My countrymen will never permit the unholy slaughter of innocent women and children, that would result from your efforts to overthrow our government and establish a wholly impossible Utopia upon the basis of an equality that is contrary to every law of life. You preach freedom to the working people in order to rob them of the freedom they already have. With visions of impossible wealth and luxurious idleness you blind them to the greater happiness that is within reach of their industry. In the name of an equality, the possibility of which your own assumed leadership denies, you incite a class hatred and breed an intolerance and envy that destroy the good feeling of comradeship and break down the noble spirit of that actual equality which we already have and which is our only salvation."

"Equality!" sneered Jake Vodell. "You have a fine equality in this America of capitalist-ridden fools who are too cowardly to say that their souls are their own. It is the equality of Adam Ward and Sam Whaley, I suppose."

"Sam Whaley is a product of your teaching, sir," the Interpreter answered. "The equality of which I speak is that of Adam Ward and Peter Martin as it is evidenced in the building up of the Mill. It is the equality that is in the comradeship of their sons, John and Charlie, who will protect and carry on the work of their fathers. It is the equality of a common citizenship—of mutual dependence of employer and employee upon the industries, that alone can save our people from want and starvation and guard our nation from the horrors you would bring upon it."

The man laughed. "Suppose you sing that pretty song to McIver, heh? What do you think he would say?"

"He would laugh, as you are laughing," returned the Interpreter, sadly.

"Tell it to Adam Ward then," jeered the other. "He will recognize his equality with Peter Martin when you explain it, heh?"

"Adam Ward is already paying a terrible price for denying it," the Interpreter answered.

Again Jake Vodell laughed with sneering triumph. "Well, then I guess you will have to preach your equality to the deaf and dumb man there. Maybe you can make him understand it. The old basket maker without any legs and the big husky who can neither hear nor talk—they are equals, I suppose, heh?"

"Billy Rand and I perfectly illustrate the equality of dependence, sir," returned the Interpreter. "Billy is as much my superior physically as I am his superior mentally.

Without my thinking and planning he would be as helpless as I would be without his good bodily strength. We are each equally dependent upon the other, and from that mutual dependence comes our comradeship in the industry which alone secures for us the necessities of life. I could not make baskets without Billy's labor—Billy could not make baskets without my planning and directing. And yet, sir, you and McIver would set us to fighting each other. You would have Billy deny his dependence upon me and use his strength to destroy me, thus depriving himself of the help he must have if he would live. McIver would have me deny my dependence upon Billy and by antagonizing him with my assumed superiority turn his strength to the destruction of our comradeship by which I also live. Your teaching of class loyalty and class hatred applied to Billy and me would result in the ruin of our basket making and in our consequent starvation."

Again the Interpreter, from his wheel chair, pointed with outstretched arm to the scene that lay with all its varied grades of life—social levels and individual interests—before them. "Look," he said, "to the inequality that is there—inequalities that are as great as the difference between Billy Rand and myself. And yet, every individual life is dependent upon all the other individual lives. The Mill yonder is the basket making of the people. All alike must look to it for life itself. The industries, without which the people cannot exist, can be carried on only by the comradeship of those who labor with their hands and those who work with their brains. In the common dependence all are equal.

"The only equality that your leadership, with its progress of destruction, can insure to American employers and employees is an equality of indescribable suffering and death."

The old basket maker paused a moment before he added, solemnly, "I wonder that you dare assume the responsibility for such a catastrophe. Have you no God, sir, to whom you must eventually account?"

The man's teeth gleamed in a grin of malicious sarcasm. "I should know that you believed in God. Bah! An old woman myth to scare fools and children. I suppose you believe in miracles also?"

"I believe in the miracle of life," the Interpreter answered; "and in the great laws of life—the law of inequality and dependence, that in its operation insures the oneness of all things."

The agitator rose to his feet, and with a shrug of contempt, said, "Very pretty, Mr. Interpreter, very pretty. You watch now from your hut here and you shall see what men who are not crippled old basket makers will do with that little bit of your America out there. It is I who will teach Peter Martin and his comrades in the Mill how to deal with your friend Adam Ward and his class."

"You are too late, sir," said the Interpreter, as the man moved toward the door.

154

Jake Vodell turned. "How, too late?" Then as he saw Billy Rand rising to his feet, his hand went quickly inside his vest.

The old basket maker smiled as he once more held out a restraining hand toward his companion. "I do not mean anything like that, sir. I told you some time ago that you were defeated in your Millsburgh campaign by Adam Ward's retirement from the Mill. You are too late because you are forced now to deal, not with Adam Ward and Peter Martin, but with their sons."

"Oh, ho! and what you should say also, is that I am really forced to deal with an old basket maker who has no legs, heh? Well, we shall see about that, too, Mr. Interpreter, when the time comes—we shall see."

CHAPTER XXI

PETER MARTIN'S PROBLEM

It was not long until the idle workmen began to feel the want of their pay envelopes. The grocers and butchers were as dependent upon those pay envelopes as were the workmen themselves.

The winter was coming on. There was a chill in the air. In the homes of the strikers the mothers and their little ones needed not only food but fuel and clothing as well. The crowds at the evening street meetings became more ominous. Through the long, idle days grim, sullen-faced men walked the streets or stood in groups on the corners watching their fellow citizens and muttering in low, guarded tones. Members of the Mill workers' union were openly branded as cowards and traitors to their class. The suffering among the women and children became acute.

But Jake Vodell was a master who demanded of his disciples most heroic loyalty, without a thought of the cost—to them.

McIver put an armed guard about his factory and boasted that he could live without work. The strikers, he declared, could either starve themselves and their families or accept his terms.

The agitator was not slow in making capital of McIver's statements.

The factory owner depended upon the suffering of the women and children to force the workmen to yield to him. Jake Vodell, the self-appointed savior of the laboring people, depended upon suffering of women and children to drive his followers to the desperate measures that would further his peculiar and personal interests.

Through all this, the Mill workers' union still refused to accept the leadership of this man whose every interest was anti-American and foreign to the principles of the loyal citizen workman. But the fire of Jake Vodell's oratory and argument was not without kindling power, even among John Ward's employees. As the feeling on both sides of the controversy grew more bitter and intolerant, the Mill men felt with increasing force the pull of their class. The taunts and jeers of the striking workers were felt. The cries of "traitor" hurt. The suffering of the innocent members of the strikers' families appealed strongly to their sympathies.

When McIver's imperialistic declaration was known, the number who were in favor of supporting Jake Vodell's campaign increased measurably.

Nearly every day now at some hour of the evening or night, Pete and Captain Charlie, with others from among their union comrades, might have been found in the hut on the cliff in earnest talk with the man in the wheel chair. The active head of the union was Captain Charlie, as his father had been before him, but it was no secret that the guiding counsel that held the men of the Mill steady cane from the old basket maker.

For John Ward the days were increasingly hard. He could not but sense the feeling of the men. He knew that if Jake Vodell could win them, such disaster as the people of Millsburgh had never seen would result. The interest and sympathy of Helen, the comradeship of Captain Charlie, and the strength of the Interpreter gave him courage and hope. But there was nothing that he could do. He felt as he had felt sometimes in France when he was called upon to stand and wait. It was a relief to help Mary as he could in her work among the sufferers. But even this activity of mercy was turned against him by both McIver and Vodell. The factory man blamed him for prolonging the strike and thus working injury to the general business interests of Millsburgh. The strike leader charged him with seeking to win the favor of the working class in order to influence his own employees against, what he called the fight for their industrial freedom.

The situation was rapidly approaching a crisis when Peter Martin and Captain Charlie, returning home from a meeting of their union laid one evening, found the door of the house locked.

The way the two men stood facing each other without a word revealed the tension of their nerves. Captain Charlie's hand shook so that his key rattled against the lock. But when they were inside and had switched on the light, a note which Mary had left on the table for them explained.

The young woman had gone to the Flats in answer to a call for help. John was with her. She had left the note so that her father and brother would not be alarmed at her absence in case they returned home before her.

In their relief, the two men laughed. They were a little ashamed of their unspoken fears.

"We might have known," said Pete, and with the words seemed to dismiss the incident from his mind.

But Captain Charlie did not recover so easily. While his father found the evening paper and, settling himself in an easy-chair by the table, cleaned his glasses and filled and lighted his pipe, the younger man went restlessly from room to room, turning on the lights, turning them off again—all apparently for no reason whatever. He finished his inspection by returning to the table and again picking up Mary's note.

When he had reread the message he said, slowly, "I thought John expected to be at the office to-night."

Something in his son's voice caused the old workman to look at him steadily, as he answered, "John probably came by on his way to the Mill and dropped in for a few minutes."

"I suppose so," returned Charlie. Then, "Father, do you think it wise for sister to be so much with John?"

The old workman laid aside his paper. "Why, I don't know—I hadn't thought much about it, son. It seems natural enough, considering the way you children was all raised together when you was youngsters."

"It's natural enough all right," returned Captain Charlie, and, with a bitterness that was very unlike his usual self, he added, "That's, the hell of it—it's too natural—too human—too right for this day and age."

Pete Martin's mind worked rather slowly but he was fully aroused now—Charlie's meaning was clear. "What makes you think that Mary and John are thinking of each other in that way, son?"

"How could they help it?" returned Captain Charlie. "Sister is exactly the kind of woman that John would choose for a wife. Don't I know what he thinks of the light-headed nonentities in the set that he is supposed to belong to? Hasn't he demonstrated his ideas of class distinctions? It would never occur to him that there was any reason why John Ward should not love Mary Martin. As for sister—when you think of the whole story of their childhood together, of how John and I were all through the war, of how he has been in the Mill since we came home, of their seeing each other here at the house so much, of the way he has been helping her with her work among the poor in the Flats—well, how could any woman like sister help loving him?"

While the older man was considering his son's presentation of the case, Captain Charlie added, with characteristic loyalty, "God may have made finer men than John Ward, but if He did they don't live around Millsburgh."

"Well, then, son," said Peter Martin, with his slow smile, "what about it? Suppose they are thinking of each other as you say?"

Captain Charlie did not answer for a long minute. And the father, watching, saw in that strong young face the shadow of a hurt which the soldier workman could not hide.

"It is all so hopeless," said Charlie, at last, in a tone that told more clearly than words could have done his own hopelessness. "I—it don't seem right for Mary to have to bear it, too."

158

"I'm sorry, son," was all that the old workman said, but Captain Charlie knew that his father understood.

After that they did not speak until they heard an automobile stop in front of the house.

"That must be Mary now," said Pete, looking at his watch. "They have never been so late before."

They heard her step on the porch. The sound of the automobile died away in the distance.

When Mary came in and they saw her face, they knew that Charlie was right. She tried to return their greetings in her usual manner but failed pitifully and hurried on to her room.

The two men looked at each other without a word.

Presently Mary returned and told them a part of her evening's experience. Soon after her father and brother had left the house for the meeting of their union, a boy from the Flats came with the word that the wife of one of Jake Vodell's followers was very ill. Mary, knowing the desperate need of the case but fearing to be alone in that neighborhood at night, had telephoned John at the Mill and he had taken her in his car to the place. The woman, in the agonies of childbirth, was alone with her three little girls. The husband and father was somewhere helping Jake Vodell in the agitator's noble effort to bring happiness to the laboring class. While Mary was doing what she could in the wretched home, John went for a doctor, and to bring fuel and blankets and food and other things that were needed. But, in spite of their efforts, the fighting methods of McIver and Vodell scored another point, that they each might claim with equal reason as in his favor—to God knows what end.

"I can't understand why you Mill men let them go on," Mary cried, with a sudden outburst of feeling, as she finished her story. "You could fight for the women and children during the war. Whenever there is a shipwreck the papers are always full of the heroism of the men who cry 'women and children first!' Why can't some one think of the women and children in these strikes? They are just as innocent as the women and children of Belgium. Why don't you talk on the streets and hold mass meetings and drive Jake Vodell and that beast McIver out of the country?"

"Jake Vodell and McIver are both hoping that some one will do just that, Mary," returned Captain Charlie. "They would like nothing better than for some one to start a riot. You see, dear, an open clash would result in bloodshed—the troops would be called in by McIver, which is exactly what he wants. Vodell would provoke an attack on the soldiers, some one would be killed, and we would have exactly the sort of war against the government that he and his brotherhood are working for."

The old workman spoke. "Charlie is right, daughter; these troubles will never be settled by McIver's way nor Vodell's way. They will be settled by the employers like John getting together and driving the McIvers out of business—and the employees like Charlie here and a lot of the men in our union getting together with John and his crowd and sending the Jake Vodells back to whatever country they came from." When her father spoke John's name, the young woman's face colored with a quick blush. The next moment, unable to control her overwrought emotions, she burst into tears and started to leave the room. But at the door Captain Charlie caught her in his arms and held her close until the first violence of her grief was over.

When she had a little of her usual calmness, her brother whispered, "I know all about it, dear."

She raised her head from his shoulder and looked at him with tearful doubt. "You know about—about John?" she said, wonderingly.

"Yes," he whispered, with an encouraging smile, "I know—father and I were talking about it before you came home. I am going to leave you with him now. You must tell father, you know. Goodnight, dear—good-night, father."

Slowly Mary turned back into the room. The old workman, sitting there in his big chair, held out his arms. With a little cry she ran to him as she had gone to him all the years of her life.

When she had told him all—how John that very evening on their way home from the Flats had asked her to be his wife—and how she, in spite of her love for him, had forced herself to answer, "No," Pete Martin sat with his head bowed as one deep in thought.

Mary, knowing her father's slow way, waited.

When the old workman spoke at last it was almost as though, unconscious of his daughter's presence, he talked to himself. "Your mother and I used to think in the old days when you children were growing up together that some time perhaps the two families would be united. But when we watched Adam getting rich and saw what his money was doing to him and to his home, we got to be rather glad that you children were separated. We were so happy ourselves in our own little home here that we envied no man. We did not want wealth even for you and Charlie when we saw all that went with it. We did not dream that Adam's success could ever stand in the way of our children's happiness like this. But I guess that is the way it is, daughter. I remember the Interpreter's saying once that no man had a right to make even himself miserable because no man could be miserable alone."

The old workman's voice grew still more reflective. "It was the new process that made Adam rich. He was no better man at the bench than I. I never considered him

160

as my superior. He happened to be born with a different kind of a brain, that is all. And he thought more of money, while I cared more for other things. But there is a good reason why his money should not be permitted to stand between his children and my children. There is a lot of truth, after all, in Jake Vodell's talk about the rights of men who work with their hands. The law upholds Adam Ward in his possessions, I know. And it would uphold him Just the same if my children were starving. But the law don't make it right. There should be some way to make a man do what is right—law or no law. You and John—"

"Father!" cried Mary, alarmed at his words. "Surely you are not going to hold with Jake Vodell about such things. What do you mean about making a man do what is right—law or no law?"

"There, there, daughter," said the old workman, smiling. "I was just thinking out loud, I guess. It will be all right for you and John. Run along to bed now, and don't let a worry come, even into your dreams."

"I would rather give John up a thousand times than have you like Jake Vodell," she said. "You shan't even *think* that way."

When she was gone, Peter Martin filled and lighted his pipe again, and for another hour sat alone.

Whether or not his thoughts bore any relation to the doctrines of Jake Vodell, they led the old workman, on the following day, to pay a visit to Adam Ward at his home on the hill.

CHAPTER XXII

OLD FRIENDS

It was Sunday morning and the church bells were ringing over the little city as the old workman climbed the hill to Adam Ward's estate.

There was a touch of frost in the air. The hillside back of the interpreter's hut was brown. But the sun was bright and warm and in every quarter of the city the people were going to their appointed places of worship. The voice of the Mill was silenced.

Pete wondered if he would find Adam at home. He had not thought about it when he left the cottage—his mind had been so filled with the object of his visit to the man who had once been his working comrade and friend.

But Adam Ward was not at church.

The Mill owner's habits of worship were very simply regulated. If the minister said things that pleased him, and showed a properly humble gratification at Adam's presence in the temple of God, Adam attended divine services. If the reverend teacher in the pulpit so far forgot himself as to say anything that jarred Adam's peculiar spiritual sensitiveness, or failed to greet this particular member of his flock with proper deference, Adam stayed at home and stopped his subscription to the cause. Nor did he ever fail to inform his pastor and the officers of the congregation as to the reason for his nonattendance; always, at the time, assuring them that whenever the minister would preach the truths that he wanted to hear, his weekly offerings to the Lord would be renewed. Thus Adam Ward was just and honest in his religious life as he was in his business dealings. He was ready always, to pay for that which he received, but, as a matter of principle, he was careful always to receive exactly what he paid for.

This Sunday morning Adam Ward was at home.

When Pete reached the entrance to the estate the heavy gates were closed. As Mary's father stood in doubt before the iron barrier a man appeared on the inside.

"Good-morning, Uncle Pete," he said, in hearty greeting, when he saw who it was that sought admittance.

"Good-morning, Henry—and what are you doing in there?" returned the workman, who had known the man from his boyhood.

The other grinned. "Oh, I'm one of the guards at this institution now."

Pete looked at him blankly. "Guards? What are you guarding, Henry?"

Standing close to the iron bars of the gate, Henry glanced over his shoulder before he answered in a low, cautious tone, "Adam."

The old workman was shocked. "What! you don't mean it!" He shook his grizzly head sadly. "I hadn't heard that he was that bad."

Henry laughed. "We're not keepin' the old boy in, Uncle Pete—not yet. So far, our orders are only to keep people out. Dangerous people, I mean—the kind that might want to run away with the castle, or steal a look at the fountain, or sneak a smell of the flowers or something—y' understand."

Pete smiled. "How do you like your job, Henry?"

"Oh, it's all right just now when the strike is on. But was you wantin' to come in, Uncle Pete, or just passing' by?"

"I wanted to see Adam if I could."

The man swung open the gate. "Help yourself, Uncle Pete, just so you don't stick a knife into him or blow him up with a bomb or poison him or something." He pointed toward that part of the grounds where Helen had watched her father from the arbor. "You'll find him over there somewhere, I think. I saw him headed that way a few minutes ago. The rest of the family are gone to church."

"Is Adam's life really threatened, Henry?" asked Pete, as he stepped inside and the gates were closed behind him.

"Search me," returned the guard, indifferently. "I expect if the truth were known it ought to be by rights. He sure enough thinks it is, though. Why, Uncle Pete, there can't a butterfly flit over these grounds that Adam ain't a yellin' how there's an aeroplane a sailin' around lookin' fer a chance to drop a monkey wrench on his head or something."

"Poor Adam!" murmured the old workman. "What a way to live!"

"Live?" echoed the guard. "It ain't livin' at all—it's just bein' in hell before your time, that's what it is—if you ask me."

* * * * *

When Peter Martin, making his slow way through the beautiful grounds, first caught sight of his old bench mate, Adam was pacing slowly to and fro across a sunny open space of lawn. As he walked, the Mill owner was talking to himself and moving his arms and hands in those continuous gestures that seemed so necessary to any expression of his thoughts. Once Pete heard him laugh. And something in the mirthless sound made the old workman pause. It was then that Adam saw him.

There was no mistaking the sudden fear that for a moment seemed to paralyze the man. His gray face turned a sickly white, his eyes were staring, his jaw dropped, his body shook as if with a chill. He looked about as if he would call for help, and started as if to seek safety in flight.

"Good-morning, Adam Ward," said Pete Martin.

And at the gentle kindliness in the workman's voice Adam's manner, with a suddenness that was startling, changed. With an elaborate show of friendliness he came eagerly forward. His gray face, twitching with nervous excitement, beamed with joyous welcome. As he hurried across the bit of lawn between them, he waved his arms and rubbed his hands together in an apparent ecstasy of gladness at this opportunity to receive such an honored guest. His voice trembled with high-pitched assurance of his happiness in the occasion. He laughed as one who could not contain himself.

"Well, well, well—to think that you have actually come to see me at last." He grasped the workman's hand in both his own with a grip that was excessive in its hearty energy. With affectionate familiarity he almost shouted, "You old scoundrel! I can't believe it is you. Where have you been keeping yourself? How are Charlie and Mary? Lord, but it's good to see you here in my own home like this."

While Pete was trying to make some adequate reply to this effusive and startling reception, Adam looked cautiously about to see if there were any chance observers lurking near.

Satisfied that no one was watching, he said, nervously, "Come on, let's sit over here where we can talk." And with his hand on Pete's arm, he led his caller to lawn chairs that were in the open, well beyond hearing of any curious ear in the shrubbery.

Giving the workman opportunity for no more than an occasional monosyllable in reply, he poured forth a flood of information about his estate: The architectural features of his house—the cost; the loveliness of his trees—the cost; the coloring of his flowers—the cost; the magnificence of his view, And all the while he studied his caller's face with sharp, furtive glances, trying to find some clew to the purpose of the workman's visit.

Peter Martin's steady eyes, save for occasional glances at the objects of Adam's interest as Adam pointed them out, were fixed on the Mill owner with a half-wondering, half-pitying expression. Adam's evident nervousness increased. He talked of his Mill—how he had built it up from nothing almost, to its present magnitude—of the city and what he had done for the people.

164

The old workman listened without comment.

At last, apparently unable to endure the suspense a moment longer, Adam Ward said, nervously, "Well, Pete, out with it! What do you want? I can guess what you are here for. We might as well get done with it."

In his slow, thoughtful manner of speech that was so different from the Mill owner's agitated expressions, the old workman said, "I have wanted for nothing, Adam. We have been contented and happy in our little home. But now," he paused as if his thoughts were loath to form themselves into words.

The last vestige of pretense left Adam Ward's face as suddenly as if he had literally dropped a mask. "It's a good thing you have been satisfied," he said, coldly. "You had better continue to be. You know that you owe everything you have in the world to me! You need not expect anything more."

"Have you not made a big profit on every hour's work that I have done in your Mill, Adam?"

"Whatever profit I have or have not made on your work is none of your business, sir," retorted Adam. "I have given you a job all these years. I could have thrown you out. You haven't a thing on earth that you did not buy with the checks you received from me. I have worn myself out—made an invalid of myself—building up the business that has enabled you and the rest of my employees to make a living. Every cent that I ever received from that new process I put back into the Mill. You have had more out of it than I ever did."

Peter Martin looked slowly about at the evidence of Adam Ward's wealth. When he again faced the owner of the estate he spoke as if doubting that he had heard him clearly. "But the Mill is yours, Adam?" he said, at last. "And all this is yours. How—where did it come from?"

"Certainly the Mill is mine. Didn't I make it what it is? As for the place here—it came from the profits of my business, of course. You know I was nothing but a common workman when I started out."

"I know," returned Pete. "And it was the new process that enabled you to get control of the Mill—to buy it and build it up—wasn't it? If you hadn't happened to have had the process the Mill would have made all this for some one else, wouldn't it? We never dreamed that the process would grow into such a big thing for anybody when we used to talk it over in the old days, did we, Adam?"

Adam Ward looked cautiously around at the shrubbery that encircled the bit of lawn. There was no one to be seen within hearing distance.

When he faced his companion again the Mill owner's eyes were blazing, but he controlled his voice by a supreme effort of will. "Look here, Pete, I'm not going even to discuss that matter with you. I have kept you on at the Mill and taken care of you all these years because of our old friendship and because I was sorry for you. But if you don't appreciate what I have done for you, if you attempt to start any talk or anything I'll throw you and Charlie out of your jobs to-morrow. And I'll fix it, too, so you will never either of you get another day's work in Millsburgh. That process is my property. No one has any interest in the patents in any way. I have it tied up so tight that all the courts in the world couldn't take it away from me. Law is law and I propose to keep what the law says is mine. I have thousands of dollars to spend in defense of my legal rights where you have dimes. You needn't whine about moral obligations either. The only obligations that are of any force in business are legal! If you haven't brains enough to look after your own interests you can't expect any one else to look after them for you."

When Adam Ward finished his countenance was distorted with hate and fear. Before this simple, kindly old workman, in whose honest soul there was no shadow of a wish to harm any one in any way, the Mill owner was like a creature of evil at bay.

"I did not come to talk of the past, Adam Ward," said Pete, sadly. "And I didn't come to threaten you or to ask anything for myself."

At the gentle sadness of his old friend's manner and words, Adam's eyes gleamed with vicious triumph. "Well, out with it!" he demanded, harshly. "What are you here for?"

"Your boy and my girl love each other, Adam."

An ugly grin twisted the gray lips of Pete's employer.

But Mary's father went on as though he had not seen. "The children were raised together, Adam. I have always thought of John almost as if he were my own son. It seems exactly right that he should want Mary and that she should want him. There is no man in the world I would rather it would be."

Adam listened, still grinning, as the old workman continued in his slow, quiet speech.

"I never cared before for all that the new process made for you. You wanted money—I didn't. But it don't seem right that what you have—considering how you got it—should stand in the way of Mary's happiness. I understand that there is nothing I can do about it, but I thought that, considering everything, you might be willing to—"

Adam Ward laughed aloud—laughed until the tears of his insane glee filled his eyes. "So that's your game," he said, at last, when he could speak. "You hadn't brains

166

enough to protect yourself to start out with and you have found out that you haven't a chance in the world against me in the courts. So you try to make it by setting your girl up to catch John."

"You must stop that sort of talk, Adam Ward." Peter Martin was on his feet, and there was that in his usually stolid countenance which made the Mill owner shrink back. "I was a fool, as you say. But my mistake was that I trusted you. I believed in your pretended friendship for me. I thought you were as honest and honorable as you seemed to be. I didn't know that your religion was all such a rotten sham. I have never cared that you grew rich while I remained poor. All these years I have been sorry for you because I have had so much of the happiness and contentment and peace that you have lost. But you must understand, sir, that there are some things that I will do in defense of my children that I would not do in defense of myself."

Adam, white and trembling, drew still farther away. "Be careful," he cried, "I can call half a dozen men before you can move."

Pete continued as if the other had not spoken. "There is no reason in the world why John and Mary should not marry."

Adam Ward's insane hatred for the workman and his evil joy over this opportunity to make his old comrade suffer was stronger even than his fear. With another snarling laugh he retorted, viciously, "There is the best reason in the world why they will never marry. *I* am the reason, Pete Martin! And I'd like to see you try to do anything about it."

Mary's father answered, slowly, "I do not understand your hatred for me, Adam. All these years I have been loyal to you. I have never talked of our affairs to any one—"

Adam interrupted him with a burst of uncontrollable rage. "*Talk*, you fool! Talk all you please. Tell everybody anything you like. Who will believe you? You will only get yourself laughed at for being the short-sighted idiot you were. That process is patented in my name. I own it. You don't need to keep still on my account, but I tell you again that if you do try to start anything I'll ruin you and I'll ruin your children." Suddenly, as if in fear that his rage would carry him too far, his manner changed and he spoke with forced coldness. "I am sorry that I cannot continue this interview, Pete. You have all that you will ever get from me—children or no children. Go on about your business as usual and you may hold your job in the Mill as long as you are able to do your work. I had thought that I might give you some sort of a little pension when you got too old to keep up your end with the rest of the men."

And then Adam Ward added the crowning insolent expression of his insane and arrogant egotism. With a pious smirk of his gray, twitching face, he said, "I want you to know, too, Pete, that you can approach me any time without any feeling of humiliation."

He turned abruptly away and a moment later the old workman, watching, saw him disappear behind some tall bushes.

As Pete Martin went slowly back to the entrance gate he did not know that the owner of the estate was watching him. From bush to bush Adam crept with the stealthy care of a wild creature, following its prey—never taking his eyes from his victim, save for quick glances here and there to see that he himself was not observed. Not until Pete had passed from sight down the hill road did Adam appear openly. Then, going to the watchman at the gate, he berated him for admitting the old workman and threatened him with the loss of his position if he so offended Again.

* * * * *

When Peter Martin arrived home he found Jake Vodell and Charlie discussing the industrial situation. The strike leader had come once more to try to enlist the support of the old workman and his son in his war against the employer class.

CHAPTER XXIII

A LAST CHANCE

Jake Vodell greeted the old workman cordially. "You have been to church this fine morning, I suppose, heh?" he said, with a sneering laugh that revealed how little his interview with Captain Charlie was contributing to his satisfaction.

"No," returned Pete. "I did not attend church this morning—I do go, though, generally."

"Oh-ho! you worship the God of your good master Adam Ward, I suppose."

But Pete Martin was in no way disturbed by the man's sarcasm. "No," he said, slowly, "I do not think that Adam and I worship the same God."

"Is it so? But when the son goes to war so bravely and fights for his masters one would expect the father to say his prayers to his masters' God, heh?"

Captain Charlie retorted, sharply, "The men who fought in the war fought for this nation—for every citizen in it. We fought for McIver just as we fought for Sam Whaley. Our loyalty in this industrial question is exactly the same. We will save the industries of this country for every citizen alike because our national life is at stake. Did you ever hear of a sailor refusing to man the pumps on a sinking ship because the vessel was not his personal property?"

"Bah!" growled Jake Vodell. "Your profession of loyalty to your country amuses me. *Your* country! It is McIver's country—Adam Ward's country, I tell you. It is my little band of live, aggressive heroes who are the loyal ones. We are the ones who will save the industries, but we will save them for the laboring people alone. And you shirkers in your Mill workers' union are willing to stand aside and let us do your fighting for you. Have you no pride for your class at all?"

"Oh, yes," returned Captain Charlie, "we have plenty of class pride. Only you see, Vodell, we don't consider ourselves in your class. You are no more loyal to the principles of our American unions than you are to the principles of our government. You don't represent our unions. You represent something foreign to the interests of every American citizen. You are trying to use our unions in your business, that is all. And because you manage to get hold of a few poor fellows like Sam Whaley, you think you can lead the working people. If you really think our loyalty to our country is a joke, drop in at an American Legion meeting some evening—bring along your foreign flag and all your foreign friends. I'll promise you a welcome that will, I think, convince you that we have some class pride after all."

The agitator rose heavily to his feet. "It is your friendship with this John Ward that makes you turn from your own class. I have known how it would be with you. But it is no matter. You shall see. We will make a demonstration in Millsburgh that will win the men of your union in spite of you and your crippled old basket maker. If you had a personal grievance against Adam Ward as so many others have you would be with me fast enough. But he and his son have made you blind with their pretended kindness."

Pete Martin spoke now with a dignity and pride that moved Captain Charlie deeply. "Mr. Vodell, you are wrong. My son is too big to be influenced in this matter by any personal consideration. Whatever there is that is personal between Charlie and John or between Adam Ward and myself will never be brought into this controversy."

Jake Vodell shrugged his heavy shoulders. "Very well—I will go now. You will see that in the end the working people will know who are for their interests and who are against them, and we will know, too, how to reward our friends and punish our enemies. I am sorry. I have given you to-day your last chance. You have a pretty little place here, heh?"

There was a look in his dark face, as he gazed about appraisingly, that made Captain Charlie go a step toward him. "*You* have given us our last chance? Is this a sample of the freedom that you offer so eloquently to the people? Instead of the imperialist McIver we are to have the imperialist Vodell, are we? Between the two of you I prefer McIver. He is at least sane enough to be constructive in his imperialism. My father and I have lived here all our lives, as most of our neighbors have. The majority of the workmen in this community own their homes just as we do. We are a part of the life of this city. What have you at stake? Where is your home and family? What is your nationality? What is your record of useful industry? Before you talk about giving a last chance to workmen like my father you will need to produce the credentials of your authority. We have your number, Jake Vodell. You may as well go back to the land where you belong, if you belong anywhere on earth. You will never hang your colors in the union Mill workers' hall. We have a flag there now that suits us. The chance you offer, last or first, is too darned big a chance for any sane American workman to monkey with."

Jake Vodell answered harshly as he turned to go. "At least I know now for sure who it is that makes the Mill workers such traitors to their class." He looked at Pete. "Your son has made his position very clear. We shall see now how bravely the noble Captain will hold his ground. As for you, well—always the old father can pray to his God for his son. It is so, heh?"

Quickly the man passed through the white gate and disappeared down the street toward the Flats.

"I am afraid that fellow means trouble, son," said Pete, slowly.

"Trouble," echoed Captain Charlie, "Jake Vodell has never meant anything but trouble."

170

* * * * *

Adam Ward did not join his family when they returned from church. A nervous headache kept him in his room.

In the afternoon John went for a long drive into the country. He felt that he must be alone—that he must think things out, for both Mary and himself.

As he looked back on it all now, it seemed to him that he had always loved this girl companion of his old-house days. In his boyhood he had accepted her as a part of his daily life just as he had accepted his sister. Those years of his schooling had been careless, thoughtless years, and followed, as they were, by his war experience, they seemed now to have had so small a part in the whole that they scarcely counted at all. His renewed comradeship with Charlie in the army had renewed also, through the letters that Charlie always shared with him, his consciousness of Mary. In the months just passed his love had ripened and become a definite thing, fixed and certain in his own mind and heart as the fact of life itself. He had no more thought of accepting as final Mary's answer than he had of turning the management of the Mill over to Jake Vodell or to Sam Whaley. But still there were things that he must think out.

On that favorite hillside spot where he and Charlie had spent so many hours discussing their industrial problems, John faced squarely the questions raised by Mary's "no."

Through the chill of the fall twilight John went home to spend the evening with his mother. But he did not speak to her of Mary. He could not, somehow, in the house that was so under the shadow of that hidden thing.

His father was still in his room.

On his way to his own apartment after his mother had retired, John stopped at his father's door to knock gently and ask if there was anything that he could do.

The answer came, "No, I will be all right—let me alone."

Later Helen returned from somewhere with McIver. Then John heard McIver leaving and Helen going to her mother for their usual good-night visit.

Seeing the light under his door, as she passed, she tapped the panel and called softly that it was tune all good little boys were fast asleep.

It was an hour, perhaps, after John had gone to bed that he was awakened by the sound of some one stealing quietly into his room. Against the dim night light in the hall, he caught the outline of an arm and shoulder as the intruder carefully closed the door. Reaching out to the lamp at the head of his bed, he snapped on the light and sprang to his feet.

"Father!"

"Sh—be careful, John, they will hear you!" Adam Ward's gray face was ghastly with nervous excitement and fear, and he was shaking as with a chill.

"No one must know I told you," he whispered, "but the new process is the source of everything we have—the Mill and everything. If it wasn't for my patent rights we would have nothing. You and I would be working in the Mill just like Pete and his boy."

John spoke soothingly. "Yes, father, I understand, but it will be all right—I'll take care of it."

Adam chuckled. "They're after it. But I've got it all sewed up so tight they can't touch it. That old fool, Pete, was here to feel me out to-day."

"Pete—here!"

Adam grinned. "While you folks were at church."

"But what did he want, father?"

"They've got a new scheme now. They've set Mary after you. They figure that if the girl can land you they'll get a chance at what I have made out of the process that way. I told him you was too smart to be caught like that. But you've got to watch them. They'll do anything."

In spite of his pity for his father, John Ward drew from him, overcome by a feeling of disgust and shame which he could not wholly control.

Adam, unconscious of his son's emotions, went on. "I've made it all in spite of them, John, but I've had to watch them. They'll be after you now that I have turned things over to you, just as they have been after me. They'll never get it, though. They'll never get a penny of it. I'll destroy the Mill and everything before I'll give up a dollar of what I've made."

John Ward could not speak. It was too monstrous—too horrible. As one in a hideous dream, he listened. What was back of it all? Why did his father in his spells of nervous excitement always rave so about the patented process? Why did he hate Pete Martin so bitterly? What was this secret thing that was driving Adam Ward insane?

172

Thinking to find an answer to these perplexing questions, if there was any answer other than the Mill owner's mental condition, John forced himself to the pretense of sharing his father's fears. He agreed with Adam's arraignment of Pete, echoed his father's expression of hatred for the old workman, thanked Adam for warning him, boasted of his own ability to see through their tricks and schemes and to protect the property his father had accumulated.

In this vein they talked in confidential whispers until John felt that he could venture the question, "Just what is it about the process that they are after, father? If I knew the exact history of the thing I would be in a much better position to handle the situation as you want, wouldn't I?"

Adam Ward's manner changed instantly. With a look of sly cunning he studied John's face. "There is nothing about the process, son," he said, steadily. "You know all there is to know about it now."

But when John, thinking that his father had regained his self-control, urged him to go back to his bed, Adam's painful agitation returned.

For some moments he paced to and fro as if in nervous indecision, then, going close to John, he said in a low, half whisper, "John, there is something else I wanted to ask you. You have been to college and over there in the war, you must have seen a lot of men die—" He paused. "Yes, yes, you must have been close to death a good many times. Tell me, John, do you believe that there is anything after—I mean anything beyond this life? Does a man's conscious existence go on when he is dead?"

"Yes," said John, wondering at this apparent change in his father's thought. "I believe in a life beyond this. You believe in it, too, don't you, father?"

"Of course," returned Adam. "We can't know, though, for sure, can we? But, anyway, a man would be foolish to risk it, wouldn't he?"

"To risk what, father?"

"To risk the chance of there being no hell," came the startling answer. "My folks raised me to believe in hell, and the preachers all teach it. And if there should be such a place of eternal torment a man would be a fool not to fix up some way to get out of it, wouldn't he?"

John did not know what to say.

Adam Ward leaned closer to his son and with an air of secrecy whispered, "That's exactly what I've done, John—I've worked out a scheme to tie God up in a contract that will force Him to save me. The old Interpreter gave me the idea. You see if it should turn out that there is no hell my plan can't do any harm and if there is a hell it makes me safe anyway."

He chuckled with insane satisfaction. "They say that God knows everything—that nobody can figure out a way to beat Him, but I have—I have worked out a deal with God that is bound to give me the best of it. I've got Him tied up so tight that He'll be bound to save me. Some people think I'm crazy, but you wait, my boy—they'll find out how crazy I am. They'll never get me into hell. I have been figuring on this ever since the Interpreter told me I had better make a contract with God. And after Pete left this morning I got it all settled. A man can't afford to take any chances with God and so I made this deal with Him. Hell or no hell, I'm safe. God don't get the best of me,—And you are safe, too, son, with the new process, if you look after your own interests, as I have done, and don't overlook any opportunities. I wanted to tell you about this so you wouldn't worry about me. I'll go back to bed now. Don't tell mother and Helen what we have been talking about. No use to worry them—they couldn't understand anyway. And don't forget, John, what Pete told me about Mary. Their scheme won't work of course. I know you are too smart for them. But just the same you've got to be on your guard against her all the time. Never take any unnecessary chances. Don't talk over a deal with a man when any one can hear. If you are careful to have no witnesses when you arrange a deal you are absolutely safe. It is what you can slip into the written contract that counts—once you get your man's signature. That's always been my way. And now I have even put one over on God."

He stole cautiously out of the room and back to his own apartment.

Outside his father's door John waited, listening, until he was convinced that sleep had at last come to the exhausted man.

Late that same Sunday evening, when the street meeting held by Jake Vodell was over, there was another meeting in the room back of the pool hall. The men who sat around that table with the agitator were not criminals—they were workmen. Sam Whaley and two others were men with families. They were all American citizens, but they were under the spell of their leader's power. They had been prepared for that leadership by the industrial policies of McIver and Adam Ward.

This meeting of that inner circle was in no way authorized by the unions. The things they said Sam Whaley would not have dared to say openly in the Mill workers' organization. The plans they proposed to carry out in the name of the unions they were compelled to make in secret. In their mad, fanatical acceptance of the dreams that Vodell wrought for them; in their blind obedience to the leadership he had so cleverly established; in their reckless disregard of the consequences under the spell of his promised protection, they were as insane, in fact, as the owner of the Mill himself.

The supreme, incredible, pitiful tragedy of it all was this: That these workmen committed themselves to the plans of Jake Vodell in the name of their country's workmen.

CHAPTER XXIV

THE FLATS

Helen Ward knew that she could not put off much longer giving McIver a definite answer. When she was with him, the things that so disturbed her mind and heart were less real—she was able to see things clearly from the point of view to which she had been trained. Her father's mental condition was nothing more than a nervous trouble resulting from overwork—John's ideals were highly creditable to his heart and she loved him dearly for them, but they were wholly impossible in a world where certain class standards must be maintained—the Mill took again its old vague, indefinite place in her life—the workman Charlie Martin must live only in her girlhood memories, those secretly sad memories that can have no part in the grown-up present and must not be permitted to enter into one's consideration of the future. In short, the presence of McIver always banished effectually the Helen of the old house: with him the daughter of Adam Ward was herself.

And Helen was tempted by this feeling of relief to speak the decisive word that would finally put an end to her indecision and bring at least the peace of certainty to her troubled mind. In the light of her education and environment, there was every reason why she should say, "Yes" to McIver's insistent pleadings. There was no shadow of a reason why she should refuse him. One word and the Helen of the old house would be banished forever—the princess lady would reign undisturbed.

And yet, for some reason, that word was not spoken. Helen told herself that she would speak it. But on each occasion she put it off. And always when the man was gone and she was alone, in spite of the return in full force of all her disturbing thoughts and emotions, she was glad that she had not committed herself irrevocably—that she was still free.

She had never felt the appeal of all that McIver meant to her as she felt it that Sunday. She had never been more disturbed and unhappy than she was the following day when John told her a little of his midnight experience with their father and how Adam's excitement had been caused by Peter Martin's visit. All of which led her, early in the afternoon, to the Interpreter.

* * * * *

She found the old basket maker working with feverish energy. Billy Rand at the bench in the corner of the room was as busy with his part of their joint industry.

It was the Interpreter's habit, when Helen was with him, to lay aside his work. But of late he had continued the occupation of his hands even as he talked with her. She had noticed this, as women always notice such things—but that was all. On this day, when the old man in the wheel chair failed to give her his undivided attention, something in his manner impressed the trivial incident more sharply on her mind.

He greeted her kindly, as always, but while she was conscious of no lack of warmth in his welcome, she felt in the deep tones of that gentle voice a sadness that moved her to quick concern. The dark eyes that never failed to light with pleasure at her coming were filled with weary pain. The strong face was thin and tired. As he bent his white head over the work in his lap he seemed to have grown suddenly very weak and old.

With an awakened mind, the young woman looked curiously about the room.

She had never seen it so filled with materials and with finished baskets. The table with the big lamp and the magazines and papers had been moved into the far corner against the book shelves, as though he had now neither time nor thought for reading. The floor was covered thick with a litter of chips and shavings. Even silent Billy's face was filled with anxiety and troubled care as he looked from Helen to his old companion in the wheel chair and slowly turned back to his work on the bench.

"What is the matter here?" she demanded, now thoroughly aroused.

"Matter?" returned the Interpreter. "Is there anything wrong here, Helen?"

"You are not well," she insisted. "You look all worn out—as if you had not slept for weeks—what is it?"

"Oh, that is nothing," he answered, with a smile. "Billy and I have been working overtime a little—that is all."

"But why?" she demanded, "why must you wear yourself out like this? Surely there is no need for you to work so hard, day and night."

He answered as if he were not sure that he had heard her aright. "No need, Helen? Surely, child, you cannot be so ignorant of the want that exists within sight of your home?"

She returned his look wonderingly. "You mean the strike?"

Bending over his work again, the old basket maker answered, sorrowfully, "Yes, Helen, I mean the strike."

There was something in the Interpreter's manner—something in the weary, drooping figure in that wheel chair—in the tired, deep-lined face—in the pain-filled eyes and the gentle voice that went to the deeps of Helen Ward's woman heart.

With her, as with every one in Millsburgh, the strike was a topic of daily conversation. She sympathized with her brother in his anxiety. She was worried over the noticeable effect of the excitement upon her father. She was interested in

176

McIver's talk of the situation. But in no vital way had her life been touched by the industrial trouble. In no way had she come in actual contact with it. The realities of the situation were to her vague, intangible, remote from her world, as indeed the Mill itself had been, before her visit with John that day. To her, the Interpreter was of all men set apart from the world. In his little hut on the cliff, with his books and his basket making, her gentle old friend's life, it seemed to her, held not one thing in common with the busy world that lay within sight of the balcony-porch. The thought that the industrial trouble could in any way touch him came to her with a distinct shock.

"Surely," she protested, at last, "the strike cannot affect you. It has nothing to do with your work."

"Every strike has to do with all work everywhere, child," returned the man in the wheel chair, while his busy fingers wove the fabric of a basket. "Every idle hand in the world, Helen, whatever the cause of its idleness, compels some other's hand to do its work. The work of the world must be done, child—somehow, by some one—the work of the world must be done. The little Maggies and Bobbies of the Flats down there must be fed, you know—and their mother too—yes, and Sam Whaley himself must be cared for. And so you see, because of the strike, Billy and I must work overtime."

Certainly there was no hint of rebuke in the old basket maker's kindly voice, but the daughter of Adam Ward felt her cheeks flush with a quick sense of shame. That her old friend in the wheel chair should so accept the responsibility of his neighbor's need and give himself thus to help them, while she—

"Is there," she faltered, "is there really so much suffering among the strikers?"

Without raising his eyes from his work, he answered, "The women and children—they are so helpless."

"I—I did not realize," she murmured. "I did not know."

"You were not ignorant of the helpless women and children who suffered in foreign lands," he returned. "Why should you not know of the mothers and babies in Millsburgh?"

"But McIver says—" she hesitated.

The Interpreter caught up her words. "McIver says that by feeding the starving families of the strikers the strike is prolonged. He relies upon the hunger and cold and sickness of the women and children for his victory. And Jake Vodell relies upon the suffering in the families of his followers for that desperate frenzy of class hatred, without which he cannot gain his end. Does McIver want for anything? No! Is Jake Vodell in need? No! It is not the imperialistic leaders in these industrial wars who

177

pay the price. It is always the little Bobbies and Maggies who pay. The people of America stood aghast with horror when an unarmed passenger ship was torpedoed or a defenseless village was bombed by order of a ruthless Kaiser; but we permit these Kaisers of capital and labor to carry on their industrial wars without a thought of the innocent ones who must suffer under their ruthless policies."

He paused; then, with no trace of bitterness, but only sadness in his voice, he added, "You say you do not know, child—and yet, you could know so easily if you would. Little Bobby and Maggie do not live in a far-off land across the seas. They live right over there in the shadow of your father's Mill—the Mill which supplies you, Helen, with every material need and luxury of your life."

As if she could bear to hear no more, Helen rose quickly and went from the room to stand on the balcony-porch.

It was not so much the Interpreter's words—it was rather the spirit in which they were spoken that moved her so deeply. By her own heart she was judged. "For every idle hand," he had said. Her hands were idle hands. Her old white-haired friend in his wheel chair was doing her work. His crippled body drooped with weariness over his task because she did nothing. His face was lined with care because she was careless of the need that burdened him. His eyes were filled with sadness and pain because she was indifferent—because she did not know—had not cared to know.

* * * * *

The sun was almost down that afternoon when Bobby Whaley came out of the wretched house that was his home to stand on the front doorstep. The dingy, unpainted buildings of the Flats—the untidy hovels and shanties—the dilapidated fences and broken sidewalks—unlovely at best, in the long shadows of the failing day, were sinister with the gloom of poverty.

High above the Mill the twisting columns of smoke from the tall stacks caught the last of the sunlight and formed slow, changing cloud-shapes—rolling hills of brightness with soft, shadowy valleys and caons of mysterious depths between— towering domes and crags and castled heights—grim, foreboding, beautiful.

The boy who stood on the steps, looking so listlessly about, was not the daring adventurer who had so boldly led his sister up the zigzag steps to the Interpreter's hut. He was not the Bobby who had ridden in such triumph beside the princess lady so far into the unknown country. His freckled face was thin and pinched. The skin was drawn tight over the high cheek bones and the eyes were wide and staring. His young body that had been so sturdy was gaunt and skeletonlike. The dirty rags that clothed him were scarcely enough to hide his nakedness. The keen autumn air that had put the flush of good red blood into the cheeks of the golfers at the country club that afternoon whirled about his bare feet and legs with stinging cruelty. His thin lips and wasted limbs were blue with cold. Turning slowly, he seemed about to

178

reenter the house, but when his hand touched the latch he paused and once more uncertainly faced toward the street. There was no help for him in his home. He knew no other place to go for food or shelter.

As the boy again looked hopelessly about the wretched neighborhood, he saw a woman coming down the street. He could tell, even at that distance, that the lady was a stranger to the Flats. Her dress, simple as it was, and her veil marked her as a resident of some district more prosperous than that grimy community in the shadow of the Mill.

A flash of momentary interest lighted the hungry eyes of the lad. But, no, it could not be one of the charity workers—the charity ladies always came earlier in the day and always in automobiles.

Then he saw the stranger stop and speak to a boy in front of a house two doors away. The neighbor boy pointed toward Bobby and the lady came on, walking quickly as if she were a little frightened at being alone amid such surroundings.

At the gap where once had been a gate in the dilapidated fence, she turned in toward the house and the wondering boy on the front step. She was within a few feet of the lad when she stopped suddenly with a low exclamation.

Bobby thought that she had discovered her mistake in coming to the wrong place. But the next moment she was coming closer, and he heard, "Bobby, is that really you! You poor child, have you been ill?"

"*I* ain't been sick, if that's what yer mean," returned the boy. "Mag is, though. She's worse to-day."

His manner was sullenly defiant, as if the warmly dressed stranger had in some way revealed herself as his enemy.

"Don't you know me, Bobby?"

"Not with yer face covered up like that, I don't."

She laughed nervously and raised her veil.

"Huh, it's you, is it? Funny—Mag's been a-talkin' about her princess lady all afternoon. What yer doin' here?"

Before this hollow-cheeked skeleton of a boy Helen Ward felt strangely like one who, conscious of guilt, is brought suddenly into the presence of a stern judge.

"Why, Bobby," she faltered, "I—I came to see you and Maggie—I was at the Interpreter's this afternoon and he told me—I mean something he said made me want to come."

"The Interpreter, he's all right," said the boy. "So's Mary Martin."

"Aren't you just a little glad to see me, Bobby?"

The boy did not seem to hear. "Funny the way Mag talks about yer all the time. She's purty sick all right. Peterson's baby, it died."

"Can't we go into the house and see Maggie? You must be nearly frozen standing out here in the cold."

"Huh, I'm used to freezin'—I guess yer can come on in though—if yer want to. Mebbe Mag 'd like to see yer."

He pushed open the door, and she followed him into the ghastly barrenness of the place that he knew as home.

Never before had the daughter of Adam Ward viewed such naked, cruel poverty. She shuddered with the horror of it. It was so unreal—so unbelievable.

A small, rusty cookstove with no fire—a rude table with no cloth—a rickety cupboard with its shelves bare save for a few dishes—two broken-backed chairs—that was all. No, it was not all—on a window ledge, beneath a bundle of rags that filled the opening left by a broken pane, was a small earthen flowerpot holding a single scraggly slip of geranium.

Helen seemed to hear again the Interpreter saying, "A girl with true instincts for the best things of life and a capacity for great happiness."

At Bobby's call, Mrs. Whaley came from another room.

The boy did not even attempt an introduction but stood sullenly aside, waiting developments, and the mother in her pitiful distress evidently failed to identify their visitor when Helen introduced herself.

"I'm pleased to meet you, ma'am," she said, mechanically, and gazed at the young woman with a stony indifference, as though her mind, deadened by fearful anxiety and physical suffering, refused even to wonder at the stranger's presence in her home.

Helen did not know what to say—in the presence of this living tragedy of motherhood she felt so helpless, so overwhelmed with the uselessness of mere words. What right had she, a stranger from another world, to intrude unasked upon the privacy of this home? And yet, something deep within her—something more potent in its authority than the conventionalities that had so far ruled her life—assured her that she had the right to be there.

"I—I called to see Bobby and Maggie," she faltered. "I met them, you know, at the Interpreter's."

As if Helen's mention of the old basket maker awakened a spark of life in her pain-deadened senses, the woman returned, "Yes, ma'am—take a chair. No, not that one—it's broke. Here—this one will hold you up, I guess."

With nervous haste she dusted the chair with her apron. "You'd best keep your things on. We don't have no fire except to cook by—when there's anything to cook."

She found a match and lighted a tiny lamp, for it was growing dark.

"Bobby tells me that little Maggie is ill," offered Helen.

Mrs. Whaley looked toward the door of that other room and wrung her thin, toil-worn hands in the agony of her mother fear. "Yes, ma'am—she's real bad, I guess. Poor child, she's been ailin' for some time. And since the strike—" Her voice broke, and her eyes, dry as if they had long since exhausted their supply of tears, were filled with hopeless misery.

"We had the doctor once before things got so bad; about the time my man quit his work in the Mill to help Jake Vodell, it was. And the doctor he said all she needed was plenty of good food and warm clothes and a chance to play in the fresh country air."

She looked grimly about the bare room. "We couldn't have the doctor no more. I don't know as it would make any difference if we could. My man, he's away most of the time. I ain't seen him since yesterday mornin'. And to-day Maggie's been a lot worse. I—I'm afraid—"

Helen wanted to cry aloud. Was it possible that she had asked the Interpreter only a few hours before if there was really much suffering in the families of the strikers? "You can see Maggie if you want," said the mother. "She's in there."

She rose as if to show her visitor to the room.

But Helen said, quickly, "In just a moment. Mrs. Whaley, won't you tell me first—is there—is there no one to help you?" She asked the question timidly, as if fearing to offend.

The other woman answered, hopelessly, "The charity ladies do a little, and the Interpreter and Mary Martin do all they can. But you see, ma'am, there's so many others just like us that there ain't near enough to go 'round."

The significance of the woman's colorless words went to Helen's heart with appalling force—"so many others just like us." This stricken home was not then an exception. With flashing vividness her mind pictured many rooms similar to the cold and barren apartment where she sat. She visioned as clearly as she saw Mrs. Whaley the many other wives and mothers with Bobbies and Maggies who were caught helplessly in the monstrous net of the strike, as these were caught. She knew now why the Interpreter and Billy Rand worked so hard. And again she felt her cheeks burn with shame as when the old basket maker had said, "For every idle hand—"

Helen Ward had been an active leader in the foreign relief work during the war. Her portrait had even been published in the papers as one who was devoted to the cause of the stricken women and children abroad. But that had all been impersonal, while this—Already in her heart she was echoing the old familiar cry of the comparative few, "If only the people knew! If only they could be made to see as she had been made to see! The people are not so cruel. They simply do not know. They are ignorant, as she was ignorant."

Aloud she was saying to Bobby, as she thrust her purse in the boy's hand, "You must run quickly, Bobby, to the nearest store and get the things that your mother needs first, and have some one telephone for a doctor to come at once."

To the mother she added, hurriedly, as if fearing a protest, "Please, Mrs. Whaley, let me help. I am so sorry I did not know before. Won't you forgive me and let me help you now?"

"Gee!" exclaimed Bobby, who had opened the purse. "Look-ee, mom! Gee!"

As one in a dream, the mother turned from the money in the boy's hand to Helen. "You ain't meanin', ma'am, for us to use all that?"

"Yes—yes—don't be afraid to get what you need—there will be more when that is gone."

The poor woman did not fill the air with loud cries of hysterical gratitude and superlative prayers to God for His blessing upon this one who had come so miraculously to her relief. For a moment she stood trembling with emotion, while her tearless eyes were fixed upon Helen's face with a look of such gratitude that the young woman was forced to turn away lest her own feeling escape her control. Then, snatching the money from the boy's hands, she said, "I had better go myself, ma'am—Bobby can come along to help carry things. If you"—she hesitated, with a look toward that other room—"if you wouldn't mind stayin' with Maggie till we get back?"

A minute later and Helen was alone in that wretched house in the Flats—alone save for the sick child in the next room.

The door to the street had scarcely closed when a wave of terror swept over her. She started to her feet. She could not do it. She would call Mrs. Whaley back. She would go herself for the needed things. But there was a strength in Helen Ward that few of her most intimate friends, even, realized; and before her hand touched the latch of the door she had command of herself once more. In much the same spirit that her brother John perhaps had faced a lonely night watch in Flanders fields, Adam Ward's daughter forced herself to do this thing that had so unexpectedly fallen to her.

For some minutes she walked the floor, listening to the noises of the neighborhood. Anxiously she opened the door and looked out into the fast, gathering darkness. No one of her own people knew where she was. She had heard terrible things of Jake Vodell and his creed of terrorism. McIver had pressed it upon her mind that the strikers were all alike in their lawlessness. What if Sam Whaley should return to find her there? She listened—listened.

A faint, moaning sound came from the next room. She went quickly to the doorway, but in the faint light she could see only the shadowy outline of a bed. Taking the lamp she entered fearfully.

Save for the bed, an old box that served as a table, and one chair, this room was as bare as the other. With the lamp in her hand Helen stood beside the bed.

The tiny form of little Maggie was lost under the ragged and dirty coverlet. The child's face in the tangled mass of her unkempt hair was so wasted and drawn, her eyes, closed under their dark lids, so deeply sunken, and her teeth so exposed by the thin fleshless lips, that she seemed scarcely human. One bony arm with its clawlike hand encircled the rag doll that she had held that day when Helen took the two children into the country.

As Helen looked all her fears vanished. She had no thought, now, of where she was or how she came there. Deep within her she felt the awakening of that mother soul which lives in every woman. She did not shrink in horror from this hideous fruit of Jake Vodell's activity. She did not cry out in pity or sorrow. She uttered no word of protest. As she put the lamp down on the box, her hand did not tremble. Very quietly she placed the chair beside the bed and sat down to watch and wait as motherhood in all ages has watched and waited.

While poor Sam Whaley was busy on some mission assigned to him by his leader, Jake Vodell, and his wife and boy were gone for the food supplied by a stranger to his household, this woman, of the class that he had been taught to hate, held alone her vigil at the bedside of the workman's little girl.

A thin, murmuring voice came from the bed. Helen leaned closer. She heard a few incoherent mutterings—then, "No—no—Bobby, yer wouldn't dast blow up the castle. Yer'd maybe kill the princess lady—yer know yer couldn't do that!"

Again the weak little voice sank into low, meaning less murmurs. The tiny, clawlike fingers plucked at the coverlet. "Tain't so, the princess lady *will* find her jewel of happiness, I tell yer, Bobby, jest like the Interpreter told us—cause her heart is kind—yer know her heart is—kind—kind—"

Silence again. Some one passed the house. A dog howled. A child in the house next door cried. Across the street a man's voice was raised in anger.

Suddenly little Maggie's eyes opened wide. "An' the princess lady is a-comin' some day to take Bobby and me away up in the sky to her beautiful palace place where there's flowers and birds an' everythin' all the time an'—an'—"

The big eyes were fixed on Helen's face as the' young woman stooped over the bed, and the light of a glorious smile transformed the wasted childish features.

"Why—why—yer—yer've come!"

CHAPTER XXV

McIVER'S OPPORTUNITY

When the politician stopped at the cigar stand late that afternoon for a box of the kind he gave his admirers, the philosopher, scratching the revenue label, remarked, "I see by the papers that McIver is still a-stayin'."

"Humph!" grunted the politician with careful diplomacy.

The bank clerk who was particular about his pipe tobacco chimed in, "McIver is a stayer all right when it comes to that."

"Natural born fighter, sir," offered the politician tentatively.

"Game sport, McIver is," agreed the undertaker, taking the place at the show case vacated by the departing bank clerk.

The philosopher, handing out the newcomer's favorite smoke, echoed his customer's admiration. "You bet he's a game sport." He punched the cash register with vigor. "Don't give a hang what it costs the other fellow."

The undertaker laughed.

"I remember one time," said the philosopher, "McIver and a bunch was goin' fishin' up the river. They stopped here early in the morning and while they was gettin' their smokes the judge—who's always handin' out some sort of poetry stuff, you know— he says: 'Well, Jim, we're goin' to have a fine day anyway. No matter whether we catch anything or not it will be worth the trip just to get out into the country.' Mac, he looked at the judge a minute as if he wanted to bite him—you know what I mean—then he says in that growlin' voice of his, 'That may do for you all right, judge, but I'm here to tell you that when *I* go fishin' *I go for fish.*'"

The cigar-store philosopher's story accurately described the dominant trait in the factory man's character. To him business was a sport, a game, a contest of absorbing interest. He entered into it with all the zest and strength of his virile manhood. Mind and body, it absorbed him. And yet, he knew nothing of that true sportsman's passion which plays the game for the joy of the game itself. McIver played to win; not for the sake of winning, but for the value of the winnings. Methods were good or bad only as they won or lost. He was incapable of experiencing those larger triumphs which come only in defeat. The Interpreter's philosophy of the "oneness of all" was to McIver the fanciful theory of an impracticable dreamer, who, too feeble to take a man's part in life, contented himself by formulating creeds of weakness that befitted his state. Men were the pieces with which he played his game—they were of varied values, certainly, as are the pieces on a chess table, but they were pieces on the chess table and nothing more. All of which does not mean that Jim McIver was

185

cruel or unkind. Indeed, he was genuinely and generously interested in many worthy charities, and many a man had appealed to him, and not in vain, for help. But to have permitted these humanitarian instincts to influence his play in the game of business would have been, to his mind, evidence of a weakness that was contemptible. The human element, he held, must, of necessity, be sternly disregarded if one would win.

While his fellow townsmen were discussing him at the cigar stand, and men everywhere in Millsburgh were commenting on his determination to break the strikers to his will at any cost, McIver, at his office, was concluding a conference with a little company of his fellow employers.

It was nearly dark when the conference finally ended and the men went their several ways. McIver, with some work of special importance waiting his attention, telephoned that he would not be home for dinner. He would finish what he had to do and would dine at the club later in the evening.

The big factory inside the high, board fence was silent. The night came on. Save for the armed men who guarded the place, the owner was alone.

Absorbed in his consideration of the business before him, the man was oblivious of everything but his game. An hour went by. He forgot that he had had no dinner. Another hour—and another.

He was interrupted at last by the entrance of a guard.

"Well, what do you want?" he said, shortly, when the man stood before him.

"There's a woman outside, sir. She insists that she must see you."

"A woman!"

"Yes, sir."

"Who is she?"

"I don't know."

"Well, what does she look like?"

"I couldn't see her face, she's got a veil on."

The factory owner considered. How did any one outside of his home know that he was in his office at that hour? These times were dangerous. "Vodell is likely to try anything," he said, aloud. "Better send her about her business."

186

"I tried to," the guard returned, "but she won't go—says she is a friend of yours and has got to see you to-night."

"A friend! Huh! How did she get here?"

"In a taxi, and the taxi beat it as soon as she got out."

Again McIver considered. Then his heavy jaw set, and he growled, "All right, bring her in—a couple of you—and see that you stand by while she is here. If this is a Vodell trick of some sort, I'll beat him to it."

Helen, escorted by two burly guards, entered the office.

McIver sprang to his feet with an exclamation of amazement, and his tender concern was unfeigned and very comforting to the young woman after the harrowing experience through which she had just passed.

Sending the guards back to their posts, he listened gravely while she told him where she had been and what she had seen.

"But, Helen," he cried, when she had finished, "it was sheer madness for you to be alone in the Flats like that—at Whaley's place and in the night, too! Good heavens, girl, don't you realize what a risk you were taking?"

"I had to go, Jim," she returned.

"You had to go?" he repeated. "Why?"

"I had to see for myself if—if things were as bad as the Interpreter said. Oh, can't you understand, Jim, I could not believe it—it all seemed so impossible. Don't you see that I had to know for sure?"

"I see that some one ought to break that meddlesome old basket maker's head as well as his legs," growled McIver indignantly. "The idea of sending you, Adam Ward's daughter, of all people, alone into that nest of murdering anarchists."

"But the Interpreter didn't send me, Jim," she protested. "He did not even know that I was going. No one knew."

"I understand all that," said McIver. "The Interpreter didn't send you—oh, no—he simply made you think that you ought to go. That's the way the tricky old scoundrel does everything, from what I am told."

She looked at him steadily. "Do you think, Jim, the Interpreter's way is such a bad way to get people to do things?"

"Forgive me," he begged humbly, "but it makes me wild to think what might have happened to you. It's all right now, though. I'll take you home, and in the future you can turn such work over to the regular charity organizations." He was crossing the room for his hat and overcoat. "Jove! I can't believe yet that you have actually been in such a mess and all by your lonesome, too."

She was about to speak when he stopped, and, as if struck by a sudden thought, said, quickly, "But Helen, you haven't told me—how did you know I was here?"

She explained hurriedly, "The doctor sent a taxi for me and I telephoned your house from a drug store. Your man told me you expected to be late at the office and would dine at the club. I phoned the club and when I learned that you were not there I came straight on. I—I had to see you to-night, Jim. And I was afraid if I phoned you here at the office you wouldn't let me come."

McIver evidently saw from her manner that there was still something in the amazing situation that they had not yet touched upon. Coming back to his desk, he said, "I don't think I understand, Helen. Why were you in such a hurry to see me? Besides, don't you know that I would have gone to you, at once, anywhere?"

"I know, Jim," she returned, slowly, as one approaching a difficult subject, "but I couldn't tell you what I had seen. I couldn't talk to you about these things at home."

"I understand," he said, gently, "and I am glad that you wanted to come to me. But you are tired and nervous and all unstrung, now. Let me take you home and to-morrow we will talk things over."

As if he had not spoken, she said, steadily, "I wanted to tell you about the terrible, terrible condition of those poor people, Jim. I thought you ought to know about them exactly as they are and not in a vague, indefinite way as I knew about them before I went to see for myself."

The man moved uneasily. "I do know about the condition of these people, Helen. It is exactly what I expected would happen."

She was listening carefully. "You expected them to—to be hungry and cold and sick like that, Jim?"

"Such conditions are always a part of every strike like this," he returned. "There is nothing unusual about it, and it is the only thing that will ever drive these cattle back to their work. They simply have to be starved to it."

"But John says—"

He interrupted. "Please, Helen—I know all about what John says. I know where he gets it, too—he gets it from the Interpreter who gave you this crazy notion of going

188

alone into the Flats to investigate personally. And John's ideas are just about as practical."

"But the mothers and children, Jim?"

"The men can go back to work whenever they are ready," he retorted.

"At your terms, you mean?" she asked.

"My terms are the only terms that will ever open this plant again. The unions will never dictate my business policies, if every family in Millsburgh starves."

She waited a moment before she said, slowly, "I must be sure that I understand, Jim—do you mean that you are actually depending upon such pitiful conditions as I have seen to-night to give you a victory over the strikers?"

The man made a gesture of impatience. "It is the principle of the thing that is at stake, Helen. If I yield in this instance it will be only the beginning of a worse trouble. If the working class wins this time there will be no end to their demands. We might as well turn all our properties over to them at once and be done with it. This strike in Millsburgh is only a small part of the general industrial situation. The entire business interests of the country are involved."

Again she waited a little before answering. Then she said, sadly, "How strange! It is hard for me to realize, Jim, that the entire business interests of this great nation are actually dependent upon the poor little Maggie Whaleys."

"Helen!" he protested, "you make me out a heartless brute."

"No, Jim, I know you are not that. But when you insist that what I saw to-night— that the suffering of these poor, helpless mothers and their children is the only thing that will enable you employers to break this strike and save the business of the country—it—it does seem a good deal like the Germans' war policy of frightfulness that we all condemned so bitterly, doesn't it?"

"These things are not matters of sentiment, Helen. Jake Vodell is not conducting his campaign by the Golden Rule."

"I know, Jim, but I could not go to Jake Vodell as I have come to you—could I? And I could not talk to the poor, foolish strikers who are so terribly deceived by him. Don't you suppose, Jim, that most of the strikers think they are right?"

The man stirred uneasily. "I can't help what they think. I can consider only the facts as they are."

"That is just what I want, Jim," she cried. "Only it seems to me that you are leaving out some of the most important facts. I can't help believing that if our great captains of industry and kings of finance and teachers of economics and labor leaders would consider *all* the facts they could find some way to settle these differences between employers and employees and save the industries of the country without starving little girls and boys and their mothers."

"If I could have my way the government would settle the difficulty in a hurry," he said, grimly.

"You mean the soldiers?"

"Yes, the government should put enough troops from the regular army in here to drive these men back to their jobs."

"But aren't these working people just as much a part of our government as you employers? Forgive me, Jim, but your plan sounds to me too much like the very imperialism that our soldiers fought against in France."

"Imperialism or not!" he retorted, "the business men of this country will never submit to the dictatorship of Jake Vodell and his kind. It would be chaos and utter ruin. Look what they are doing in other countries."

"Of course it would," she agreed, "but the Interpreter says that if the business men and employers and the better class of employees like Peter Martin would get together as—as John and Charlie Martin are—that Jake Vodell and his kind would be powerless."

He did not answer, and she continued, "As I understand brother and the Interpreter, this man Vodell does not represent the unions at all—he merely uses some of the unions, wherever he can, through such men as Sam Whaley. Isn't that so, Jim?"

"Whether it is so or not, the result is the same," he answered. "If the unions of the laboring classes permit themselves to be used as tools by men like Jake Vodell they must take the consequences."

He rose to his feet as one who would end an unprofitable discussion. "Come, Helen, it is useless for you to make yourself ill over these questions. You are worn out now. Come, you really must let me take you home."

"I suppose I must," she answered, wearily.

He went to her. "It is wonderful for you to do what you have done to-night, and for you to come to me like this. Helen—won't you give me my answer—won't you—?"

She put out her hands with a little gesture of protest. "Please, Jim, let's not talk about ourselves to-night. I—I can't."

Silently he turned away to take up his hat and coat. Silently she stood waiting.

But when he was ready, she said, "Jim, there is just one thing more."

"What is it, Helen?"

"Tell me truly: you *could* stop this strike, couldn't you? I mean if you would come to some agreement with your factory men, all the others would go back to work, too, wouldn't they?"

"Yes," he said, "I could."

She hesitated—then falteringly, "Jim, if I—if I promise to be your wife will you—will you stop the strike? For the sake of the mothers and children who are cold and hungry and sick, Jim—will you—will you stop the strike?"

For a long minute, Jim McIver could not answer. He wanted this woman as a man of his strength wants the woman he has chosen. At the beginning of their acquaintance his interest in Helen had been largely stimulated by the business possibilities of a combination of his factory and Adam Ward's Mill. But as their friendship had grown he had come to love her sincerely, and the more material consideration of their union had faded into the background. Men like McIver, who are capable of playing their games of business with such intensity and passion, are capable of great and enduring love. They are capable, too, of great sacrifices to principle. As he considered her words and grasped the full force of her question his face went white and his nerves were tense with the emotional strain.

At last he said, gently, "Helen, dear, I love you. I want you for my wife. I want you more than I ever wanted anything. Nothing in the world is of any value to me compared with your love. But, dear girl, don't you see that I can't take you like this? You cannot sell yourself to me—even for such a price. I cannot buy you." He turned away.

"Forgive me, Jim," she cried. "I did not realize what I was saying. I—I was thinking of little Maggie—I—I know you would not do what you are doing if you did not think you were right. Take me home now, please, Jim."

* * * * *

Silently they went out to his automobile. Tenderly he helped her into the car and tucked the robe about her. The guards swung open the big gates, and they swept away into the night. Past the big Mill and the Flats, through the silent business district and up the hill they glided swiftly—steadily. And no word passed between them.

They were nearing the gate to the Ward estate when Helen suddenly grasped her companion's arm with a low exclamation.

At the same moment McIver instinctively checked the speed of his car.

They had both seen the shadowy form of a man walking slowly past the entrance to Helen's home.

To Helen, there was something strangely familiar in the dim outlines of the moving figure. As they drove slowly on, passing the man who was now in the deeper shadows of the trees and bushes which, at this spot grew close to the fence, she turned her head, keeping her eyes upon him.

Suddenly a flash of light stabbed the darkness. A shot rang out. And another.

Helen saw the man she was watching fall.

With a cry, she started from her seat; and before McIver, who had involuntarily stopped the car, could check her, she had leaped from her place beside him and was running toward the fallen man.

With a shout "Helen!" McIver followed.

As she knelt beside the form on the ground McIver put his hand on her shoulder. "Helen," he said, sharply, as if to bring her to her senses, "you must not—here, let me—"

Without moving from her position she turned her face up to him. "Don't you understand, Jim? It is Captain Charlie."

Two watchmen on the Ward estate, who had heard the shots, came running up.

McIver tried to insist that Helen go with him in his roadster to the house for help and a larger car, but she refused.

When he returned with John, the chauffeur and one of the big Ward machines, after telephoning the police and the doctor, Helen was kneeling over the wounded man just as he had left her.

She did not raise her head when they stood beside her and seemed unconscious of their presence. But when John lifted her up and she heard her brother's voice, she cried out and clung to him like a frightened child.

192

The doctor arrived just as they were carrying Captain Charlie into the room to which Mrs. Ward herself led them. The police came a moment later.

While the physician, with John's assistance, was caring for his patient, McIver gave the officers what information he could and went with them to the scene of the shooting.

He returned to the house after the officers had completed their examination of the spot and the immediate vicinity just in time to meet John, who was going out. Helen and her mother were with the doctor at the bedside of the assassin's victim.

McIver wondered at the anguish in John Ward's face. But Captain Charlie's comrade only asked, steadily, "Did the police find anything, Jim?"

"Not a thing," McIver answered. "What does the doctor say, John?"

John turned away as if to hide his emotion and for a moment did not answer. Then he spoke those words so familiar to the men of Flanders' fields, "Charlie is going West, Jim. I must bring his father and sister. Would you mind waiting here until I return? Something might develop, you know."

"Certainly, I will stay, John—anything that I can do—command me, won't you?"

"Thank you, Jim—I'll not be long."

* * * * *

While he waited there alone, Jim McIver's mind went back over the strange incidents of the evening: Helen's visit to the Whaley home and her coming to him. Swiftly he reviewed their conversation. What was it that had so awakened Helen's deep concern for the laboring class? He had before noticed her unusual interest in the strike and in the general industrial situation—but to-night—he had never dreamed that she would go so far. Why had she continued to refuse an answer to his pleading? What was Charlie Martin doing in that neighborhood at that hour? How had Helen recognized him so quickly and surely in the darkness? The man, as these and many other unanswerable questions crowded upon him, felt a strange foreboding. Mighty forces beyond his understanding seemed stirring about him. As one feels the gathering of a storm in the night, he felt the mysterious movements of elements beyond his control.

He was disturbed suddenly by the opening of an outer door behind him. Turning quickly, he faced Adam Ward.

Before McIver could speak, the Mill owner motioned him to be silent.

Wondering, McIver obeyed and watched with amazement as the master of that house closed the door with cautious care and stole softly toward him. To his family Adam Ward's manner would not have appeared so strange, but McIver had never seen the man under one of his attacks of nervous excitement.

"I'm glad you are here, Jim," Adam said, in a shaking whisper. "You understand these things. John is a fool—he don't believe when I tell him they are after us. But you know what to do. You have the right idea about handling these unions. Kill the leaders; and if the men won't work, turn the soldiers loose on them. You said the right thing, 'Drive them to their jobs with bayonets.' Pete Martin's boy was one of them, and he got what was coming to him to-night. And John and Helen brought him right here into my house. They've got him upstairs there now. They think I'll stand for it, but you'll see—I'll show them! What was he hanging around my place for in the night like this? I know what he was after. But he got what he wasn't looking for this time and Pete will get his too, if he—"

"Father!"

Unnoticed, Helen had come into the room behind them. In pacing the open door she had seen her father and had realized instantly his condition. But the little she had heard him say was not at all unusual to her, and she attached no special importance to his words.

Adam Ward was like a child, abashed in her presence.

She looked at McIver appealingly. "Father is excited and nervous, Jim. He is not at all well, you know."

McIver spoke with gentle authority, "If you will permit me, I will go with him to his room for a little quiet talk. And then, perhaps, he can sleep. What do you say, Mr. Ward?"

"Yes—yes," agreed Adam, hurriedly.

Helen looked her gratitude and McIver led the Mill owner away.

When they were in Adam's own apartment and the door was shut McIver's manner changed with startling abruptness. With all the masterful power of his strong-willed nature he faced his trembling host, and his heavy voice was charged with the force of his dominating personality.

"Listen to me, Adam Ward. You must stop this crazy nonsense. If you act and talk like this the police will have the handcuffs on you before you know where you are."

Adam cringed before him. "Jim—I—I—do they think that I—"

194

"Shut up!" growled McIver. "I don't want to hear another word. I have heard too much now. Charlie Martin stays right here in this house and your family will give him every attention. His father and sister will be here, too, and you'll not open your mouth against them. Do you understand?"

"Yes—yes," whispered the now thoroughly frightened Adam.

"Don't you dare even to speak to Mrs. Ward or John or Helen as you have to me. And for God's sake pull yourself together and remember—you don't know any more than the rest of us about this business—you were in your room when you heard the shots."

"Yes, of course, Jim—but I—I—"

"Shut up! You are not to talk, I tell you—even to me."

Adam Ward whimpered like a child.

For another moment McIver glared at him; then, "Don't forget that I saw this affair and that I went over the ground with the police. I'm going back downstairs now. You go to bed where you belong and stay there."

He turned abruptly and left the room.

But as he went down the stairway McIver drew his handkerchief from his pocket and wiped the perspiration from his brow.

"What in God's name," he asked himself, "did Adam Ward's excited fears mean? What terrible thing gave birth to his mad words? What awful pattern was this that the unseen forces were weaving? And what part was he, with his love for Helen, destined to fill in it all?" That his life was being somehow woven into the design he felt certain—but how and to what end? And again the man in all his strength felt that dread foreboding.

* * * * *

When Peter Martin and his daughter arrived with John at the big house on the hill, Mrs. Ward met them at the door.

The old workman betrayed no consciousness of the distance the years of Adam Ward's material prosperity had placed between these two families that in the old-house days had lived in such intimacy.

Mary hesitated. It must have been that to the girl, who saw it between herself and the happy fulfillment of her womanhood, the distance seemed even greater than it actually was.

But her hesitation was only for an instant. One full look into the gentle face that was so marked by the years of uncomplaining disappointment and patient unhappiness and Mary knew that in the heart of John Ward's mother the separation had brought no change. In the arms of her own mother's dearest friend the young woman found, even as a child, the love she needed to sustain her in that hour.

When they entered the room where Captain Charlie lay unconscious, Helen rose from her watch beside the bed and held out her hands to her girlhood playmate. And in her gesture there was a full surrender—a plea for pardon. Humbly she offered— lovingly she invited—while she held her place beside the man who was slowly passing into that shadow where all class forms are lost, as if she claimed the right before a court higher than the petty courts of human customs. No word was spoken—no word was needed. The daughter of Peter Martin and the daughter of Adam Ward knew that the bond of their sisterhood was sealed.

In that wretched home in the Flats, little Maggie Whaley smiled in her sleep as she dreamed of her princess lady.

The armed guards at their stations around McIver's dark and silent factory kept their watch.

The Mill, under the cloud of smoke, sang the deep-voiced song of its industry as the night shift carried on.

In the room back of the pool hall, Jake Vodell whispered with two of his disciples.

In the window of the Interpreter's hut on the cliff a lamp gleamed starlike above the darkness below.

CHAPTER XXVI

AT THE CALL OF THE WHISTLE

Everywhere in Millsburgh the shooting of Captain Charlie was the one topic of conversation. As the patrons of the cigar stand came and went they talked with the philosopher of nothing else. The dry-goods pessimist delivered his dark predictions to a group of his fellow citizens and listened with grave shakes of his head to the counter opinions of the real-estate agent. The grocer questioned the garage man and the lawyer discussed the known details of the tragedy with the postmaster, the hotel keeper and the politician. The barber asked the banker for his views and reviewed the financier's opinion to the judge while a farmer and a preacher listened. The milliner told her customers about it and the stenographer discussed it with the bookkeeper. In the homes, on the streets, and, later in the day, throughout the country, the shock of the crime was felt.

Meanwhile, the efforts of the police to find the assassin were fruitless. The most careful search revealed nothing in the nature of a clew.

Millsburgh had been very proud of Captain Martin and the honors he had won in France, as Millsburgh was proud of Adam Ward and his success—only with a different pride. The people had known Charlie from his birth, as they had known his father and mother all their years. There had been nothing in the young workman's life—as every one remarked—to lead to such an end.

It is doubtful if in the entire community there was a single soul that did not secretly or openly think of the tragedy as being in some dark way an outcome of the strike. And, gradually, as the day passed, the conjectures, opinions and views crystallized into two opposing theories—each with its natural advocates.

One division of the people held that the deed was committed by some one of Jake Vodell's followers, because of the workman's known opposition to a sympathetic strike of the Mill workers' union. Captain Charlie's leadership of the Mill men was recognized by all, and it was conceded generally that it was his active influence, guided by the Interpreter's counsel, that was keeping John Ward's employees at work. Without the assistance of the Mill men the strike leader could not hope for victory. With Captain Charlie's personal influence no longer a factor, it was thought that the agitator might win the majority of the Mill workers and so force the union into line with the strikers.

This opinion was held by many of the business men and by the more thoughtful members of the unions, who had watched with grave apprehension the increasing bitterness of the agitator's hatred of Captain Charlie, because of the workman's successful opposition to his schemes.

The opposing theory, which was skillfully advanced by Jake Vodell himself and fostered by his followers, was that the mysterious assassin was an agent of McIver's and that the deed was committed for the very purpose of charging the strikers with the crime and thus turning public sympathy against them.

This view, so plausible to the minds of the strikers, prepared, as they were, by hardship and suffering, found many champions among the Mill men themselves. Not a few of those who had stood with Charlie in his opposition to the agitator and against their union joining the strike now spoke openly with bitter feeling against the employer class. The weeks of agitation—the constant pounding of Vodell's arguments—the steady fire of his oratory and the continual appeal to their class loyalty made it easy for them to stand with their fellow workmen, now that the issue was being so clearly forced.

So the lines of the industrial battle were drawn closer—the opposing forces were massed in more definite formation—the feeling was more intense and bitter. In the gloom and hush of the impending desperate struggle that was forced upon it by the emissary of an alien organization, this little American city waited the coming of the dark messenger to Captain Charlie. It was felt by all alike that the workman's death would precipitate the crisis.

And through it all the question most often asked was this, "Why was the workman, Charlie Martin, at the gate to Adam Ward's estate at that hour of the night?"

To this question no one ventured even the suggestion of a satisfactory answer.

All that long day Helen kept her watch beside the wounded man. Others were there in the room with her, but she seemed unconscious of their presence. She made no attempt, now, to hide her love. There was no pretense—no evasion. Openly, before them all, she silently acknowledged him—her man—and to his claim upon her surrendered herself without reserve.

James McIver called but she would not see him.

When they urged her to retire and rest, she answered always with the same words: "I must be here when he awakens—I must."

And they, loving her, understood.

It was as if the assassin's hand had torn aside the curtain of material circumstances and revealed suddenly the realities of their inner lives. They realized now that this man, who had in their old-house days won the first woman love of his girl playmate, had held that love against all the outward changes that had taken her from him. John and his mother knew, now, why Helen had never said "Yes" to Jim McIver. Peter Martin and Mary knew why, in Captain Charlie's heart, there had seemed to be no place for any woman save his sister.

At intervals the man on the bed moved uneasily, muttering low words and disconnected fragments of speech. Army words—some of them were—as if his spirit lived for the moment again in the fields of France. At other times the half-formed phrases were of his work—the strike—his home. Again he spoke his sister's name or murmured, "Father," or "John." But not once did Helen catch the word she longed to hear him speak. It was as if, even in his unconscious mental wanderings, the man still guarded the name that in secret he had held most dear.

Three times during the day he opened his eyes and looked about—wonderingly at first—then as though he understood. As one contented and at peace, he smiled and drifted again into the shadows. But now at times his hand went out toward her with a little movement, as though he were feeling for her in the dark.

About midnight he seemed to be sleeping so naturally that they persuaded Helen to rest. At daybreak she was again at her post.

Mrs. Ward and Mary had gone, in their turn, for an hour or two of sorely needed rest. Peter Martin was within call downstairs. John, who was watching with his sister, had left the room for the moment and Helen was at the bedside alone.

Suddenly through the quiet morning air came the deep-toned call of the Mill whistle.

As a soldier awakens at the sound of the morning bugle, Captain Charlie opened his eyes.

Instantly she was bending over him. As he looked up into her face she called his name softly. She saw the light of recognition come into his eyes. She saw the glory of his love.

"Helen," he said—and again, "Helen."

It was as if the death that claimed him had come also for her.

For the first time in many months the voice of the Mill was not heard by the Interpreter in his little hut on the cliff. Above the silent buildings the smoke cloud hung like a pall. From his wheel chair the old basket maker watched the long procession moving slowly down the hill.

There were no uniforms in that procession—no military band with muffled drums led that solemn march—no regimental colors in honor of the dead. There were no trappings of war—no martial ceremony. And yet, to the Interpreter, Captain Charlie died in the service of his country as truly as if he had been killed on the field of battle.

Long after the funeral procession had passed beyond his sight, the Interpreter sat there at the window, motionless, absorbed in thought. Twice silent Billy came to stand beside his chair, but he did not heed. His head was bowed. His great shoulders stooped. His hands were idle.

There was a sound of some one knocking at the door.

The Interpreter did not hear.

The sound was repeated, and this time he raised his head questioningly.

Again it came and the old basket maker called, "Come in."

The door opened. Jim McIver entered.

CHAPTER XXVII

JAKE VODELL'S MISTAKE

Since that night of the tragedy McIver had struggled to grasp the hidden meaning of the strange series of incidents. But the more he tried to understand, the more he was confused and troubled. Nor had he been able, strong-willed as he was, to shake off the feeling that he was in the midst of unseen forces—that about him mysterious influences were moving steadily to some fixed and certain end.

In constant touch, through his agents, with the strike situation, he had watched the swiftly forming sentiment of the public. He knew that the turning point of the industrial war was near. He did not deceive himself. He knew Jake Vodell's power. He knew the temper of the strikers. He saw clearly that if the assassin who killed Captain Charlie was not speedily discovered the community would suffer under a reign of terror such as the people had never conceived. And, what was of more vital importance to McIver, perhaps, if the truth was not soon revealed, Jake Vodell's charges that the murder was inspired by McIver himself would become, in the minds of many, an established fact. With the full realization of all that would result to the community and to himself if the identity of the murderer was not soon established, McIver was certain in his own mind that he alone knew the guilty man.

To reveal what he believed to be the truth of the tragedy would be to save the community and himself—and to lose, for all time, the woman he loved. McIver did not know that through the tragedy Helen was already lost to him.

In his extremity the factory owner had come at last to the man who was said to wield such a powerful influence over the minds of the people. He had never before seen the interior of that hut on the cliff nor met the man who for so many years had been confined there. Standing just outside the door, he looked curiously about the room with the unconscious insolence of his strength.

The man in the wheel chair did not speak. When Billy looked at him he signaled his wishes in their silent language, and, watching his visitor, waited.

For a long moment McIver gazed at the old basket maker as if estimating his peculiar strength, then he said with an unintentional touch of contempt in his heavy voice, "So *you* are the Interpreter."

"And you," returned the man in the wheel chair, gently, "are McIver."

McIver was startled. "How did you know my name?"

"Is McIver's name a secret also?" came the strange reply.

McIver's eyes flashed with a light that those who sat opposite him in the game of business had often seen. With perfect self-control he said, coolly, "I have been told often that I should come to see you but—" he paused and again looked curiously about the room.

The Interpreter, smiling, caught up the unfinished sentence. "But you do not see how an old, poverty-stricken and crippled maker of baskets can be of any use to you."

McIver spoke as one measuring his words. "They tell me you help people who are in trouble."

"Are you then in trouble?" asked the Interpreter, kindly.

The other did not answer, and the man in the wheel chair continued, still kindly, "What trouble can the great and powerful McIver have? You have never been hungry—you have never felt the cold—you have no children to starve—no son to be killed."

"I suppose you hold me personally responsible for the strike and for all the hardships that the strikers have brought upon themselves and their families?" said McIver. "You fellows who teach this brotherhood-of-man rot and never have more than one meal ahead yourselves always blame men like me for all the suffering in the world."

The Interpreter replied with a dignity that impressed even McIver. "Who am I that I should assume to blame any one? Who are you, sir, that assume the power implied by either your acceptance or your denial of the responsibility? You are only a part of the whole, as I am a part. You, in your life place, are no less a creature of circumstances—an accident—than I, here in my wheel chair—than Jake Vodell. We are all—you and I, Jake Vodell, Adam Ward, Peter Martin, Sam Whaley—we are all but parts of the great oneness of life. The want, the misery, the suffering, the unhappiness of humanity is of that unity no less than is the prosperity, peace and happiness of the people. Before we can hope to bring order out of this industrial chaos we must recognize our mutual dependence upon the whole and acknowledge the equality of our guilt in the wretched conditions that now exist."

As the Interpreter spoke, James McIver again felt the movement of those unseen forces that were about him. His presence in that little hut on the cliff seemed, now, a part of some plan that was not of his making. He was awed by the sudden conviction that he had not come to the Interpreter of his own volition, but had been led there by something beyond his understanding.

"Why should your fellow workmen not hate you, sir?" continued the old basket maker. "You hold yourself apart, superior, of a class distinct and separate. Your creed of class is intolerance. Your very business policy is a declaration of class war. Your boast that you can live without the working people is madness. You can no more live without them than they can live without you. You can no more deny the mutual dependence of employer and employee with safety to yourself than Samson of old could pull down the pillars of the temple without being himself buried in the ruins."

By an effort of will McIver strove to throw off the feeling that possessed him. He spoke as one determined to assert himself. "We cannot recognize the rights of Jake Vodell and his lawless followers to dictate to us in our business. It would mean ruin, not only of our industries, but of our government."

"Exactly so," agreed the Interpreter. "And yet, sir, you claim for yourself the right to live by the same spirit of imperialism that animates Vodell. You make the identical class distinction that he makes. You appeal to the same class intolerance and hatred. You and Jake Vodell have together brought about this industrial war in Millsburgh. The community itself—labor unions and business men alike—is responsible for tolerating the imperialism that you and this alien agitator, in opposition to each other, advocate. The community is paying the price."

The factory owner flushed. "Of course you would say these things to Jake Vodell."

"I do," returned the Interpreter, gently.

"Oh, you *are* in touch with him then?"

"He comes here sometimes. He is coming this afternoon—at four o'clock. Will you not stay and meet him, Mr. McIver?" McIver hesitated. He decided to ignore the invitation. With more respect in his manner than he had so far shown, he said, courteously, "May I ask why Jake Vodell comes to you?"

The Interpreter replied, sadly, as one who accepts the fact of his failure, "For the same reason that McIver came."

McIver started with surprise. "You know why I came to you?"

The man in the wheel chair looked steadily into his visitor's eyes. "I know that you are not personally responsible for the death of the workman, Captain Martin."

McIver sprang to his feet. He fairly gasped as the flood of questions raised by the Interpreter's words swept over him.

"You—you know who killed Charlie Martin?" he demanded at last.

The old basket maker did not answer.

"If you know," cried McIver, "why in God's name do you not tell the people? Surely, sir, you are not ignorant of the danger that threatens this community. The death of this union man has given Vodell just the opportunity he needed and he is using it. If you dare to shield the guilty man—whoever he is—you will—"

"Peace, McIver! This community will not be plunged into the horrors of a class war such as you rightly fear. There are yet enough sane and loyal American citizens in Millsburgh to extinguish the fire that you and Jake Vodell have started."

* * * * *

When Jake Vodell came to the Interpreter's hut shortly after McIver had left, he was clearly in a state of nervous excitement.

"Well," he said, shortly, "I am here—what do you want—why did you send for me?"

The Interpreter spoke deliberately with his eyes fixed upon the dark face of the agitator. "Vodell, I have told you twice that your campaign in Millsburgh was a failure. Your coming to this community was a mistake. Your refusal to recognize the power of the thing that made your defeat certain was a mistake. You have now made your third and final mistake."

"A mistake! Hah—that is what you think. You do not know. I tell you that I have turned a trick that will win for me the game. Already the people are rallying to me. I have put McIver at last in a hole from which he will not escape. The Mill workers are ready *now* to do anything I say. You will see—to-morrow I will have these employers and all their capitalist class eating out of my hand. To me they shall beg for mercy. I—I will dictate the terms to them and they will pay. You may take my word—they will pay."

The man paced to and fro with the triumphant air of a conqueror, and his voice rang with his exultation.

"No, Jake Vodell," said the Interpreter, calmly. "You are deceiving yourself. Your dreams are as vain as your mistake is fatal."

The man faced the old basket maker suddenly, as if arrested by a possible meaning in the Interpreter's words that had not at first caught his attention.

"And what is this mistake that I have made?" he growled.

The answer came with solemn portent. "You have killed the wrong man."

The agitator was stunned. His mouth opened as if he would speak, but no word came from his trembling lips. He drew back as if to escape.

204

The old man in the wheel chair continued, sadly, "*I* am the one you should have killed—I am the cause of your failure to gain the support of the Mill workers' union."

The strike leader recovered himself with a shrug of his heavy shoulders.

"So that is it," he sneered; "you would accuse me of shooting your Captain Charlie, heh?"

"You have accused yourself, sir."

"But how?"

"By the use you are making of Captain Charlie's death. If you did not know who committed the crime—if you did not feel sure that the identity of the assassin would remain a mystery to the people—you would not dare risk charging the employers with it."

With an oath the other returned, "I tell you that McIver or his hired gunmen did it so they could lay the blame on the strikers and so turn the Mill workers' union against us. That is what the Mill men believe."

"That is what you want them to believe. It is an old trick, Vodell. You have used it before."

The agitator's eyes narrowed under his scowling brows. "Look here," he growled, "I do not like this talk of yours. Perhaps you had better prove what you charge, heh?"

"Please God, I will prove it," came the calm answer.

Jake Vodell, as he looked down upon the seemingly helpless old man in the wheel chair, was thinking, "It would be safer if this old basket maker were not permitted to speak these things to others—his influence, after all, is a thing to consider."

"No, Jake Vodell," said the Interpreter gently, "you won't do it. Billy Rand is watching us. If you make a move to do what you are thinking, Billy will kill you."

The Interpreter raised his hand and his silent companion came quickly to stand beside his chair.

With a shrug of his shoulders Vodell drew back a few steps toward the door.

"Bah! Why should I waste my time with a crippled old basket maker—I have work to do. If you watch from the window of your shanty you will see to-morrow whether or not the Mill workers are with me. I will make for you a demonstration that will be known through the country. I told you at the first that the working people would find out who is their friend. Now you shall see what they will do to the enemies of their class. Who can say, Mr. Interpreter, perhaps your miserable hut so high up here would make a good torch to signal the beginning of the show, heh?"

When the door had closed behind Jake Vodell, the Interpreter said, aloud, "So he has set to-morrow night for his demonstration. We must work fast, Billy—there is no time to lose."

With his hands he asked his companion for paper and pencil. When Billy brought them he wrote a few words and folding the message gave it to the big man who stood waiting.

For a few minutes they talked together in their silent way. Then Billy Rand put the Interpreter's message carefully in his pocket and hurriedly left the hut.

* * * * *

That evening Jake Vodell addressed the largest crowd that had yet assembled at his street meetings. With characteristic eloquence the agitator pictured Captain Charlie as a martyr to the unprincipled schemes of the employer class.

"McIver and his crew are charging the strikers with this crime in order to set our union brothers against us," he shouted. "They think that by setting up a division among us they can win. They know that if the working people stand together, true to their class, loyal to their comrades, they will rule the world. Why don't the police produce the murderer of Captain Charlie? I will tell you the answer, my brother workmen: it is because the law and the officers of the law are under the control of those who do not want the murderer produced—that is why. They dare not produce him. The life of a poor working man—what is that to these masters of crime who acknowledge no law but the laws they make for themselves. You workers have no laws. A slave knows no justice but the whim of his master. Think of the mothers and children in your homes—you slaves who create the wealth of your lords and masters. And now they have taken the life of one of your truest and most loyal union leaders. Where will they stop? If you do not stand like men against these cruel outrages what have you to hope for? You know as well as I that no workman in Millsburgh would raise his hand against such a fellow worker as Captain Charlie Martin."

While the agitator was speaking, Billy Rand moved quickly here and there through the crowd, as if searching for some one.

After the mass meeting on the street there was a meeting of the Mill workers' union.

Later, Vodell's inner circle met in the room back of Dago Bill's pool hall.

206

It was midnight when Billy Rand finally returned to the waiting Interpreter.

Evidently he had failed in the mission entrusted to him by the old basket maker.

The next morning, Billy Rand again went forth with the Interpreter's message.

CHAPTER XXVIII

THE MOB AND THE MILL

On the morning following the day of the funeral scarcely half of the usual force of workmen appeared at the Mill. The men who did choose to work were forced to pass a picket line of strikers who with jeers and threats and arguments sought to turn them from their purpose.

The death of Captain Charlie, by defining more clearly the two lines of public sentiment, had increased Jake Vodell's strength materially, but the Mill workers' union had not yet officially declared for the sympathetic strike that would deliver the community wholly into the hands of the agitator. The Mill men, who were still opposed to Jake Vodell's leadership and coolly refused to hold the employers guilty of the death of Captain Charlie upon the mere unsupported assertions of the strike leader, were therefore free to continue their work. This action of the members of the Mill workers' union who were loyal to John, however, quite naturally increased the feeling of their comrades who had accepted Vodell's version of the murder. Thus, the final crisis of the industrial battle centered about the Mill.

Every hour that John Ward could keep the Mill running lessened Vodell's chances of final victory. The strike leader knew that if these days immediately following Captain Charlie's death passed without closing the Mill, his cause was lost. The workmen were now aroused to the highest pitch of excitement. The agitator realized that if they were not committed by some action to his cause before the fever of their madness began to abate, his followers would, day by day, in ever increasing numbers go back to work under John. The successful operation of the Mill was a demonstration to the public that Vodell's campaign against the employers was not endorsed by the better and stronger element of employees. To the mind of the strike leader a counter demonstration was imperative. To that immediate end the man now bent every effort.

All day the members of the agitator's inner circle were active. When evening came, a small company of men gathered in a vacant store building not far from the Mill. There was little talk among them. When one did speak it was to utter a mere commonplace or perhaps to greet some newcomer. They were as men who meet at a given place by agreement to carry out some definite and carefully laid plan. Moment by moment the company grew in numbers until the gathering assumed such proportions that it overflowed the building and filled the street. And now, scattered through the steadily growing crowd, the members of that inner circle were busy with exhortations and arguments preparing the workmen for what was to follow.

Presently from the direction of the strike headquarters came another company with Jake Vodell himself in their midst. These had assembled at the strike headquarters. Without pausing they swept on down the street toward the Mill, taking with them the crowd that was waiting at the old store. Scarcely had they reached the front of the large main building when they were joined by still another crowd that had been gathering in the neighborhood of McIver's factory. Thus, with startling suddenness, a great company of workmen was assembled at the Mill.

But a large part of that company had yet to be molded to Vodell's purpose. Many had gone to the designated places in response to the simple announcement that a labor meeting would be held there. Only those of the agitator's trusted inner circle had known of the plan to unite these smaller gatherings in one great mass meeting. Only these chosen few knew the real purpose of that meeting. There were hundreds of workmen in that throng who were opposed to Vodell and his methods, but they were unorganized, with no knowledge of the strike leader's plans. And so it had been easy for the members of that inner circle to lead these separate smaller gatherings to the larger assembly in front of the Mill.

To accomplish the full purpose of his demonstration against the employer class, the strike leader must make it appear to the public as the united action of the working people of Millsburgh. The requirements of his profession made Jake Vodell a master of mob psychology. With the leaven of his chosen inner circle and the temper of the many strikers whose nerves were already strained to the breaking point by their weeks of privation, the agitator was confident that he could bend the assembled multitude to his will. Those who were opposed to his leadership and to his methods—disorganized and taken by surprise as they were—would be helpless. At the same time their presence in the mob would appear to give their sanction and support to whatever was accomplished.

Quickly word of the gathering spread throughout the community. From every direction—from the Flats, from the neighborhood of the Martin home—and from the more distant parts of the city—men were moving toward the Mill. With every moment the crowd increased in size. Everywhere among the mass of men Vodell's helpers were busy.

A block away an automobile stopped at the curb in front of a deserted house. A man left the car, and, keeping well out of the light from the street lamps, walked swiftly to the outskirts of the mob. With his face hidden by the turned-up collar of his overcoat and the brim of his hat pulled low, he moved here and there in the thin edge of the multitude.

The agitator, standing on a goods box on the street opposite the big doors of the main Mill building, began his address. As one man, the hundreds of assembled workmen turned toward the leader of the strike. A hush fell over them. But there was one in that great crowd to whom the words of Jake Vodell meant nothing. Silent Billy Rand, pushing his way through the press of men, searched face after face with simple, untiring purpose.

A squad of police arrived. Vodell, calling attention to them, facetiously invited the guardians of the law to a seat of honor on the rostrum. The crowd laughed.

At that moment Billy Rand caught sight of the face he was seeking. When the Interpreter's messenger grasped his arm, the man, who was standing well back in the edge of the crowd, started with fear. Billy thrust the note into his hand. As he read the message he shook so that the paper rattled in his fingers. Helplessly he looked about. He seemed paralyzed with horror. Again Billy Rand grasped his arm and this time drew him aside, out of the crowd.

Helpless and shaken, the man made no effort to resist, as the Interpreter's deaf and dumb companion hurried him away down the street.

At the foot of the zigzag stairway Billy's charge sank down on the lower step, as if he had no strength to go on. Without a moment's pause Billy lifted him to his feet and almost carried him up the stairs and into the hut to place him, cowering and whimpering, before the man in the wheel chair.

* * * * *

John and Helen had gone to the Martin cottage that evening to spend an hour with the old workman and his daughter. They had just arrived when the telephone rang.

It was the watchman at the Mill. He had called John at the Ward home, and Mrs. Ward had directed him to call the cottage.

In a few words John told the others of the crowd at the Mill. He must go at once.

"But not alone, boy," said Peter Martin. "This is no more your job than 'tis mine."

As they were leaving, John said hurriedly to Helen, "Telephone Tom to come for you at once and take Mary home with you. Mother may need you, and Mary must not be left here alone. I'll bring Uncle Pete home with me."

A moment later the old workman and the general manager, in John's roadster, were on their way to the Mill.

When Tom arrived at the cottage with Helen's car the two young women were ready. They were entering the automobile when Billy Rand appeared. It was evident from his labored breathing that he had been running, but his face betrayed no excitement. With a pleased smile, as one who would say, "Luckily I got here just in time," he handed a folded paper to Mary.

By the light of the automobile lamp she read the Interpreter's message aloud to Helen."

"Telephone John to come to me at once with a big car. If you can't get John tell Helen."

For an instant they looked at each other questioningly. Then Helen spoke to the chauffeur. "To the Interpreter's, Tom." She indicated to Billy Rand that he was to go with them.

* * * * *

It was not Jake Vodell's purpose to call openly in his address to the assembled workmen for an attack on the Mill. Such a demonstration against the employer class was indeed the purpose of the gathering, but it must come as the spontaneous outburst from the men themselves. His speech was planned merely to lay the kindling for the fire. The actual lighting of the blaze would follow later. The conflagration, too, would be started simultaneously from so many different points in the crowd that no one individual could be singled out as having incited the riot.

The agitator was still speaking when John and Peter Martin arrived on the scene. Quietly and carefully John drove through the outskirts of the crowd to a point close to the wall and not far from the main door of the building, nearly opposite the speaker. Stopping the motor the two men sat in the car listening to Vodell's address.

The agitator did not call attention to the presence of the manager of the Mill as he had to the police, nor was there any noticeable break in his speech. But throughout the great throng there was a movement—a ripple of excitement—as the men looked toward John and the old workman, and turned each to his neighbor with low-spoken comments. And then, from every part of the crowd, the agitator saw individuals moving quietly toward the manager's car until between the two men in the automobile and the main body of the speaker's audience a small compact group of workmen stood shoulder to shoulder. They were the men of the Mill workers' union who had refused to follow Jake Vodell. And every man, as he took his place, greeted John and the old workman with a low word, or a nod and a smile. The agitator concluded his address, and amid the shouts and applause left his place on the goods box to move about among his followers.

Presently, a low murmur arose like a growling undertone. Now and then a voice was raised sharply in characteristic threat or epithet against the employer class. The murmur swelled into a heavy menacing roar. The crowd, shaken by some invisible inner force, swayed to and fro. A shrill yell rang out and at the signal scores of hoarse voices were raised in shouts of mad defiance—threats and calls for action. As the whirling waters of a maelstrom are drawn to the central point, the mob was massed before the doors of the Mill.

The little squad of police was struggling forward. John Ward sprang to his feet. The loyal union men about the car stood fast.

At the sound of the manager's voice the mob hesitated. In all that maddened crowd there was not a soul in ignorance of John Ward's comradeship with his fellow workmen. In spite of Jake Vodell's careful teaching—in spite of his devilish skill in using McIver as an example in his appeals and arguments inciting their hatred

211

against all employers as a class, they were checked in their madness by the presence of Captain Charlie's friend.

But it was only for the moment. The members of Vodell's inner circle were at work among them. John had spoken but a few sentences when he was interrupted by voices from the crowd.

"Tell us where your old man got this Mill that he says is his?"

"Where did Adam get his castle on the hill?"

"We and our families live in shanties."

"Who paid for your automobile, John?"

"We and our children walk."

As the manager, ignoring the voices, continued his appeal, the interruptions came with more frequency, accompanied now by groans, shouts, hisses and derisive laughter.

"You're all right, John, but you're in with the wrong bunch."

"We're going to run things for a while now and give you a chance to do some real work."

The police pleaded with them. The mob jeered, "Go get a job with McIver's gunmen. Go find the man who murdered Captain Charlie."

Once more the growling undertones swelled into a roar. "Come on—come on—-we've had enough talk—let's do something."

As the crowd surged again toward the Mill doors, there was a forward movement of the close-packed group of workmen about the ear. John, leaning over them, said, sharply, "No—no—not that—men, not that!"

Then suddenly the movement of the mob toward the Mill was again checked as Peter Martin raised his voice. "If you won't listen to Mr. Ward," said the old man, when he had caught their attention, "perhaps you'll not mind hearin' me."

In the stillness of the uncertain moment, a voice answered, "Go ahead, Uncle Pete!"

Standing on the seat of the automobile, the kindly old workman looked down into the grim faces of his comrades. And, as they saw him there and thought of Captain Charlie, a deep breath of feeling swept over the throng.

212

In his slow, thoughtful way the veteran of the Mill spoke. "There'll be no one among you, I'm thinkin', that'll dare say as how I don't belong to the workin' class. An' there'll be no man that'll deny my right to be heard in any meeting of Millsburgh working men. I helped the Interpreter to organize the first union that was ever started in this city—and so far we've managed to carry on our union work without any help from outsiders who have no real right to call themselves American citizens even—much less to dictate to us American workmen."

There was a stir among Vodell's followers. A voice rose but was silenced by the muttered protest which it caused. Jake Vodell, quick to grasp the feeling of the crowd, was making his way toward his goods box rostrum. Here and there he paused a moment to whisper to one of his inner circle.

The old workman continued, "You all know the principles that my boy Charlie stood for. You know that he was just as much against employers like McIver as he was against men like this agitator who is leading you into this trouble here to-night. Jake Vodell has made you believe that my boy was killed by the employer class. But I tell you men that Charlie had no better friend in the world than his employer, John Ward. And I tell you that John and Charlie were working together here for the best interests of us all—just as they were together in France. You know what my boy would say if he was here to-night. He would say just what I am saying. He would tell you that we workmen have got to stand by the employers who stand by us. He would tell you that we American union workmen must protect ourselves and our country against this anarchy and lawlessness that has got you men here to-night so all excited and beside yourselves that you don't know what you're doing. In Captain Charlie's name I ask you men to break up this mob and go quietly to your homes where you can think this thing over. We—"

From his position across the street Jake Vodell suddenly interrupted the old workman with a rapid fire of questions and insinuations and appeals to the mob.

Peter Martin, poorly equipped for a duel of words with such a master of the art, was silenced.

Slowly the mob swung again to the agitator. Under the spell of his influence they were responding once more to his call, when a big automobile rolled swiftly up to the edge of the crowd and stopped.

John Ward was the first to recognize his sister's car. With a word to the men near him he sprang to the ground and ran forward. The loyal workmen went with him.

In the surprise of the moment, not knowing what was about to happen, Jake Vodell stood silent. In breathless suspense every eye in the crowd was fixed upon that little group about Helen's car.

Another moment and the assembled workmen witnessed a sight that they will never forget. Down the lane that opened as if by magic through the mass of men came the loyal members of the Mill workers' union. High on their shoulders they carried the Interpreter.

In a silence, deep as the stillness of death, they bore him through those close-packed walls of humanity, straight to the big doors of the Mill. With their backs against the building they held him high—face to face with Jake Vodell and the mob that the agitator was swaying to his will.

The old basket maker's head was bare and against the dark background of the dingy walls his venerable face with its crown of silvery hair was as the face of a prophet.

They did not cheer. In silent awe they stood with tense, upturned faces.

A voice, low but clear and distinct, cut the stillness.

"Hats off!"

As one man, they uncovered their heads.

The Interpreter's deep voice—kindly but charged with strange authority—swept over them.

"Workmen—what are you doing here? Are you toys that you give yourselves as playthings into the hands of this man who chooses to use you in his game? Are you children to be led by his idle words and moved by his foolish dreams? Are you men or are you cattle to be stampeded by him, without reason, to your own destruction? Would you, at this stranger's bidding, dig a pit for your fancied enemies and fall into it yourselves?"

Not a man in that great crowd of workmen moved. In breathless silence they stood awed by the majesty of the old basket maker's presence—hushed by the sorrowful authority of his voice.

Solemnly the Interpreter continued, "The one who took the life of your comrade workman, Captain Charlie, was not a tool in the hands of your employers as you have been led to believe. Neither was that dreadful act inspired by the workmen of Millsburgh. Captain Charlie was killed by a poor, foolish weakling who was under the same spell that to-night has so nearly led you into this blind folly of destroying that which should be your glory and your pride. Sam Whaley has confessed to me. He has surrendered himself to the proper authorities. But the instigator of the crime—the one who planned, ordered and directed it—the leader who dominated and drove his poor tool to the deed is this man Jake Vodell."

The sound of the Interpreter's voice ceased. For a moment longer that dead silence held—then as the full import of the old basket maker's words went home to them, the crowd with a roar of fury turned toward the spot where the agitator had stood when the arrival of the Interpreter interrupted his address.

But Jake Vodell had disappeared.

CHAPTER XXIX

CONTRACTS

They had carried the Interpreter back to his wheel chair in the hut on the cliff.

John, Peter Martin and the two young women were bidding the old basket maker goodnight when suddenly they were silenced by the dull, heavy sound of a distant explosion.

A moment they stood gazing at one another, then John voiced the thoughts that had gripped the minds of every one in that little group:

"The Mill!"

Springing to the door that opened on to the balcony porch, John threw it open and they went out, taking the Interpreter in his chair. In breathless silence they strained their eyes toward the dark mass of the Mill with its forest of stacks and its many lights.

"Everything seems to be all right there," murmured John.

But as the last word left his lips a chorus of exclamations came from the others. Farther up the river a dull red glow flushed the sky.

"McIver's!"

"The factory!"

The Interpreter said, quietly, "Jake Vodell."

With every second the red glow grew brighter—reaching higher and higher—spreading wider and wider over the midnight sky. Then they could see the flames—threadlike streaks and flashes in the dark cloud of smoke at first but increasing in volume, climbing and climbing in writhing, twisting columns of red fury. The wild, long-drawn shriek of the fire whistles, the clanging roar of the engines, the frantic rush of speeding automobiles awoke the echoes of the cliffs and aroused the sleeping creatures on the hillsides. The volume of the leaping, whirling mass of flames increased until the red glare shut out the stars.

The officers of the law who were hunting Jake Vodell heard that explosion and telephoned their stations for orders. The business men of the little city, awakened from their sleep, looked from their windows, muttered drowsy conjectures and returned to their beds. Mothers and children in their homes heard and turned uneasily in their dreams. The dwellers in the Flats heard and wondered fearfully.

216

Before morning dawned the telegraph wires would carry the word throughout the land. In every corner of our country the people would read, as they have all too often read of similar explosions. They would read, offer idle comments, perhaps, and straightway forget. That is the wonder and the shame of it—that with these frequent warnings ringing in our ears we are not warned. With these things continually forced upon our attention we do not heed. With the demonstration before our eyes we are not convinced. We are not aroused to the meaning of it all.

In his cell in the county jail, Sam Whaley heard that explosion and knew what it was.

The Interpreter was right when he said, "Jake Vodell."

It was an hour, perhaps, after the Interpreter's friends had left the hut when the old basket maker, who was still sitting at the window watching the burning factory, heard an automobile approaching at a frightful pace from the direction of the fire. The noise of the speeding machine ceased with startling suddenness at the foot of the stairway, and the Interpreter heard some one running up the steps with headlong haste. Without pausing to knock, Adam Ward burst into the room and stood panting and shaking with mad excitement before the man in the wheel chair.

The Mill owner's condition was pitiful. By his eyes that were glittering with wild, unnatural light, by the gray, twitching features, the grotesque gestures, the trembling, jerking limbs, the Interpreter knew that the last flickering gleam of reason had gone out. The hour toward which the man himself had looked with such dread had come. Adam Ward was insane.

With a leering grin of triumph the madman went closer to the old basket maker. "I got away again. They were right after me but they couldn't catch me. That roadster of mine is the fastest car in the county—cost me four thousand dollars. I knew if I could get here I would be safe. They wouldn't think of looking for me here in your shanty, would they? They can't get in anyway if they should come. You wouldn't—you wouldn't let them get me, would you?"

"Peace, Adam Ward! You are safe here."

The insane man chuckled. "The folks at the house think I am in my room asleep. They don't know that I never sleep. I'll tell you something. If a man sleeps he goes to hell—hell—hell—" His voice rose almost to a scream and he shook with terror.

"Did you see it? Did you see when hell broke out to-night over there where McIver's factory used to be? I did—I was there and I heard them roaring in the fibres of torment and screaming in the flames. They called for me but I laughed and came here. They'll never get Adam Ward into hell. They don't know it yet, but I've got a contract with God. I fixed it up myself just like you told me to and God signed it without reading it just as Peter Martin did. I'll show them! It'll take more than God to get the best of Adam Ward in a deal."

He walked about the room, waving his arms and laughing in hideous triumph, muttering mad boasts and mumbling to himself or taunting the phantom creatures of his disordered brain.

The helpless Interpreter could only wait silently for whatever was to follow.

At last the madman turned again to the old basket maker. Placing a chair close in front of the Interpreter, he seated himself and in a confidential whisper said, "Did you know that everybody thinks I am going insane? Well, I am not. Nobody knows it, but it's not me that's crazy—it's John. He's been that way ever since he got home from France. The poor boy thinks the world is still at war and that he can run the Mill just as he fought the Germans over there. There's another thing that you ought to know, too—you are crazy yourself. Don't be afraid, I won't tell anybody else. But you ought to know it. If a man knows it when he is going crazy it gives him a chance to fix things up with God so they can't get him into hell for all eternity, you see. So I thought I had better tell you."

The Interpreter spoke in a calm, matter-of-fact tone. "Thank you, Adam, I appreciate your kindness."

"I was there at the Mill tonight," Adam continued, "and I heard you tell them who killed Charlie Martin. And then those crazy fools went tearing off to hunt Jake Vodell." He chuckled and laughed. "What difference does it make who killed Charlie Martin? I own the patented process. I am the man they want. But they can't touch me. I hired the best lawyers in the country and I've got it sewed up tight. I put one over on Pete Martin in that deal and I've put one over on God, too. I've got God sewed up tight, I tell you, just like I sewed up Peter Martin. They can howl their heads off but they'll never get me into hell."

He leaned back in his chair with the satisfied air of a business man crediting himself with having closed a successful transaction.

Then, with a manner and voice that was apparently normal, he said, "Did I ever tell you about how I got that patented process of mine, Wallace?" The Interpreter knew by his use of that name, so seldom heard in these later years, that Adam's mind was back in the old days when, with Peter Martin, they had worked side by side at the same bench in the Mill.

Hoping to calm him, the old basket maker returned indifferently, "No, Adam, I don't remember that you ever told me, but don't you think some other time would be better perhaps than to-night? It is getting late and you—"

The other interrupted with a wave of his hand. "Oh, that's all right. It's safe enough to talk about it now. Besides," he added, with a cunning leer, "nobody would believe you if you should tell them the truth. You're nothing but a crazy old basket maker and I am Adam Ward, don't forget that for a minute." He glared threateningly at the man in the wheel chair, and the Interpreter, fearing another outburst, said, soothingly, "Certainly, Adam, I understand. I will not forget."

With the manner of one relating an interesting story in which he himself figured with great personal credit, Adam Ward said:

"It was Pete Martin, you see, who actually discovered the new process. But, luckily for me, I was the first one he told about it. He had worked it all out and I persuaded him not to say a thing to any one else until the patents were secured. Pete didn't really know the value of what he had. But I knew—I saw from the first that it would revolutionize the whole business, and I knew it would make a fortune for the man that owned the patents.

"Pete and I were pretty good friends in those days, but friendship don't go far in business. I never had a friend in my life that I couldn't use some way. So I had Pete over to my house every evening and made a lot over him and talked over his new process and made suggestions how he should handle it, until finally he offered to give me a half interest if I would look after the business details. That, of course, was exactly what I was playing for. And all this time, you see, I took mighty good care that not a soul was around when Pete and I talked things over. So we fixed it all up between us—with no one to hear us, mind you—that we were to share equally—half and half—in whatever the new process brought.

"After that, I went ahead and got all the patents good and tight and then I fixed up a nice little document for Pete to sign. But I waited and I didn't say a word to Pete until one evening when he and his wife were studying and figuring out the plans for the house they were going to build. I sat and planned with them a while until I saw how Pete's mind was all on his new house, and then all at once I put my little document down on the table in front of him and said, 'By the way, Pete, those patents will be coming along pretty soon and I have had a little contract fixed up just as a matter of form—you know how we planned it all. Here's where you sign—'"

Adam Ward paused to laugh with insane glee. "Pete did just what I knew he'd do—he signed that document without even reading a line of it and went on with his house planning and figuring as if nothing had happened. But something had happened—something big had happened. Instead of the way we had planned it together when we were talking alone with nobody to witness it, Pete signed to me outright for one dollar all his rights and interests in that new patented process."

Again the madman laughed triumphantly. "Pete never even found out what he'd done until nearly a year later. And then he wouldn't believe it until the lawyers made him. He couldn't do anything of course. I had it sewed up too tight. That process is mine, I tell you—mine by all the laws in the country. What if I did take advantage of him! That's business. A man ought to have sense enough to read what he puts his signature to. You don't catch me trusting anybody far enough to sign anything he puts before me without reading it. Why—why—what are you crying for?"

Adam Ward was not mistaken—the Interpreter's eyes were wet with tears.

The sight of the old basket maker's grief sent the insane man off on another tangent. "Don't you worry about me. Helen and John and their mother worry a lot about me. They think I'm going to hell."

He sprang to his feet with a hoarse inarticulate cry. "They'll never get me into hell! God has got to keep His contracts and I've fixed it all up so He'll have to save me whether He wants to or not. The papers are all signed and everything. My lawyer has got them in his safe. God can't help Himself. You told me I'd better do it and I have. I'm not afraid to meet God now! I'll show Him just like I showed Pete."

He rushed from the room as abruptly as he had entered. The Interpreter heard him plunging down the stairs. The roar of his automobile died away in the distance.

In an early morning extra edition, the Millsburgh *Clarion* announced the death of two of the most prominent citizens.

James McIver was killed in the explosion that burned his factory.

Adam Ward's body was found in a secluded corner of his beautiful estate. He died by his own hand.

The cigar-store philosopher put his paper down and reached into the show case for the box that the judge wanted. "It looks like McIver played the wrong cards in his little game with Jake Vodell," he remarked, as the judge made a careful selection.

"I am afraid so," returned the judge.

The postmaster took a handful from the same box and said, as he dropped a dollar on the top of the show case, "I see Sam Whaley has confessed that the blowing up of the factory was all set as part of their program. Their plan was to wreck the Mill first then McIver's place. Where do you suppose Jake Vodell got away to?"

"Hard to guess," said the judge.

The philosopher put the proper change before them. "There's one thing sure—the people of these here United States had better get good and busy findin' out where he is."

It was significant that neither the philosopher nor his customers mentioned the passing of Adam Ward.

BOOK IV

THE OLD HOUSE

"Tell them, O Guns, that we have heard their call,

That we have sworn, and will not turn aside, That we will onward till we win or fall,

That we will keep the faith for which they died_."

CHAPTER XXX

"JEST LIKE THE INTERPRETER SAID"

It is doubtful if in all Millsburgh there was a soul who felt a personal loss in the passing of their "esteemed citizen" Adam Ward. During the years that followed his betrayal of Peter Martin's friendship the man had never made a friend who loved him for himself—who believed in him or trusted him. In business circles his reputation for deals that were always carefully legal but often obviously dishonest had caused the men he met to accept him only so far as their affairs made the contact necessary. Because of the power he had through his possession of the patented process he was known. His place in the community had been fixed by what he took from the community. His habit of boasting of his possessions, of his power, and of his business triumphs, and his way of considering the people as his personal debtors had been a never-failing subject of laughing comment. Men spoke of his death in a jocular vein—made jests about it—wondering what he was really worth. But one and all invariably concluded their comments with some word of sincere sympathy for his family.

Because of the people's estimation of the Mill owner's character, the publication of his will created a sensation the like of which was never before known in the community.

One half of his estate, including the Mill, Adam Ward gave to his family. The other half he gave to his old workman friend, Peter Martin.

Millsburgh was stunned, stupefied with amazement and wonder. But no one outside the two families, save the Interpreter, ever knew the real reason for the bequest. The old basket maker alone understood that this was Adam Ward's deal with God—it was the contract by which he was to escape the hell of his religious fears—the horrors of which he had so often suffered in his dreams and the dread of which had so preyed upon his diseased mind.

When the necessary time for the legal processes in the settlement of Adam Ward's estate had passed, John called the Mill workers together. In his notice of the meeting, the manager stated simply that it was to consider the mutual interests of the employers and employees by safeguarding the future of the industry. When the workmen had assembled, they wondered to see on the platform with their general manager, Helen and her mother, Mary and Peter Martin, the city mayor, with representative men from the labor unions and from the business circles of the community, and, sitting in his wheel chair, the Interpreter.

To the employees in the Mill and to the representatives of the people the announcement of the final disposition of Adam Ward's estate was made.

The house on the hill with the beautiful grounds surrounding it became in effect the property of the people—with an endowment fixed for its maintenance. It was to be converted into a center of community interest, one feature of which was to be an institute for the study of patriotism.

"We have foundations for the promotion of the sciences, of art and of business," said the legal gentleman who made the announcements. "Why not an institution for the study and promotion of patriotism—research in the fields of social and industrial life that are peculiarly American—lectures, classes, and literature on the true Americanization of those who come to us from foreign countries—the promotion of true American principles and standards of citizenship in our public schools and educational institutions and among our people—the collection and study of authentic data from the many industrial and social experiments that are being carried on—these are some of the proposed activities."

This Institute of American Patriotism would be under the leadership of the Interpreter and would stand as a memorial to the memory of Captain Charlie Martin.

When the mayor, in behalf of the people, had made a fitting response to this presentation, John told the Mill men that their employer, Pete Martin, would make an announcement.

The old workman was greeted with cheers. Some one in the crowd called, good-naturedly, "How does it feel to be an owner, Uncle Pete?" Everybody laughed and the veteran himself grinned.

"I guess I'm too old to change my feelings much, Bill Sewold," he answered. "And that's about what I was going to tell you. The lawyers say that I own half of our Mill here and that I can do what I please with it. But I can't some way make it seem any more mine than it always was. Mary and I are agreed that we'd like to do what we know Charlie would be in for if he was here, and we've talked it over with John and his folks and they feel just like we do about it.

"The lawyers can explain the workin's of the plan to you better than I can; but this is the main idea: The whole thing has been made over into a company with John and his mother and sister owning one half and me the other. What John wants me to tell you is that he and his folks are turning one half of their interest and Mary and me are turning one half of our interest back to you workmen. So that from now on all the employees of the Mill will be employers—and all the employers will be employees. With John and me and our folks owning one half, you can see that we're figuring on keeping the management in the proper hands, John will be in the office where he belongs and the rest of us will be where we belong. Considering our recent demonstration, I guess you'll all agree that a lot of us need to be protected by the rest of us from all of us. And now all we have to do is to work. And I'd like to see Jake Vodell or any other foreign agitator try to start another industrial war in Millsburgh."

It was the Interpreter who asked the assembled workmen to endorse a petition to the governor asking clemency for Sam Whaley. The ground upon which the petition was based was that the guilty principal in the crime was still at liberty—that others, still unknown, were involved with him—that Sam Whaley by his confession had saved the Mill and the community from the full horrors planned by the agitator, and that under the new standard of industrial citizenship the former follower of the anarchist might in time become a useful member of society.

A solemn hush fell over the company when Peter Martin, Mary, John and Helen were the first to sign the petition.

The old house is no longer empty, deserted and forlorn. Repaired and repainted from the front gate to the back-yard fence—with well-kept lawn, flowers and garden—it impresses the passer-by with its air of modest home happiness. To Helen and her mother who live there, to John and his wife, Mary, and to the old workman who live in the cottage next door, the spirit of the old days has returned.

The neighbors in passing always stop for a word with the gray-haired woman who works among her flowers just as she used to do before the discovery of the new process, or with her sweet-faced daughter. The workmen going to or from the Mill always have a smile or a word of greeting for the mother and the sister of their comrade manager.

Nor is there a man or woman in all the city or in the country round about who does not know and love this Helen of the old house, who is giving herself so without reserve to the people's need, who has, as the Interpreter says, "found herself in service."

But when the deep tones of the Mill whistle sound over the city, the valley and the hillsides, there is a look in Helen's eyes that only those who know her best understand.

And often in these days the neighborhood of the old house rings with the merry voices of Bobby and Maggie and their playmates. From the Flats—from the tenement houses—from the homes of the laborers, they come, these children, to this beautiful woman who loves them all and who calls them, somewhat fancifully, her "jewels of happiness."

"Yer see," explained little Maggie, "the princess lady, she jest couldn't help findin' them there happiness jewels—'cause her heart was so kind—jest like the Interpreter said."

THE END

477358

Made in the USA